The Scroll

Toby

Miriam Feinberg Vamosh

The Scroll

The Toby Press

The Scroll
First Toby Press Edition, 2018

The Toby Press LLC
POB 8531, New Milford, CT 06776–8531, USA
POB 2455, London W1A 5WY, England
POB 4044, Jerusalem 91040

www.tobypress.com

The photograph of the writ of divorce on the cover appears by permission of the Israel Antiquities Authority

ISBN 978-1-59264-511-4, *paperback*

Printed and bound in the United States

Foreword and Acknowledgments

The Jewish divorce decree that spurred the idea for this book was in fact discovered in a cave in Wadi Murabba'at in the Judean Desert.[1] The document is dated to the equivalent of what many scholars believe to be 71–72 CE. That means it was composed toward the end of the Sicarii community at Masada, shortly before the fortress was captured by the Romans. The document records the husband's name as Joseph and the wife's – like mine – Miriam. Both are among the most common names in the Second Temple period. Out of respect for Joseph and Miriam of Masada, I have kept their true names, although I concede, this book emerged partly out of the desire to explore how a present-day Miriam might have responded to the devastating choices an ancient Miriam faced. How they came to be divorced, and how the scroll recording their divorce reached the Judean desert cave where it was found by archaeologists some 2,000 years later, I drew from my imagination.

1. R. de Vaux, J. T. Milik, and P. Benoit, *Les Grottes de Murabaʿat,* Discoveries in the Judean Desert II (Oxford, 1961); H. M. Cotton and A. Yardeni, *The Aramaic and Greek Documents from Nahal Hever and Other Sites* (Oxford, 1997).

My deepest thanks go to Arik, Maya and Nili for devotion and encouragement at every turn, and to Tania, Paul and Maya who read the manuscript and offered loving and priceless counsel. Thanks to Brian Schultz, who read and critiqued the manuscript when he was a student in Jerusalem. I am also grateful to Michal O'Dwyer for listening and offering suggestions, and to Ashirah Yosefah and Chaim Natan Firszt for editing the book. Special thanks to Eva Marie Everson for her friendship and expert guidance, and to Linda Shepherd and Cheri Cowell. The ancient document pictured on the cover is the writ of divorce from which the plot of this book emerged. The photograph appears by permission of the Israel Antiquities Authority, with thanks to Yael Barschak for her cooperation.

Prologue

JAN. 21, 1951, BETHLEHEM

Two battered Fords, their Jordanian police markings barely visible under a layer of couscous-colored mud from the last rainstorm, maneuvered slowly out a narrow alleyway and emerged on the edge of town. In the lead car were Hannan Farhan and Hassan 'Id of the Ta'amirah Bedouin tribe. Following close behind, in the second car, were Father Roland de Vaux, head of Jerusalem's École Biblique, and Gerald Lankester Harding, director of the Jordanian Department of Antiquities.

"Does he *aim* for the potholes, I wonder?" Harding mused aloud, grabbing on to the door handle in an attempt to stabilize his angular frame. In response, De Vaux raised his palms in mock surrender to the bone-jarring bumps that were by now so familiar he thought he might give them names. Names whose origins would one day be forgotten, like those the Arabs gave the biblical mountains around them.

The little convoy made its way eastward, past the last of the greening wheat and barley fields, toward the prearranged meeting place at Jabal Muntar, the "mountain of the guards" where, thousands of years ago, the Temple priests in Jerusalem would dispatch the doomed ritual scapegoat that bore the sins of Israel.

Two more mounted *shurta* were waiting to take over the task of escorting and protecting the foreign scholars. The mode of transportation changed at this point too. The motorcars were left behind, and the

Dominican priest and the British scholar mounted donkeys for the next leg of the journey. Three hours into the trip the donkeys, too, became useless. From that point on, the trail that wound treacherously through Wadi Murabba'at could be navigated only on foot.

Since the Ta'amira Bedouin had stumbled across the first of the Dead Sea Scrolls at Qumran four years before, the number of brittle fragments in the Scrollery in the basement of the Rockefeller Museum had increased from a few dozen to several hundred. The international team of scholars, Abbeys Starchy, Milik and Barthelemy, Professor Allegro and the others were hard at work on the laborious task of piecing them together in order to properly transcribe and finally, translate them without access to those who, in some other world, would be the most natural of de Vaux's colleagues, among them the Hebrew University's Professor Sukenik, two miles and a universe away on the other side of the barbed wire and minefields that divided Jerusalem between the Hashemite Kingdom of Jordan and the newborn State of Israel.

But two months ago, the Parisian-born De Vaux had received a visitor. It was Khalil Iskander Sharir, better known as Kando, the Bethlehem antiquities dealer who had, some three years before, mediated between the ivory towers of Jerusalem and the tents of the Judean Desert Bedouin for the purchase of the original batch of Dead Sea Scrolls. The houseman showed Kando directly to De Vaux's study.

After the requisite Middle Eastern amenities had been disposed of, and the houseman had set two tiny cups of steaming aromatic coffee before them, Kando finally announced the reason for his visit.

"I have some more fragments from Qumran."

The gaunt merchant proceeded to unwrap a layer of newspaper, damp with the vapors of a Jerusalem winter morning, from around a cardboard box. Wordlessly, he pushed it across the table at De Vaux. He waited while the priest took in the contents: a few blackened fragments of leather and several shreds of darkened papyrus. De Vaux raised one aristocratic eyebrow. The game had begun, or rather, it continued.

"From the first cave at Qumran? Really?" De Vaux responded dryly, making no attempt to disguise the doubt in his voice.

"That is an unexpected windfall indeed," the scholar continued. The Qumran fragments had become De Vaux's oldest and most intimate friends; one glance at Kando's offering was enough to tell him: these were not from Qumran. His expression still bland, he removed a handkerchief from the pocket of his white cassock, peeled off his horned-rim glasses, polishing imaginary smudges away with slow, deliberate motions. He peered into the box again, showing just the right, slight amount of interest. Finally, he spoke.

"I am not sure that the Department of Antiquities can afford another purchase at this stage."

Kando's own inscrutable visage did justice to his skill as a merchant, developed over years of negotiating under just such circumstances. He folded his arms, leaned one elbow on the table, and cupped his chin in one hand. A long index finger came to rest on his small mustache, groomed to a careful square covering the space beneath his nostrils. He made no move to rise or take the box back.

"Of course," said De Vaux, "if it should turn out that these finds originated in another location, and if we could be shown that location, I imagine that would put a different light on things."

More cups of coffee, more roundabout discussion. Finally Kando was persuaded to reveal the true source of his latest find. It was Wadi Murabḅa'at, eleven miles south of the first cave of Qumran. Negotiations had moved toward to a quick and favorable conclusion from that point on, and so here they were at Wadi Murabba'at, one of the most inaccessible places in Jordan's Judean Desert. And yet, on this January morning as the sun rose higher on the little party rounding the last curve in the trail, they saw they were not alone. Harding rubbed his eyes in disbelief, but insisted on counting as thirty-four Bedouin burst out of a cave on the north flank of the wadi like a flock of startled starlings, scattering in every direction. Harding came across the last of the diggers still energetically going at it, in the depths of the cave, abandoned by his fellow raiders and too busy earning his living to be aware of the arrival of the dignitaries from Jerusalem.

From January 21 until March 1, a narrow rock ledge fronting the caves that became known as Murabba'at 1, 2, 3, and 4 was home to De Vaux and Harding, together with eight laborers from Bethlehem and two foremen from the Rockefeller Museum. The winter of 1951 was a wet one. The clouds that had formed over the Mediterranean floated heavily eastward, crossing the watershed in Jerusalem still potent with rain. The rainfall turned the desert into an intricately designed and riotously colored oriental carpet of wildflowers and grasses. But it also washed out the trail by which the men had reached Wadi Murabba'at, turning the three-hour trip back to civilization into a perilous daylong trek. It loosened rocks from the cliff above them and brought them crashing down on their two-man tents, set precariously on the rocky porch. Sometimes, a gray Judean sky left them an offering – crystal ponds of drinking water. More than once it turned the streambed below them into a raging river. Food came by truck via Jerusalem twice a week as far as it could go, with donkeys at the ready to bear the burden until the point when only two-legged porters would do.

Just west of Cave I was the grotto where Kando had told them the fragments in the cardboard box had been found. The cave's main chamber was a muscle-cramping four feet high, lower in places where the ceiling had collapsed in a long-ago earthquake. Sure enough, even before their eyes had become used to the dark, they saw fragments of papyrus lying everywhere, on the rocks, or just under them. Many were chewed to pieces by the coneys that had turned them into nests. Their immediate task was to carefully scour the entrance chamber, hoping to find a corner or a boulder neglected by the energetic "excavators" that had preceded them.

The gloom of what soon proved to be a labyrinth beckoned. A narrow rock chimney was one of two that the Bedouin had transformed into a busy route of passage between the main vault of the cave and what turned out to be its lower level. The archaeologists took the better part of an hour to inch their way through it. As they regained their bearings, the dim light of their kerosene lamp revealed a level of black soil, above which was a layer of ash. De Vaux knelt down and probed the ash gently. "More Chalcolithic fragments here," he said, opening his hand to reveal a few potsherds to Harding. Harding, close behind, muttered in agreement.

"Wait a minute," said De Vaux, his practiced eye falling on another item. The tip of his thumb and forefinger once again disappeared into the ancient layer. When they withdrew, they were holding an Egyptian scarab. De Vaux and Harding looked at one another in amazement.

"This is going to take some explaining," Harding finally said. De Vaux placed the scarab carefully in the rucksack slung over one shoulder. But the familiar flutter of anticipation he had felt when he dropped from the chimney to the lower chamber had been replaced by resignation. The impossible mix of artifacts, which 4,000 years of history should have separated by several feet of soil and debris, told him what he needed to know.

"No it won't. They've gotten to everything," De Vaux stated flatly.

The Frenchman's eyes roamed restlessly over the chamber, frustrated by the poor light. But Harding urged him back to the mound of soil and ash.

"*Ta'alu,*" Harding shouted up the chimney, ordering the waiting laborers to come down. Two more hours of work brought them to another layer of black soil. Then, a foot-thick layer of Roman-era antiquities: the gift of an unmistakably undisturbed stratum. Fragments of pottery, pieces of leather and cloth and wood, as well as the rarest treasure of all. No, neither precious metal nor stones, but a find of infinitely greater value – a document. They were to discover that it had been inscribed, by an ancient and forgotten hand, with the dry details of the divorce agreement between one Joseph and his wife Miriam – issued at Masada in 71 CE, two years before the fall of the doomed fortress and the death of its inhabitants. From that document, the story you are about to read was born, bringing the ill-fated Joseph and the bold and determined Miriam, and her descendants, back to life.

Chapter 1

OCTOBER 71 CE

The flame of the single clay lamp in its niche was tiny, but it cast a monstrous shadow against the plastered stone wall, mimicking Joseph's every move as he placed the scroll into the shaking hands of his wife. His own hands, warm in spite of the chill of the ebbing night, remained cupped tightly around hers. Miriam locked his eyes with her own, willing him to let her go so she could unroll the parchment for one last time.

She knew its terms. Her dowry was to be returned to her, together with fourfold compensation for lost or damaged property. She had declared no such property, but the scribe they had engaged insisted on writing out this additional clause with all the self-importance he could muster.

"And at any time that you say to me, I shall replace for you the document, as long as I am alive." Joseph had been adamant about the inclusion of this sentence. Miriam remembered the scribe, bent low over the document as he took down Joseph's dictation, glancing up with surprise when he heard these words. Now, as the words danced in the flicker of the lamplight, the finality of their meaning coiled itself around Miriam's heart like a viper poised to strike. In spite of her promise to herself, her green-gold eyes glittered with tears.

Joseph saw her falter, and he seized her firmly by the shoulders, just as he had done when he first suggested the idea to her.

"But why, why must you do it this way?" Miriam had cried out in anguish then, when he revealed his plan.

"Because," he had answered quietly, "when I leave the fortress, I will never return. I do not know if there is anyone left in Jerusalem to help me fulfill the mission Elazar has entrusted to me. If our enemies among our own people are the only ones to have survived, I will not last out the day I am discovered, and no one will care whether our community ever finds out what happened to me. You would become *aguna*."

Such a woman, her husband's whereabouts unknown, was doomed to disgrace, robbed of her future. She could remarry only if her husband reappeared to divorce her, or if his death could be proven beyond all doubt. Though a widow for all intents and purposes, she would remain chained – *aguna* – to her husband for the rest of her life.

Joseph released her as suddenly as he had grabbed hold of her, breaking abruptly into her thoughts of the past.

"It is time."

He bent to fasten the final knot on his woven cord carry-basket, hoisting it onto his shoulder. He turned to face his wife and slipped his arms through hers. Lacing his fingers together at the small of her back, he pulled her toward him in the embrace she knew so well. But this time it was she who broke away, lowering her head to hide the tears.

"Away now, or first light will be upon you before you reach the bottom of the path," she choked out. Daylight was a familiar, pitiless adversary, and Joseph instinctively placed his hand against the folds of his broad belt, feeling beneath his woolen cloak for the *sica*, the dagger that all the warriors carried. He turned, thrust aside the door curtain, and stepped over the threshold of the two-room dwelling the couple shared with Miriam's mother.

Joseph's back was tall as he crossed the courtyard, stepped through the outer door and disappeared from view.

Chapter 2

66 CE

Miriam had been so small when it all started. As often as her father Jonathan would let her, she had accompanied him to the Court of Israel in the Holy Temple, her hand proudly held in his. Wedged tightly among a forest of legs, she listened, absorbing more than anyone would have believed her child's mind could grasp as opinions on the Law, the Prophets and events of the day darted and flew over her head like swallows in the pink evening sky. People would sigh at the cleverness of one man's point, grumble with disapproval at another's, and the incense-perfumed air of the Temple court seemed to glow with the vigor of the debate.

Discussion always moved, all too quickly, from the sacred scriptures to the burning question of the day: How should the Jews respond to the daily indignities and oppression of their people by their Roman overlords? Boisterous dialogue would quickly deteriorate into angry dispute. Too soft-spoken a speaker would be drowned out by the Zealots and the even more severe Sicarii, bellowing the words of Jeremiah, "a curse on him who keeps his sword from bloodshed!" The upraised fists and the downturned mouths, the fulminating eyes and seething tones of these men were more than enough to make a little girl cower more deeply within the folds of her father's robe. Sometimes, his hand would unobtrusively slip down to cover her ears, which served only to amplify the sound of an expletive left hanging ominously in the air at the end of more than one debate. Friends who found themselves on opposite sides of the issues would force themselves to part from each other more civilly, with only a shrug and a sigh. By the time Miriam was five, she could make a rueful smile appear on the faces of her elders when, in her singsong child's voice, she mimicked the most popular saying of the day: "One must pronounce a blessing for evil as well as good."

They had all heard these words often enough. Most of the sages refused to sanction the anger that surged among the people. Without doubt, they said, the Holy Scriptures taught that neither political maneuvering nor armed resistance would bring redemption. And that was the polar opposite of what Miriam's father Jonathan and the other Sicarii saw in the sacred texts.

Shortly after Passover of Miriam's sixteenth year, their visits to the Temple ceased. By that time, she no longer had need of what her exasperated father used to call "Miriam's favorite question": *Why*. She knew. The screams that tore out of the Upper City market for days on end, when no one dared leave the house, told her. The family passed those terrible days together in the *triclinium*. In this room, where fine meals had once been served, the family stared at each other across an empty table. The servants, who had perfected the art of waiting, immobile as the conquerors' statues until called upon, now jumped at every sound.

When the noise finally abated, the housekeeper booted two terrified kitchen maids out the door to seek food. They returned with tales that made Miriam's empty stomach churn. Crows, they reported frantically to the rest of the servants, not caring that their young mistress was within earshot, were pecking the desiccated eyes from the broken bodies that hung from the crucifixes lining the streets. It seemed that Rome's avaricious governor Florus would have his revenge against the Jews for the riots that had destroyed the market, riots that he had gleefully instructed his own agents to instigate.

Their queen, Berenice herself, went to Florus. She had begged him to cease and desist, but she had barely escaped with her life from her audience with the madman. As spring wore into summer, there were only a few days when anyone dared leave the house. Florus dogged his subordinates to find any excuse, to use any means, to extract money and profit from his subjects. People making their way from home to market or synagogue were attacked and left for dead, or whole households and workshops were plundered in the dead of night. Some feared to leave their homes; many who dared to venture forth were never seen again.

Jonathan himself braved the bleeding streets only once that summer – to hear King Agrippa speak to the people at the old Hasmonean palace courtyard. Miriam had never seen her father's face as dark with anger as when he returned from that assembly. Over nearly bare bowls at the dining table that night, he told what he had heard.

"The king thinks we should consider ourselves no better than the Gauls or the Germans," he fumed. "I could not believe my ears when I heard him: 'What confidence is it that elevates you to oppose the Romans?' he said! What about confidence in God, Whom alone we seek to serve? That is of no consequence? But what can we expect of the man who continues the traitorous line of his great-grandfather, who transformed obeisance to the conqueror into his greatest skill! Agrippa and his sister-queen were *weeping*. It was a sickening sight. People would have said anything to comfort them."

"And no one protested?" Elisheva asked.

"Oh, yes, people protested – they protested that all we really wanted was to rid ourselves of Florus, not of the Romans."

"And what of our party?"

Jonathan lowered his voice and glanced around furtively. Even in their own home. "The Sicarii will respond when the time is right."

For a while, though, it seemed that rebellion was to be averted. Jonathan was often away, seeing, he told Elisheva, to the renewal of his business interests as calm seemed to be returning to the city. Jerusalem's citizens had begun to rebuild the homes and shops that had been damaged in the riots, and Jewish officials were appointed to collect the tribute demanded by Florus. Elisheva never ceased to worry. She had good reason. Jonathan was even then making his first acquaintance with the fortress of Masada.

Unlike others of his social status, Jonathan was impatient for war against the Romans to break out. Despite the risk to his fortune, he had devoted himself to the greater cause, and he yearned to show the peacemongers that there was no compromising with Rome. He did not have long to wait. Just before the middle of Av, the hottest month of the summer, Eleazar son of Ananias the High Priest convinced the priests to end the long-standing custom of sacrifice for the wellbeing of the emperor, and took control of the Temple. This the men in power among the Jews, the supporters of Agrippa, could not abide. Supported by the Romans, they took up positions in the Upper City.

The battle raged for over two weeks. Jew against Roman, Jew against Jew. Jonathan had left to join the fighters, and Miriam, Elisheva, and the servants cowered in the inner rooms of the house, unable even there to shut out the din of the clashing of swords and lances and the crashing of ballistae missiles hurled from the Roman catapults that smashed the buildings held by the rebels in the Lower City. But the rebels gained constant ground, setting fire to the high priest's mansion and to the royal palace, the symbol of capitulation to Rome. They even burned the archives containing records of debts of poor Jews, who then looked upon the Sicarii with more adoration than ever, and flocked to their cause. Finally the Romans fled to regroup outside the city, leaving the Jews to fight each other. There seemed no end in sight.

Then one morning, Miriam's mother burst into her sleeping chamber and shook her awake excitedly. She had covered her hair as she always did for an outing. Even with the sand of sleep still in her eyes, Miriam could see the fine purple linen peeping out from under Elisheva's cloak her Temple finery.

"Hurry, Daughter, up! Up! Your father is home. We are going up to the Temple! The fighting is over! Jerusalem is ours!" Every sentence was accompanied by more excited shaking until she saw by her daughter's eyes, wide with amazement, that her words had sunk in. "We will wait for you at the door. Hurry!" Miriam barely caught the cloak her mother removed from the hook in the wall and flung at her as she left the room.

After days of confinement, the sunlight blinded Miriam momentarily as she joined her parents and the servants outside. Dust swirled through the air, kicked up by hundreds of people streaming by on their way to the Temple. Some chattered with furious gaiety of the offerings they would bring to the Temple now that the capitulators among their own people had been defeated and the days of sacrificing in the emperor's name had finally and forever ended. Others moved their lips silently in prayers of thanksgiving that they had survived the slaughter.

By the time they entered the eastern gate, the Women's Court was almost full. People jostled each other, jockeying for a better position. Everyone's eyes were on the magnificent Nicanor Gates, gleaming in all of their bronze glory. But it was not the beauty of the gates that riveted them. It was the figure that had stepped over the monumental threshold.

The man stood motionless. Row by row, family by family, as people realized who he was, waves of silence engulfed the crowd. Miriam dodged a big man in front of her until she found a crack in the wall of people. Squinting through it, she saw the king, in his most magnificent robes, dwarfed by the gigantic doorway. The king? How could it be? Questions hurled through the crowd. The king had been ignominiously dethroned by the righteous among the people. He would not dare show his face here today. But then who could it be?

"Who is it, Father?" Miriam tugged at her father's robe impatiently.

"It is our leader, Menahem ben Judah," Jonathan answered, his voice full of reverence. Jonathan was one of the few wealthy allies of the aging hero of the Sicarii who now stood before the people. He had fought side by side every hour of the past month with Menahem, who had drawn his first Roman blood sixty years ago fighting Governor Quirinius. Before the people could recover from their shock, Menahem spoke.

"My brothers and sisters, hear my words! Ananias the High Priest wanted nothing more than to give our beloved Temple to the Romans. Now justice has been served and Ananias has been executed. But know this: his son Eleazar has betrayed you no less. He has already begun to negotiate to give our hard-won freedom away, back to the conqueror. And what could anyone believe that will bring us? Temporary tranquility that is nothing more than permanent servitude! Follow me, and I will lead you to the true freedom you deserve!" Menahem punctuated each sentence with effusive gestures and paced intentionally so that with every move his garments sparkled majestically in the sun.

The High Priest was dead? At the hands of fellow Jews, Menahem and the Sicarii? The crowd murmured and seethed, and began to surge forward. Jonathan had begun to move forward too, to reach Menahem and help shepherd him to safety. Some people around them, who knew

Jonathan of Hanablata and his affinities all too well, glared at him. He met their gaze unflinchingly.

Elisheva acted. She grabbed Jonathan with one hand and Miriam with the other.

"Jonathan," Elisheva said sharply to her husband. "The girl. Please." The pleading look in his wife's eyes and the steady pressure of her hand on his arm thwarted his intention to help his leader. The crowd continued to propel them for ward moving inexorably toward the Nicanor Gates and the hapless Menahem. The family broke away through a side door of the Women's Court, together with a scattering of other escapees. The tap-tap of their fleeing footsteps echoed sharply against the high walls of the Hulda Gates exit tunnel.

It was only later, after they and the other Sicarii refugees from Jerusalem had reached Masada, that Miriam learned the outcome of that dreadful day. The mob had dragged Menahem from the Temple courts to the Kidron Valley, stripped him of his kingly garments and beaten him to a bloody pulp.

Chapter 3

MASADA, 67 CE

"Under no condition or circumstance! I said no!" Jonathan was bellowing again. He rearranged his robes haughtily around him, upsetting the clay bowl full of parched wheat perched on the mat separating Miriam's mother from her father.

"Jonathan, be careful, please! That is the last of the parched wheat until the New Moon!"

Without taking her eyes off her husband, Elisheva motioned to Miriam to sweep the wheat back into the bowl. The louder he bellowed, the closer she was to getting her wish. At least that was the way it had been in their old life.

The fabled hanging palace of Herod was still magnificent, though no one other than a few soldiers serving his great-grandson Agrippa at this lonely desert outpost had been inside for nearly one hundred years. What could possibly be wrong with a few comforts, especially for the leadership? Was it a crime to live in pleasant surroundings? It was worth incurring her husband's wrath, Elisheva thought, to try one last time to get her wish.

"It is hard enough to lead some sort of normal life on this dry tabletop of a mountain, without Miriam and the other youngsters having to lift and carry the rocks to build rooms for us. Especially not when there are perfectly good quarters to be had in this and the other old palace. And the casemate walls are fine as living quarters almost just as they are."

"No." Jonathan's voice had gone quiet with determination. For the rebel leader, the discussion was clearly not about whether the roof over their heads was to be aristocratic red tiles or simple mud and straw.

"I have had my fill of luxurious houses. What good did our fine house in Jerusalem do us? We should have left it all behind years ago, before we were forced to flee like rats. Living as we did in Jerusalem, we were no better than some of our leaders, drunk with their power over us, and the sages, with their fine talk of "moral improvement" – here Jonathan's voice dripped with sarcasm – "while they misled the people into believing that they could continue living as loyal Jews under the Romans."

Jonathan's face soured at the memory, as if the food he had just eaten had been sprinkled with too much sumaq.

"Bah." He spat the word out, making Miriam and Elisheva jump before launching into the monologue they already knew by heart.

"*They* could continue living under the Romans, as long as they kept their fine houses and their audiences in the Temple courts. Even now, they probably spend their days weeping in the streets of Jerusalem instead of keeping up the struggle, whining that our fighting amongst ourselves was our downfall. *They* and their weak posturing before the enemy were our true downfall. But thank God that, although we have lost Menahem, we still have Elazar to lead us. We must set an example, not bring shame upon your own nephew by living better than others here."

"Enough, Father, stop arguing," came the clear young voice.

Only Miriam could talk to her father in this way.

"We know what old King Herod's palaces mean to you." She soothed. "You are right, they are not for us. I will do my part, as you wish, to build rooms for us on the south side of the fortress, as far as you like from the palaces. But please, no more arguing."

Jonathan watched for that stubborn set of his daughter's jaw that told him that he was about to face another pointless standoff against her. Sometimes he thought her skill at taking the other side of whatever subject was under discussion would put him in his grave. He continued to eye his daughter warily from beneath his bushy brows. But she was uncharacteristically silent, and her slender hand reached out to cover his gnarled one. He coughed, rose with difficulty, and left the room. Miriam knew he was mollified, and was stealing some pleasure from the moment, until her mother spoke sharply to her.

"You will not bring back your father's beloved Jerusalem by pretending to be something you are not, Daughter. Let him continue to argue with you. Some things, at least, should not change." Miriam looked wordlessly at her mother.

She knew that everything already had.

But it was not to be an argument with his headstrong daughter that put Jonathan into his grave. It happened the following year. In spite of his standing as a senior leader of the community, and his advanced age, he refused to give up the chance to go out with the younger men to seek supplies for the community. While they were herding back the goats they had taken from the flocks of the Judean highland villagers, a misstep sent Jonathan plunging to his death from the heights of a barren wilderness crag. His broken body was retrieved by the other members of the raiding party, and laid to rest in a low-browed cavity in the rock above the trail in sight of the fortress.

When they returned to Masada, the men broke the news to Jonathan's wife and daughter. His companions took Miriam up to a tower in the western fortress wall and pointed out to her the cave where Jonathan lay. It was one among dozens that riddled the scarp. But Miriam never forgot which one it was. Its dark eye gazed steadily back at her whenever she turned toward it.

Chapter 4

Elazar ben Yair, the leader of their little community, and Miriam's cousin, was her guardian now. And he did not intend to let either the nature of their lives on the desert plateau or his position, deter him from the most important of a guardian's missions. One day, after the initial month-long mourning period for her father was over, Elazar stalked into the little courtyard Miriam and Elisheva shared with four other families. He found Miriam bent over her bundle of burnet sprigs, sweeping the dust from the courtyard. He was silent until she had unfolded her elegant form to its full height. Miriam was almost as tall as her cousin and unconsciously, he pulled himself up a little straighter.

"I have found you a husband," he announced. Looking down at her, he continued, "He knows of your great intellect and the fine education your father, may his memory be a blessing, has provided you. In spite of this, and although you are nearly seventeen, not as young as some, he has agreed to wed you. It is a good match."

Miriam should have been used to it, but she could not help wincing at the bite of her cousin's words. She knew that he could not understand why she continued to surround herself with the scrolls of law and wisdom, astronomy, and mathematics that her father had long ago introduced her to. Elazar had always laughed at her clumsy efforts at anything when she was a child, and as she grew older, long after her efforts were clumsy no more, he never missed an opportunity to disparage her. Her insistence on airing her opinions, behavior that her father had accepted with loving exasperation and secret pride, Elazar saw as undermining his authority. Miriam was a thorn in his side. Anxious to see her busied with the bearing and raising of children, Elazar would have begun his campaign to place her under some other man's protection the day after Jonathan's death, if custom had permitted it.

But there was Elisheva, Miriam's mother, elder sister to Elazar's father, to contend with. Elisheva had adamantly refused to allow Miriam to be married off to any of the men Elazar suggested when he first broached the subject. "My husband Jonathan, peace be upon him," she would intone piously, "liked to tell the story of Samson's marriage – how both of his parents went with him in search of a bride. My poor dead Jonathan would not want a groom that I did not approve of." Enlisting the authority of her dead husband, so soon after his passing, especially with head bowed and thin wringing hands clasped sorrowfully over her concave breasts, had the desired effect on Elazar. For a few weeks, he dropped the matter.

But life had become too uncertain to allow the young woman the same freedom she had enjoyed when her father was alive to protect her. This Miriam realized when she saw the determination in her cousin's cold eyes as she faced him in the courtyard that morning.

"Who is this groom to be?" Miriam asked warily.

"It is Joseph son of Naqsan," her cousin replied.

Elazar added that, as custom allowed, Miriam could wait one year, until she was eighteen years old, to move into her new husband's home, when the marriage would be consummated. He turned on his heel and left without another word.

Miriam began immediately to take stock of her situation. She knew who this Joseph was. He had been with Elazar and Menahem the Galilean since the beginning, and had risked his life with her father and Elazar when they came to Masada the first time. Disguised as Roman legionaries, they had taken over the fortress, overpowering and outnumbering the fortress guards, who had been dozing at the main gate or scattered uselessly through the complex. They broke all the weapons they needed out of King Herod's old storehouses and returned to Jerusalem to take back the Holy City from the Romans. After Menahem's murder, and Elazar's retreat to Masada, Miriam recalled hearing that this man Joseph had stayed on in Jerusalem, but only long enough to convince the other Sicarii that Masada – a towering desert plateau where no power on earth could reach them – was the perfect base of operations from which to continue their struggle against Rome, and anyone who stood in their way.

Miriam had even exchanged a few words with Joseph from time to time, when necessary, neither more nor less than with anyone else in their crowded community. But now that a marriage had been arranged and the *ketuba* signed, things were very different. During the months of their engagement, Joseph became a regular guest at their Sabbath table. Miriam soon understood that with the death of her father, these meals were another part of her life that had changed beyond recognition. Elazar now occupied the host's seat, flanked by his subordinates, and instead of the lively banter that despite their circumstances had still sometimes flowed when her father had sat there, their food was seasoned with bitter discourse and a sour aroma of dread wafted over it.

One particular Sabbath eve, Miriam said aloud for the first time what until that moment had only been whispered – and never at this table. "Elazar, what if the legion comes?" Joseph had only begun to realize what his future bride was capable of saying or doing, but he knew his commander very well. He watched as Miriam's words roused Elazar into a froth of invective. Joseph decided to take a sudden and intense interest in the remnants of the Sabbath meal on his plate, as if the bones of the dried fish from Herod's old stores had suddenly begun swimming in the delectable fish sauce none of them had seen for years now. He stole a glance upward in time to see that Elisheva was gasping open-mouthed as her nephew spewed a stream of obscenities at the Romans.

Elisheva finally recovered her composure. This was *her* home. "Elazar, it is the Sabbath," she interrupted firmly.

Her nephew made no overt sign that he heard her. But he rose and left the table, signaling his lieutenants to follow. Very little that went on in the fortress escaped his notice. Miriam had only voiced what he knew others were thinking. It was time for the work to begin.

The men followed Elazar to the synagogue, empty at this late hour of the Sabbath eve. First, as always, he swore them to secrecy. Then he began to instruct them on the reinforcement of the king's old fortifications. He knew the weaknesses and strengths of every sector of wall as he knew those of each of his lieutenants. The western side of the fortress was most crucial. Here, like everywhere else, it towered over the valley floor. But months before Elazar had drawn the men's attention to the point on the west where the desert slopes below crept fatefully close to the base of the plateau. That, he had told them, was where the Roman army would show off its legendary siege tactics, which for once would prove useless. With God on their side, and their position superior, the conqueror's battering rams would come to naught and the Roman soldiers would dash themselves to pieces against the iron will of the rebels. Imbued with new hope and strength of purpose, Elazar's commanders left the synagogue and headed to their homes.

After Elazar's abrupt departure, Miriam tried to escape the echo of her cousin's vitriolic words by busying herself with the mundane task of helping Elisheva clear away the dishes. She then shook out the eating mat, rolled it up and stored it under the bench. But her mind was racing. Her elder cousin's eruption had suddenly made it easier for her reconsider her initial response to his plan that she marry young Joseph. Life, any life, which lay ahead of her outside of this household would be one in which she would for the first time be under Elazar's thumb at least no more than anyone else in the community. That alone would be a relief. Her life would be built around supporting the work of this Joseph, who had, after all, always been soft-spoken and courteous to her. In fact, Joseph seemed the opposite of Elazar in everything but the driven, fiery dedication to the cause. And she could, she had to, continue to embrace that cause for as long as it took to break out of the fortress and head to Jerusalem to help restore it to its former glory. Then, she had not the slightest doubt, they would rebuild their lives and the life of their people in the Holy City. She lost no time in reporting her change of heart to Elazar as soon as she saw him the next day. Still fuming over the liberties she had taken at the Sabbath table, a slight tilt of his head was his only indication that he heard her.

Now she set about cultivating positive feelings for her future husband. But as her affection for Joseph grew deeper, so did the fear that she might not see her wedding day. Sometimes, without warning, her intended would disappear for days. From the talk of the women, Miriam learned that he and a few of the most daring of the men had gone up to the west country to lie in wait for passing Roman patrols.

The most talked-about of Joseph's raids had happened during Passover, the year after Miriam's family had come to Masada. He and his small band of warriors had traveled northward to the oasis-town of Ein Gedi. Though the Jews who owned the balsam groves now worked their own land as tenants for Procurator Flavius Silva and his cronies, they could still make a fine profit thanks to their exclusive knowhow in manufacturing the lucrative salve from the sap of their precious trees. Indeed, Joseph and his men had returned from Ein Gedi laden with food and money, and even jars full of the prized salve itself, which Elazar ordered placed under lock and key in the king's old storehouses. Unfortunately, the raiders reported, they had met with resistance; some of their own had died and they had had to kill some of the Ein Gedi men. But everyone was satisfied with the additions to their larder, and no one sought further details.

Two of the young women of their community had lost their own grooms in just such a raid. Miriam had had to listen to the same humiliation in the voice of each as they told her how her cousin Elazar had entered their homes in the company of the elders. He had come to inform them, he had said in his typical bullish manner, of a new ruling: Since a betrothed virgin was permitted to her groom from the day of their engagement, and because their grooms had died before the wedding ceremony, the bride would have to wait at least three months before remarrying to determine if their union had produced issue.

By the blush of the first young woman as she told Miriam her tale, Miriam knew that such a waiting period might actually be necessary. But the second young woman had shyly confided that "issue" was not even a remote possibility. "In this, we are sisters," Miriam thought wryly to herself, for hardly a word had been exchanged between her and Joseph during the year of their engagement, much less any intimacies.

But it was now almost thirteen months since the day their marriage document was signed and her wedding night had arrived. She was accompanied to her husband's room by Elisheva and some of the other older women, singing softly the ancient words, "a voice of joy, a voice of gladness, the voice of the bridegroom, the voice of the bride." It was a pale shadow of the joyful, lamp-lit marriage celebration she had imagined as a girl, but in keeping with the austerity Elazar had imposed on the community as the months passed.

The months since that night, which had ended in the gray chill of her husband's dawn departure had flown by as swiftly as migrating storks. Perhaps that was why all Miriam could remember now of Joseph were his eyes, black as ravens' wings, and the love that radiated from them that still had the power to warm her soul.

In the early months after his departure, Miriam would stand on the northern ramparts, where she had a good view of the roads from both west and north. Word had come that he had sailed to Alexandria, to expand the circle of the rebellion even to that great city. But still, she hoped he would return. Shielding her eyes, she would squint into the sunlight, imagining a hundred times that she could see him, a tiny figure in the distance, exhausted, perhaps even injured, on his way home to her. But her hopes were dashed when, one day as she looked out at the road, it was not Joseph she saw approaching, but Rome's thundering legion, pouring, cohort after cohort down through the wilderness. Then came the relentless construction, and within a few short months, the enemy had thrown a siege wall around the base of the plateau. For the first time, the fortress-dwellers were completely cut off from the outside world.

Nothing could stop the conqueror's forces. Not even the advent of the desert winter, when the rock-fanged gorges around Masada flooded without warning, taking the lives of hundreds of legionaries at a time. Still the enemy persisted. Eventually, they not only encircled the entire base of the mountain with a wall, but also constructed a cyclopean earthen ramp, which rose to attach itself to the base of their western fortress wall. As the grasses and flowers of winter withered on the slopes, the enemy pushed and pulled their monstrous battering ram to the top of the ramp.

Mothers forbade their children to leave their dwellings to preserve them from the enemy arrows and spears that now rained down upon them from the tower atop the battering ram.

From the day the ram began its unremitting bombardment of the wall, Elazar saw to it that every member of the community was involved in some aspect of fortress defense. During the last few days, with Herod's old western periphery wall trembling with each blow of the ram, Elazar added a new, backbreaking labor: Every able-bodied person was to help rip the wooden rafters out of the western palace roof, run with them to the wall and pile them against it to shore it up. At the same time, another team worked to raise a parallel wall of rafters a short three *ammas* from it within the fortress. The women ran back and forth to their small gardens, filling baskets with soil that until only the week before they had patiently goaded into producing radishes, chicory, mallows and turnips. The beds now lay churned and desolate, robbed to fill the space between the two wooden walls.

It was working, people told each other, as the battering ram continued to land its blows on the outer wall, shifting the earth in their inner wall into what they believed was a solid, impenetrable mass.

Chapter 5

15 NISSAN (APRIL) 73 CE

Just as Miriam had done every morning since she saw her husband for the last time, she bent to the task of kindling the fire. Her calloused fingertips no longer felt the prick of the dry, thorn-studded, prickly burnet, and in no time she had a well-placed pile of twigs in the base of the cone-shaped mud and straw oven. A few skilled turns of the fire-stick had sparks flying. The fire smoked dully in the moist air, then caught. One by one, Miriam placed small acacia branches on the kindling. She nursed the fire until dancing flames were reflected in the depths of her amber-olive eyes.

The steady whisper-whistle of her mother's breathing floated out from their sleeping quarters and told her she still had a few more minutes for her scrolls. She pulled aside the curtain from a wall niche, and selected one from among those that lined the wooden shelf within. Cradling it, she lowered herself with unconscious grace onto the rough-cut wooden bench nearest the doorway. Miriam unrolled the scroll, and before the Hebrew letters of the book of Genesis could come into focus, like a prayer, she invited thoughts of her father, Jonathan of Hanablata, who had given her the gift of learning, and to whom no farewell was ever said.

Thanks to Jonathan, Miriam's education had begun long before her family reached the fortress of Masada, back in the days when their lives in Jerusalem still resembled those of all other Jewish Jerusalemites.

Miriam's life, though, had always differed in one respect. Other girls worked their tongues in gossip faster than they worked the shuttle they passed back and forth through the linen garment taking shape at their looms. Their favorite subject: the husband their father would choose for them and what it would mean for their families.

Miriam's father used to hurry her through her daily tasks; he became irritated, she recalled with a smile, if her mother would set her any additional chores. It was not her household skills that interested him, but the world of her mind, which he exhorted her to explore and hone. He tried never to forgo his daily session with her, even when he began to be called away for what he called "consultations." He sat with her patiently as she poured over the small wax tablet on which she etched her first Hebrew letters, her chubby hand grasping the stylus earnestly. How pleased he had been as she grew into young womanhood, and her letters began to flow gracefully across the valuable parchment to which she had eventually graduated.

The daring and beautiful Judith and the courageous Tobit, heroes whom she met in her father's scrolls, became her closest companions. So did the Maccabees, who had wrested their beloved Temple from the clutches of the Seleucid Greeks, restoring it to the worship of the Almighty. Thus Miriam grew up, strong in the knowledge that she too would be valiant and do battle for the Lord.

At Masada, lonely in the wake of Joseph's disappearance, Miriam had made Scripture her own inner wall, a rampart against hopelessness and helplessness. In recent weeks too, until the sun rose and the ram landed its first blows of the day, the scrolls had still given her some measure of comfort. But the moment when the day's thunderous butting began, as it did now, causing even the earthen floor beneath her feet to shudder, her inner wall was breached. Rolling the scroll back up and putting it back in its place she thought sorrowfully that today's flood of memories had not even allowed her a moment to focus on Scripture. That night, Passover would begin. People were waiting for her. She removed the cover from the top of the small oven, and saw the coals glowing red within, ready for her mother to bake the unleavened bread for the Passover feast. "I am leaving now, Mother," she called over her shoulder to the frail figure across the room, which had just begun to stir.

Miriam left their quarters, allowing the placid mask she wore each day to settle over her features as she made her way to the storerooms, to which Elazar had assigned her. Since her marriage, and even more so since Joseph had left, Elazar's attitude toward her had softened considerably. He had grudgingly begun to appreciate the value of her quickness of mind and her way with people. He had turned responsibility over to her for disbursing supplies, which, thanks to the raids on the highland villages to the west, never seemed to run out, even at the height of the siege.

After handing Miriam the pottery sherd inscribed with their name that served as their coupon of entitlement, people would often sit for a few moments to talk. Miriam would pour out the requisite amount of oil, wheat, or barley, and they would pour out their grievances. She knew that Elazar would not hear her out in front of his men – that would have been too much to expect from her obstinate cousin. But when his lieutenants had left him alone in his quarters, Miriam took to bringing these complaints before Elazar in what had become their regular nightly meetings.

At the end of this day's work, too, Miriam went to Elazar, calling his name softly through the curtain that separated his sleeping quarters from his private courtyard. His gruff voice responded instantly. "Come!"

Pulling aside the curtain, Miriam peered into the dimness and found Elazar in his usual place: seated on the only chair in the small room, up against the back wall. The chair was adorned with leather armrests and back, the single concession to her cousin's leadership status. Elazar was leaning forward, elbows on thighs, as if the menacing forces now at the top of the siege ramp were a physical weight on his back. His long hair would have suited a wealthy man with servants to wash and style it, Miriam could not help thinking, if it were not now falling over his face in thin, sooty cords. He cradled a neglected, half-filled cup of wine. Miriam set down the small basket of dried figs she had brought with her on a small stone tray. Lifting the tray together with its wooden tripod, she moved it closer to Elazar. Extricating the cup from his hands, she placed it on the table and sat down on the wooden bench that stood against the opposite wall of the small room.

When he spoke again, his voice scraped the air like a blacksmith's sharpening iron. It was a voice worn raw from past few days' continuous shouted exhortations to the people to complete the new inner wall, convincing them that it would be their salvation. "The people feel strong," Elazar opened, once he became aware of Miriam's presence. "They know the Romans will lose heart when they find that, thanks to the new wall, even their mighty ram cannot prevail against us."

It was Elazar's usual bluster. But no, there was a difference, she thought. Those eyes, whose piercing passion Miriam had seen get a man to throw himself unarmed at a hundred legionaries, now refused to meet her own.

"They believe in you, Elazar. They believe you can lead them to victory," Miriam responded, with as much encouragement as she could muster. But her words sounded hollow and she knew it. Every day this week, their warriors had fallen to the arrows of the legion's sharpshooters stationed in the tower above the battering ram. Elazar raised his head. He smiled crookedly, looking at her from beneath lids as low as executioner's hoods. His next words shocked her.

"But I cannot, dear cousin. I cannot lead them to victory. The enemy will storm Masada any day now. God has taken the victory from us. Surely you, who have never spared me the sting of your tongue, will not now tell me otherwise."

Elazar was oddly calm. He braced his hands against his thighs before rising to his full height, in the manner Miriam had come to recognize meant a decision had been made.

"We shall continue the fight *as if* we can be victorious – until it is abundantly clear to the whole community that the victory will not be ours."

Softly, too softly, he continued. "But I swear by the service in the Holy Temple, I have not fought this long to let my people die by the hand of these wild boars who snort and paw at our walls. I will not be paraded through the streets of the capital of the wicked kingdom like the animals they bring from distant lands to fight before the crowds in the amphitheater."

"Elazar..." Miriam began, uncertain how to proceed. He silenced her with one raised hand. He turned his head away as he spoke.

"God has removed His favor from us. With Jew fighting against Jew, how could it be otherwise? We were warned that this would happen – from the day Menahem strutted in the Temple precincts, the final betrayal of the purity of our cause. I know something now that I did not know then: I cannot escape God's will for us as easily as your husband and I hid from the mob that day. We are His always, as long as we have breath to serve Him.

"This is what I have decided: Before the enemy launches his final onslaught, I want us all to take our own lives. I want us to give them to God."

Miriam had never heard Elazar, or anyone else for that matter, speak in such terms. Confused, she took refuge in silence.

"We shall take our own lives and the lives of our families," he continued, almost crooning. "Does the enemy believe he can already taste the fine vintage of his victory? It will yet turn to gall in his mouth. And from beyond the grave we will have avenged the destruction of God's Holy Temple."

Miriam's thick, dark brows now came together in a single slash of consternation. She rose and backed away from him. "How can you be so certain that God wants us to take our own lives when neither you nor anyone else can say for sure that our lives will be taken by our captors? You will never convince the others to follow this path, Elazar," she hissed.

An image from the writings of the Greeks that her father taught her came to her mind, and as usual, immediately thereafter to her lips. "You are like the captain of a boat at sea, Elazar, who sees a red sky at night and resolves to sink his ship before the storm comes."

"Ahhh, there's that blade of a tongue of yours. I almost thought not to hear it this night, for a change."

"Don't speak to me as if I were a child. This thing you say you want is impossible."

"And why is that?"

"Because no one will go along with it. I certainly will not, and neither will my mother." She stopped, apprehension stealing her breath away. She had never opposed Elazar so openly before.

Elazar seemed not to hear her. He eyed the basket of fruit on the table next to him. Deliberately he selected the largest date, glistening in its own honey. He popped it into his mouth and licked the sweet syrup meticulously from his fingers. He looked at his hands, first the backs, then the palms. He wove his fingers together, continuing to eye them almost idly. Miriam followed his gaze. She had never noticed before how the jagged edges of his fingernails ended in bleeding gashes below the quick. As she turned away to leave, he spoke.

"We shall see what the others say to my plan once they see… when they are in the midst of 'the storm,' as you put it," he said, to her back. "And as for you, I have no intention of asking you to participate.

"For you, I have other plans. You will have a chance to use that brilliant memory of yours. After I am gone, cousin, you will still be here."

She turned around again to face him, tendrils of her dark hair whipping across her face. Her almond eyes narrowed.

"What do you mean?"

"You are to remain behind as a witness," Elazar said, snaring her eyes with his own. "Your mother, too. No one need know that I have spared you. No one will come looking for you because I alone am responsible for you and Elisheva. I cannot ask any of the other leaders to spare their own – even if one was to be found as suitable as you for the task – for if we must choose between one man's kin and another's, the resolve of some may weaken.

"If we are to wrench victory from the enemy, our deed must be made known. It will be the shame of our conquerors for all ages to come," he finished triumphantly.

At these words, the despair that had begun to creep over Miriam enveloped her completely. She crossed the few remaining steps to the doorway, choosing her parting words with uncharacteristic care. Her back was to Elazar.

"These words never passed between us, cousin," she announced, focusing her eyes at an invisible point in midair. "It will be as you said at first. We will continue to fight until victory is ours," she said, purposely distorting his words. Without waiting for a response, she jerked aside the curtain with one strong arm, and ducked out the door.

Returning to their quarters, Miriam found Elisheva and some of the other older women sitting cross-legged on the ground nearby, their backs against the wall, rolling the edges of woven cloth into finished garments, bone needles flying in their habitual race against the fading light, everything deceptively ordinary. Even now there were children to be scolded or comforted, chickens to be shooed aside as they pecked at imaginary food among piles of straw and wood. Only the complete absence of all the younger men and women, who continued to work frantically to shore up the wall, not 200 *ammas* away, betrayed the community's nearness to disaster.

"Will you be going to draw the evening's water now, dear?" Elisheva asked her daughter.

Miriam blinked in amazement. Her mother had lived among the Sicarii all her life, and was wise in so many things. Had she the slightest inkling of what awaited them, perhaps only a few hours from now? Did her innocent question, one she asked every day of their lives, mean that her faith in Elazar remained unshaken? Was that true for all these women, so industriously going about their work? She did not answer; it was all she could do to keep her pace sedate and her face expressionless until she escaped to the darkness of her room. The broad shoulders that normally bore her tall frame proudly hunched forward as she leaned heavily against the whitewashed wall and bowed her head into cupped hands.

Thought tumbled upon bewildering thought. Was Elazar right about their fate if they fell into Roman hands? From the earliest days of the war everyone knew there was little hope for Jewish captives. She remembered the news that had come to them of a Zealot leader, Yehuda Ben Ari, who had escaped from Jerusalem with a band of his followers. A detachment of Roman cavalry had pursued them to the Yardes Forest. While they still lived, the soldiers sliced off their hands and feet, then their arms and legs. They were left to die like the stumps of the surrounding trees, chopped down to make a path for the infantry. Would God not want to spare the community at Masada such unimaginable pain?

She knew though, that not all captives were killed. A captive slave was a valuable commodity. But what of their life in captivity? Anyone standing atop the fortress walls could see the fate of the Jewish slaves who served the Romans in the camps below. Bent nearly double under the weight of skins bulging with water they were forbidden to taste, they would trudge the murderous three parasangs to the nearest spring every day, until they fell dead against the sun-scorched rocks.

To live such a life as this, blessing God when he finally let them breathe their last, would go against everything her father had taught her. "No master but the Holy One, blessed be He! Remember, Miriam, we will acknowledge no master but God!" She could still hear her father's voice ringing out triumphantly. Two sons of the great warrior Judah the Galilean had been crucified with those very words on their lips, Jonathan had told his daughter when she was still young enough to sit on his lap and hear his thrilling stories.

And then there was the third son, Menahem. Little did anyone realize, she thought bitterly, that with his ill-fated appearance in the Temple courts seven springs ago, he had sowed the seeds for the destruction of everything his father and brothers, and Miriam's father, had lived and died for.

No! Miriam stifled the scream that threatened to tear out of her throat. Joseph's comrades died fighting to regain our freedom! But to take our own lives, the lives of little children, of our own aged parents?

And Elazar expected her to chronicle this deed? That thought seemed as obscene to her as the deed itself. But a verse of Psalms threaded itself into her thoughts. "The dead cannot praise the Lord." She had heard these words often enough from the lips of those who argued with her father against the Sicari way. Miriam used to think they claimed this verse to mask their fear of dying in battle. The dead cannot praise the Lord. The dead cannot praise the Lord. The words meant something different to her now.

Suddenly, a screaming knot of men burst into their little courtyard, shouting at the women and children to take shelter indoors. Miriam's mother appeared at the door, her arms full of skeins of wool. One look at the sallow tinge that had stolen the burnished copper from her daughter's high, sculpted cheeks, told her something more was amiss than the frenzy created by the young men barking their orders.

"What has Elazar been telling you, my daughter?" Elisheva's voice had completely lost its placid tone.

"What has happened, Mother, what are the men saying?" she countered evasively, breathlessness hiding the catch in her throat.

"I think I heard talk of a fire," answered her mother without taking her eyes off Miriam. We are to keep to our rooms until it has been put out." A fire in the compound rated no more than passing attention in these chaotic days, of little importance compared to the anguish Elisheva saw in her daughter's eyes. Elisheva had often seen Miriam return restless from her talks with Elazar, but she had not seen her daughter this distraught in the two years since Joseph had placed the *get* in her hands.

"Mother…" Miriam started, pulling Elisheva down onto the low, roughhewn wooden bench next to her. "Mother… what would Father… Elazar thinks…" Miriam could not continue. Escaping her mother's attempt to embrace her, she made for the door.

"I must go and see what help I can give."

Outside, Miriam cocked her head. Something had changed. For the first time in days, the frightful thud of the stone-throwing engines and the battering ram were not heard. A new, terrible sound had taken its place. It was the rush and crackle of a scorching wind, which struck Miriam full in the face as she spurted across the compound to the breach in the wall.

An acrid smell pierced her nostrils. Then, when she reached the broken-down rampart, she saw them: human torches whirling and darting in the evil luminosity of the blaze that now consumed their makeshift wood-and-soil reinforcement. Ghastly shrieks filled the air. Roman short swords, claimed as trophies last week or last month, were now thrust piteously at an enemy that only a cruel trick of firelight and shadow brought anywhere near their range.

The sizzling flames extinguished life after life, while Miriam remained rooted to the ground in helpless fascination with the scene. But then, she saw that some of the survivors had paused in their frenzy and were looking toward the rampart. She followed their gaze: The tongues of fire that had been licking so relentlessly at their last-ditch support wall now stood upright in air that had become perfectly, impossibly, still. Then, a wind churned up out of nowhere, pounced on the flames, and whipped them onto the enemy's wooden siege machines.

"God has harnessed the wind!"

"He is with us!"

The triumphant cries mingled with the agonized curses of the Romans from just beyond the wall. It was as if the warriors' will to resist had not been lost after all, but had been driven into the flames themselves, now the instrument of their tormentors' destruction.

The legionaries, who only moments before had been cheering as the rebels writhed in flaming agony, were now fleeing the fire's reach, most ended their lives as bright projectiles, flinging themselves from the blazing towers into the night sky.

Then, all at once, the desert wind changed sides again. It fanned every glowing ember until once again Masada's ramparts were a solid, raging wall of fire. Flamethrowers, catapults, the gigantic ballistae – none would be needed further this night, the few soldiers left on the tower saw, as they watched the surviving rebels scurry away like so many rats, dragging the screaming wounded behind them. First light, the officers told their men, would be soon enough to complete the breach of these cursed walls. Exhausted and bloodied, eyes gleaming dully from behind sooty masks, they made their way back to camp below, each contemplating the booty that would be his by this time the next day.

As men and buildings undulated in the searing heat, Miriam caught a glimpse of Elazar darting among the warriors. He was shouting at some, dragging others away from their hapless attempts to put out the blaze or to pull a comrade from its grasp. A group of men was detaching itself from the inferno.

Miriam could guess what was happening the moment she saw Elazar's most trusted lieutenants, wait for each other, surround him and stride off toward the synagogue. These were the men, she thought grimly, who would plunge readily after Elazar into the abyss of self-destruction that was his vision of freedom.

As soon as they disappeared from view, Miriam raced down the path that connected her quarters with the apartments on the far side of the breach and beyond them, to the synagogue. Unwittingly, she had already begun to play the part Elazar had devised for her: court historian in a kingdom of 900 ghosts.

Chapter 6

Shouts of "God forbid!" burst from the doorway and nearly drowned out the incessant murmur of Elazar's voice. The only light came from a round clay lamp with seven wicks protruding from its raised edges, perched on a tall iron tripod against the far wall of the chamber. Amidst the flickering shadows, Miriam slipped into the spacious room undetected and curled herself into the corner next to the door.

Elazar was speaking long and heatedly of the bitter fate of Jews in other places in the empire. The men were clustered together on the plastered stone bleachers that girdled the room. They squirmed as he baited them, goading them with sarcasm into questioning their own courage in continuing the fight, since, he told them, the battle was clearly lost.

But God, he offered, had readied an answer to their quandary. God had presented them with this defeat in order to demand a sacrifice. One immeasurably greater than any they had ever given in the Holy Temple. Clearly, they had committed the worst possible sin against God, he said, fighting brother against brother. God would not forgive them unless they lay this sacrifice before Him. This time it was not a calf or sheaves of wheat, but their own lives that God required in recompense.

Miriam saw that her prediction – was it only earlier that evening? – had been right: The men were having none of it. They had renewed their shouted protests. Elazar allowed the last shout to fade away and finally, silence reigned. When he spoke again, his voice was almost pleading. "Let our wives die unabused, our children with no knowledge of slavery." On and on he talked, describing the horrors that awaited them at the hands of an infuriated enemy, horrors that none had allowed himself to dwell on except in the blackest of his private moments.

Groans of desperation filled the room. Elazar had them now. He did not mention again God's desire of this sacrifice from them – for just as Miriam had warned him, he had realized the men would not accept this grotesque idea. But Miriam should have known he would find a way to win them over; his appeal to them as fathers and husbands was as inescapable as the hunter's net thrown over forest partridges. Further struggle was useless.

One last time he was drowned out, but this time it was by a babble of agitated voices raised in accord.

The appalling details were quickly hammered out. A family's last moments were to be spent together. Fathers would be the executioners; mothers would not know the fate of their children, nor children the fate of their mother, until the last possible moment. The men's voices reached a frenzied pitch as they argued over which one of them would be responsible for the killing of the other men. The sound of a clay pot crashing to the floor ended the strident debate.

Miriam squinted, puzzled, into the dappling shadows. "We will cast lots," she heard Elazar say. Bending down to retrieve several pieces of the pot he had just smashed, he laid them carefully side by side on a bench. They looked no different than the chits Miriam had accepted before handing out food in the storerooms, or the fragments of old kitchen pots that long ago her father had first given her on which to practice her letters. But never was a new pot broken to provide writing material. The sherds from the pot Elazar had smashed were to become gaming pieces in a malevolent lottery.

From that point the proceedings continued in silence, broken only by the scratching of the reed quill. Then came Elazar's voice again. "We will burn all of our possessions. The enemy will have nothing, neither our living bodies nor our goods, to parade in victory. Our business here is at an end."

Miriam's ears roared and the room seemed to pulse with the hammering of her heart. She must not be seen! In one smooth movement she slipped out the door and around the corner of the building and sank into the darkness.

She need not have feared discovery; the men who stepped out over the threshold were staring straight ahead, walking as if invisible hands were bearing down on their shoulders, propelling them along the path.

For the sake of the mission to which she now found herself bound, concealment was of the essence. The synagogue was now her refuge; she made her way to the back wall and lowered herself into a sitting position.

At her feet was the evidence Elazar's resolve. She leaned over and picked up the sherds, one by one. On them, in the flickering lamplight, she could see the names inscribed of the men who had been her Joseph's closest companions for these past years.

Tzaida, "the hunter" was the nickname for Shimon ben Yosef, who in the days before the revolt, people said, had been second to none when it came to felling the deer that roamed the oak forests of his native Galilee. And here was "Yoav," whose real name had been forgotten by most after he took the name of King David's chief-of-staff. That long-ago Yoav had been first to engage the Jebusites in the battle for Jerusalem; this Yoav had always wanted to be just as fearless. Yoav's favorite stratagem had been for his band to pose as deserters in possession of valuable strategic information in order to gain an audience with a Roman camp's commander. By the time guards came investigate the suspiciously long silence within their commander's tent, Yoav's men would have the head start they needed to escape unscathed, high-ranking Roman blood already drying on their knives.

Then there was Ben K'navon, "the son of a round cake." Almost as wide as he was tall, it seemed that at any moment Masada's merciless sun would melt the perspiring rolls of flesh that encased his body. But no one taunted him. For he was a priest, and guardian of the tithes he insisted all continue to contribute to the community's coffers. He embodied the hope of their liberation and the renewal of their sacred traditions. When the work of the rebuilding of the Temple began, he told the community, the tithes he so faithfully guarded would be sorely needed.

"Gerida" was true to the meaning of his nickname as well, Miriam thought, her lips pursing disapprovingly even now. No better description could suit this rude character than "rough ground." After he had been in Gerida's company, Elazar always seemed even more brusque than usual – the man's coarseness seemed to cling to her cousin like the stink of tannin to the tanner. And Elazar's meetings with the man were all too frequent, for Gerida was responsible for the iron-smelting operations that produced and repaired their weapons. She put Gerida's sherd aside and picked up the last one in the pile.

It bore Elazar's name. The letters wavered through the tears that now stung her eyes. Tears for a leader bereft of every decision but how to lead the way to death. Tears for everyone she knew and loved, all of whom this man had condemned with a few well-chosen words.

Make me strong, O God of Israel, let me understand Your will for my people, she prayed silently as she entered the back room of the synagogue where the Holy Scriptures were kept. She groped in the near-darkness and her hand closed around one of the scrolls stored on the wooden shelves that lined the wall. Clasping it to her, she brought the tightly rolled parchment toward the flickering light and opened it. The letters rushed over her like a wave of the Great Sea, filling her mind and her heart with their power.

"The hand of the Lord came upon me. He took me out by the spirit of the Lord and set me down in the valley. It was full of bones. He led me all around them; there were very many of them spread over the valley and they were very dry. He said to me 'O mortal, can these bones live again?' I replied: 'O Lord God, only you know.' And he said to me, 'Prophesy over these bones and say to them, O dry bones, hear the word of the Lord.' Thus said the Lord God to these bones: 'I will cause breath to enter you and you shall live again. I will lay sinews upon you, and cover you with flesh, and form skin over you. And I will put breath into you, and you shall live again. And you shall know that I am the Lord!' I prophesied as I had been commanded. And while I was prophesying, suddenly there was a sound of rattling, and the bones came together, bone matching bone. I looked, and there were sinews on them, and flesh had grown, and skin had formed over them; but there was no breath in

them. Then He said to me, 'Prophesy to the breath, prophesy, O mortal! Say to the breath, thus said the Lord, God, Come O breath, from the four winds, and breathe into these slain, that they may live again.' I prophesied as He commanded me. The breath entered them, and they came to live and stood up on their feet, a vast multitude. And He said to me, 'O mortal, these bones are the whole House of Israel. They say, our bones are dried up, our hope is gone; we are doomed. Prophesy, therefore and say to them, thus said the Lord God: I am going to open your graves and lift you out of your graves, O My people, and bring you to the Land of Israel. You shall know, O My people, that I am the Lord, when I have opened your graves and lift you out of your graves. I will put My breath into you and you shall live again and I will set you on your own soil. Then you shall know that I the Lord have spoken and acted."

Ezekiel! Across the abyss of the years, the words came to her in her father's best Scripture-reading voice. Time and time again he had spoken of the awesome power of the very passage Miriam had opened to by chance this night. "Some of the sages are now teaching that the bones rose only for a moment, and then fell back dead," he had once told her – in later years she realized – just to test her reaction to this bizarre notion.

"Why, Father, would people say such a bad thing about such a great miracle?" she heard her petulant child's voice demand.

"They do not see themselves as not believing in the greatness of the miracle, Daughter. No – they fear that it is we, the Sicarii, who do that very thing. Some sages even teach that we Sicarii believe *we* will be the *only ones* to rise from the dead!" Jonathan had bantered, unable, even in conversation with his young daughter, to avoid the bitter tone that always crept into his voice when he spoke of those who turned their backs on the battle. "Now they, on the other hand, intend to *prove* that Ezekiel proposed to see all of us rise. By appeasing the wicked kingdom at every turn, they will be the death of us all, just to see if they are right about the manner of our resurrection! She had not understood everything at the time, but it was enough to teach her what her father wanted her to know of God. And as she got older, he had explained more.

"Know, Daughter, that the argument with our brethren, even the fight to the death we have been forced to fight against our own, cannot change the eternity of the promise," she remembered he had once told her. "The appeasers are wrong about what we believe. We know the promise of the resurrection is for all people. And at the end of this struggle we will again live free, and be masters of the land God gave us."

Jonathan had never lived to see town after town in Judea and Galilee crushed in the jaws of the conqueror; the wise slaughtered with the ignorant, zealots with moderates, the courageous and the cowardly sharing one mass, unmarked grave. But Miriam had. Now, in the darkness of the synagogue, she stood suspended between past and future. At Masada she thought, they, who had resisted to the last, had become the guardians of Ezekiel's promise to the generations.

The answer to her prayer and the sealing of her destiny had both come to her in Ezekiel's promise. It would give her the strength to bear witness. But it would not be for Elazar's reasons. It would be so that the generations to come would know of the choice they had made on the mountain as they looked to the future Ezekiel had promised them, toward a time when no other human being would ever have to make that choice again.

Slowly she rose, cradling the sacred scroll. In the last act of her old life, she knelt down and laid it gently in the shallow pit dug in the packed earth, where scrolls too worn to use were placed. It was in perfect condition, but she knew that soon no one would be left to care for it. Before the end came, she wanted it safely sealed away.

With the scroll, Miriam was also consigning to the past that of herself that remembered how things once were, or agonized about anything that would be. To survive, and to fulfill her mission, she knew she would have to live wholly in the vortex of the present, which would sweep her up the moment she left the sanctuary.

Some inner voice commanded her to safeguard the evidence of what had just transpired here. She scooped up the inscribed sherds, hastily tying them off into a corner of her cloak, and stepped out the door.

Chapter 7

A fearsome clamor floated through the night from the northern palace. She conquered her first instinct to run toward the sound, and shrank into the shadows to make sure she was not seen.

But someone had been watching, after all. She felt herself being pulled aside roughly. Losing her balance, she threw her arms up in front of her face in panic. The sherds she had been holding flew out of her hands and fell to the ground as she felt a strong pair of arms go around her.

"Daughter! Elazar has sent me to you." Elisheva was shouting to break through to her daughter. "Elazar has sent you?" Miriam repeated flatly. Elisheva saw that Miriam had the sleepwalker's determination to head for a destination no waking person could see.

"Miriam!" Elisheva cried again, "Daughter!" She shook Miriam harshly by the shoulders. Miriam focused. Here was her mother. Mother must be afraid. Miriam could comfort her now.

"You will be safe, Mother. Elazar promised me," Miriam mumbled.

"It is not my safety that concerns me, Daughter. It is what lies ahead for you. I see what is happening, I know my nephew, and what he has asked of you, and I feel your doubts. Your father and I brought you to this place because we believed our cause was just. We never expected it to end this way. Elazar has made a monstrous choice for us. We cannot now escape, but it is right that one of our own – you – be left behind to record it. You will tell our story! Not our enemy, who will surely twist what we have done and obscure our last hours, perhaps even deny that it even happened. And I will not leave you," Elisheva finished firmly.

Miriam found herself standing with her mother just above one of Masada's cave-quarries. Her head cleared. Her mother needed her, and she needed her mother. Miriam was beginning to rally. "Go down to the quarry, Mother, and wait for me to return," she said.

"No – I should be with you," her mother countered immediately. But the glint in her daughter's eye told Elisheva that Miriam's familiar obstinacy was back. Further argument was pointless. Elisheva allowed Miriam to steer her onto the path leading down to the cave. Miriam watched as her mother was swallowed up in the cavern's darkness. Then she strode off to the palace.

The palace – how it had dazzled them when they had first come to Masada. The palace, where Jonathan had refused to set foot. When they explored the rooms, they discovered that, true to rumor, they were more opulent than even King Herod's royal residence in Jerusalem. It was carved out of the rock of the northern face of Masada, yet it seemed to hang effortlessly in the air. Now the larger chambers, once home to a single member of the royal family when occupied at all, had been subdivided by the Sicarii, and several families lived in the magnificent colonnaded halls on the two lower levels. Miriam was close to one of the families that lived in the middle level of the palace, and it was there that she headed first.

A faint moaning sigh crept up the marble-covered entrance stairs toward her. She climbed down, and crossed the chamber's deserted foyer. Down the corridor, near the doorway, she stepped into a puddle and absently shook the drops from her sandal. But when she put her foot down again, a sticky wetness remained trapped between her toes and the leather thongs of her sandals. Looking down again she saw that her feet were covered with blood. The moaning stopped. Her eye lit on a steady trickle of blood that came from the room and had collected in a hollow in the floor just outside the doorway. The trail ended where a man lay, quivering in death-throes. Next to him a woman lay on her belly, her face turned sideways, her outstretched arms embracing three children lying crumpled beneath her. All had their throats cut cleanly from ear to ear. The man lay face-down, his sword protruding from his torso. Miriam doubled over, retching dryly.

The woman's visage was as gray and scored as the ash-coated logs of the dying Sabbath fire. It bore so little resemblance to the woman Miriam knew that she could not bring herself to attach a name to it, or to any of the empty shells that lay before her. With her back to the wall, she inched around the bodies and made her way to the staircase that led downward to the lowest level of the palace where her friend Marta had made her home. Marta had arrived at Masada the previous year in the company of her older brother, Joshua, and a younger brother, Simon. After their parents had been killed in the siege on Jerusalem, Joshua had given free rein to his Sicari sympathies, deciding that the only place for him and his surviving siblings was with the fortress rebels.

There he lay, ostentatious in death as in life: He was clad, as always, in the silvery, red, and bronze scales of parade armor he made sure everyone knew he had stripped from a Roman officer he had slain on a daring highland raid. Marta lay sprawled in the center of the floor, her lifeless body flanked by those of her two brothers.

Miriam had seen enough to know that Elazar's directive was being carried out with the same vengeful passion with which he had held sway over their lives for the past seven years. She had no doubt this scene was replaying itself in every corner of the fortress. She dragged herself back up the interminable flights of stairs and out into the open plaza that stood to the south of the palace. The night was bright with blazing fires. In the jagged pain of her loss it seemed that in the smoke that hung over everything were the souls of all the people who until that night had been her whole world.

Miriam repulsed the urge to seek survivors in the carnage that greeted her as she looked into courtyards and doorways; she knew there would be none. She moved quickly across the compound toward their own courtyard. Stepping inside, she quickly surveyed the scene to find a sharp implement that would serve her need. Her mother's loom leaned against the far wall. Next to it was a basket, containing the wool her mother had left there just a few short hours before. Also in the basket were her mother's iron wool shears.

Seizing the tool without breaking her step, Miriam stepped across the threshold of their room and knelt down at the base of the wall. She jabbed and scraped the wall repeatedly until the last bits of plaster between the stones were flicked away.

The stone was loose and she pried it out easily. Behind it lay a small bronze box, whose top was beaten into a delicate chain of rosettes. Inside was a leather pouch holding the tightly rolled parchment scroll that was her *get*. Beside the *get* was a purse with the twelve silver shekels with which her mother had entrusted her after her father was killed. It would easily pay the first three months' rent on the house in which they would live after they left Masada, her mother had said – triumphant, of course, Elisheva had added, after the last of the conqueror's soldiers had left Judea forever. More than two years had passed since she had last opened the coin purse. It had had no value for her on the mountain. Neither did a single little bronze coin, minted in the white-hot forge of the revolt, brought to the fortress by refugees from the fallen city. Now it gleamed dully at her when she opened up the purse. Its inscription "Jerusalem the Holy," seemed to mock her.

Miriam lifted the pouch with the *get* from the box. Shifting aside her long shawl she inserted the document firmly into the waistband that cinched her tunic. Next, she picked out the silver shekels from the other pouch, hastily, two and three at a time. Her hand darted out to grasp the bronze coin, and stopped midway. No. It would not go with her. In the early, heady days of freedom the Sicarii were the only ones, even among the rebel groups, who insisted upon using that currency exclusively. It certainly could buy nothing of value in the place she would go when day dawned. If found in her possession, it could only serve to further implicate her in crimes against Rome.

But what was she thinking? The silver denarii were just as dangerous for her as any worthless rebel currency. Why was she taking them? To rent a house? To buy a field? Before she could do that, the coins would give every petty thief who crossed her path reason to murder her.

Reluctantly the shekels headed back to the box. But her tightly closed fist refused to release them. The life force within her did not allow her to believe that there would be no house, no field. She placed the box back in its hiding place behind the loose stone, and the silver coins, every last one of them, went into the purse with the *get.*

Chapter 8

It seemed that only moments had passed since Miriam came upon the ghastly scene in the palace. But the sky told a different story. The stars in the east had already begun to disappear into a pale stain in the darkness above the mountains of Moab. A bituminous haze from fires that seemed loath to burn out now shrouded the opening of the cave where she had left her mother.

The sound of pebbles scattering beneath Miriam's sandals cut off the odd, urgent whispering she could hear coming from within the cave. "Daughter!" Elisheva cried out in relief when Miriam's tall, angular form appeared at the entrance to the cave, silhouetted against the wan light. The dark woolen scarf that now covered Elisheva's head and shoulders protected more than just a lone old woman from the chill of the night. From within its folds, five pairs of frightened eyes stared wildly at Miriam. "Don't be frightened, children," Elisheva said, her warm tones concealing her impatience to hear from her daughter what had transpired beyond her shelter. "Here is Miriam, to fetch us all, just as I told you she would be."

"You were not the only one with doubts about Elazar's decision." Elisheva said in answer to the silent question in Miriam's eyes as they swept over the children. "The parents of these little ones must have cast them out and hoped they would find their own way, and that way led to me. They are ours to care for now," Elisheva declared, fully the matriarch in making this particular decision. Disentangling herself from the embrace of her newly discovered brood, she arose, and with her back to the children asked in a low voice, "What will the little ones see outside?"

"They will see nothing, because we will not let them see. We must leave right away. The enemy will be seeking survivors."

But Elisheva had other ideas. They were lucid and direct, belying Miriam's earlier doubts about her mother's grasp of reality. "Daughter, you are not thinking clearly. Any way out of here that does *not* lead through the Romans leads to certain death for all of us. We must stand and face them! Surely they will leave us alive long enough to record what happened here. After that, who knows? At least let us try to choose life, if only for the sake of these children."

Before Miriam could respond, Elisheva led the children out of the cave and headed in the direction of the smoldering breach in the wall. Miriam ran behind to beg her at least to conceal herself until they could see the Romans before the Romans saw them. Then, without warning, a crushing force brought her hard to the ground.

Miriam fought helplessly against the darkening of her vision. A fetid blend of sweat and leather returned her quickly to consciousness. She gritted her teeth as strips of beaten-iron body armor cut into her skin. The Latin her father had taught her, in which she had once read the works of Homer and Virgil, were of no use in decoding the rough triumphant bellowing of the legionary that held her pinned beneath him.

A small detachment of soldiers rushed in the direction of the shouting to find Elisheva and her brood rooted to the spot. Their commander stepped out in front of them, his eyes fixed on the prey trapped beneath the legionary's stocky peasant frame. Here was one simple soldier, the centurion thought, whose clumsy maneuver would earn him promotion from lowly *pedes* to *eques cohortis*. Probably a generous pay raise, too, for landing such a prize – the first live captives from this accursed nest of rebel vipers.

All well and good. The centurion had never been one to begrudge his subordinates the prizes due them. He – Centurion Cassius Dorus – who had led the force that was first over the walls of the fortress that had finally been made to kneel before Rome's might, could look forward to receiving his own reward, the coveted golden *corona muralis*. In his mind's eye he could already see it perched firmly on his head, gleaming in the sun at every parade that would grace the many high points of his future military career.

Cassius strode toward the still-prone Miriam, his right hand resting cautiously on the short sword belted at his side. As his commander approached, the foot soldier untangled himself from his captive and quickly put distance between them, uncertain of what would happen next.

The centurion's next gesture was the least anticipated of anything he could have imagined.

Cassius was reaching his hand out toward the Jewess, gently motioning her to grasp it. Miriam recoiled – touching hands befouled with idol worship was as physically impossible for her as turning her skin inside out. Shrinking as far as she could from the Roman, she struggled to a sitting position.

"Don't you think our hostess has a strange sense of hospitality, Rufus?" Cassius hissed. Bending down, he jerked Miriam roughly to her feet. "Where are the men, where are the others?" Miriam understood every word of this man's educated Latin but responded only with an angry flash of her eyes.

Shouted curses rose from several nearby buildings. Cassius pushed her back into the grasp of his subordinate and advanced on the closest one.

When he reappeared, his face was the color of desert dust. He followed the sound of his soldiers' voices to the next courtyard, and the next. By that time the sun had risen high enough so that voices were no longer needed to announce what lay in every courtyard and behind every closed door. The stench of decay hung over the rapidly warming air, drawing flies whose incessant buzzing grew ever louder as they spread the news of this unexpected bounty.

Shouts of disbelief soon turned into low snarls of frustration, like those of a panther pawing at a kit of foxes unreachable in its lair. Reward for the long months of siege on this accursed plateau would be greater for the hordes of hungry flies than for them. Visions of profit from the sale of the hundreds of captives were rapidly dissipating in the reeking air. The troops nosed closer to where Miriam, Elisheva, and the children now stood in a tight cluster, guarded by four legionaries, their long, iron-tipped spears only inches from the women's bodies.

"They must not be harmed," Cassius warned his men. "They are the only ones who can tell us what happened here. Bring them down to headquarters. Valerius Felix will interrogate them and decide their fate."

Sullenly, the detachment complied, pushing and prodding the captives toward the ramp. Others, meanwhile, vented their fury on the corpses. The living captives were beyond their reach. But at least they could deprive the dead of the one thing they had heard was so valued by this accursed race – a proper burial.

The soldiers dragged body after body from rooms and courtyards to the edge of the plateau. Forming a human chain, they pushed and pulled their bloody burdens up and over the breach in King Herod's old wall and flung them into the gorge below. The circling buzzards by day and the hyenas by night would soon succeed where six thousand legionaries had failed: the last traces of Masada's rebels would be wiped off the face of the earth and forgotten.

Miriam and Elisheva turned the children's heads toward their skirts with gentle hands so they would not see the rapidly mounting piles of corpses by the walkways as they were herded to the smoking breach. The soldiers still stationed in the ten-story tower above the battering ram watched the progress of the captives, calling out half-hearted obscenities as they spied the detail removing the bodies and began to realize what it meant for them. The women and children were manhandled down the steep earthworks and to the headquarters of the Tenth Legion Fretensis.

Chapter 9

It was a full two hours before the prisoners stood at the gate of the great command headquarters. Their tongues licked at their cracked and bleeding lips, and even the children's whimpering had ceased. Each step Miriam took she felt was the last before the abyss of the step that followed.

The guards at the gate stood aside to let them pass, curious eyes darkening malevolently as they guessed the identity of these women and children. The prisoners were jostled by soldiers running to and fro as rumors began to trickle down from above. Slaves and camp-followers looked at them, then past them, well-practiced neutrality sealing their faces.

The guards hustled them into a spacious tent that stood by itself in a walled-off area. Grateful for the relative coolness of the interior, Miriam and Elisheva were not so much thrown down by their guards as fell upon the tapestries covering the stony desert floor.

At first they seemed to be alone. The children, although weakened by thirst, began to whimper again. Miriam did not bother to silence them. A rustle of movement in the dim interior soon told them someone else was here. Then, a young man appeared out of the shadows. His short, coarse tunic was bunched at the waist with a cord and fastened at the top with an acacia thorn. His bare feet immediately identified him as a slave.

In that mysterious way slaves have, Julius, manservant to Senior Tribune Valerius Felix, already knew the identity of the two women and five children who now awaited the arrival of his master. He approached the little group with a bronze *askos* of water in his hand. "You must rest," he said softly, pouring the cool liquid from the jug into a clay cup. He handed the cup to the younger woman, who at once passed it to the children. There was little more he could offer them.

Despite Valerius Felix' high rank as the most senior aide to the Legatus Flavius Silva, his tent held little in the way of creature comforts. Here, too, the air was ripe with the stink of hastily cured leather mounted on low stone supports – the camp *scaenicus* had stopped offering his top quality tenting as soon as he realized that the campaign was limping so badly that he was unlikely to ever be paid. This tent differed from the triangular tents of junior officers and the men only in its larger size, square shape, and carpeted floors. Julius shepherded them into a corner, where they could rest against the low stone walls. He knew that any curiosity or pity that he might show would be of no help either to them or to him. He turned his back, focusing on applying a bees' wax sheen to his master's leather gherkins with measured, circular motions.

Suddenly, the tent's flap flew aside and Valerius Felix appeared. His eyes darted around the room until they rested on the two women and the children. "Stand up!" Valerius' voice was cold. But he could hardly contain his fury since learning that he had been deprived of any gain from this campaign against the dregs of Rome's most odious enemy in this generation.

"You have a great deal to share with me," he said, addressing Miriam and Elisheva, coming so close to them that Miriam could smell the last sour draught of wine on his breath. The children moved behind the women's skirts. "I will know all there is to be known about these dead." He was already picturing the audience that awaited him later that night with Flavius Silva. He knew the legatus well enough to realize that Silva would blame his officers – Valerius Felix first and foremost – for every mishap, real or imagined, that had allowed the legion to rot here month after month while the rebels effortlessly held the high ground, and for the final humiliation – neither captives nor other booty to show for it. Valerius knew he would need to couch his report in the most careful terms. For a man who had spent his life honing his skills on every armament under the sun, it enraged him that the only weapon left at his disposal was information.

Valerius glared at Miriam. Then he broke the gaze, his eyes moving to Elisheva, and back to Miriam. Without warning, his hand came up and struck Elisheva full in the face. Blood spurted from the older women's nose and mouth as she fell to the ground.

"I am told Bacchus is a god much revered by your race," Valerius said, repeating a rumor popular among the men. "Perhaps you imbibe so much wine that you are even immune to pain. I will soon have the answer to that, even if I learn nothing else from you."

His hands plunged into Miriam's thick curls, pulling at them, his fingers flexing like a scorpion's claws. They moved to her shoulders and down her body, pausing at her breasts, probing around them, searching, without passion. Moving down to her waist, he discovered the bulge of the leather pouch that hung from her belt. He jerked her robe aside and tore away the pouch. Pulling out the scroll, he tossed it aside on the table behind him and pawed his way frantically to the bottom like a magician's apprentice failing his master at his first public performance. A few coins were all he found.

"The god revered by our people…" Miriam spoke, if only to distract the officer from the scroll. She haltingly repeated his Latin, but her voice faded as the scene in the synagogue less than 36 hours before intruded into her thoughts. What did God have to do with what had taken place since those moments?

"Do you not speak the language of Rome? Only that barbarous Judean singsong?" Valerius' head danced from side to side as he mimicked her accent. "I see I may require the services of an interpreter. Perhaps this lady can help us." A cracking sound, then a scream, as Valerius delivered a vicious kick to the fallen Elisheva with his greave-clad right shin. Experience told him a broken rib was a good start. Pain inflicted on the old woman, and then on the children, could not help but induce the flow of information he required.

"The leader of my people ordered the men to... take from life the women and the children, and then end each other's," gasped Miriam, torn with her mother's pain, as Elisheva writhed on the floor.

Valerius' eyes narrowed as he absorbed what he had just heard. It did not matter that this woman did not know the proper term for the collective act of suicide it appeared these people had committed. He understood. Faced with overwhelming odds, they had heeded the call of the Stoics. Military history had taught him that it was the same choice Cato Uticensis had made after receiving news of Caesar's resounding victory at Thapsus. It had been the choice of Brutus and Cassius after their defeat at Philippi. He had also studied the mass suicide at Zanthos in southern Asia Minor after the hopes of the people there of victory over Brutus had been dashed. One of Valerius' own ancestors, finding himself on the wrong side of Caesar, had committed suicide to avoid a death sentence. That noble step had allowed his family to inherit his wealth. One might say it was that very self-sacrifice that had enabled Valerius, so many years later, to purchase his education and promotion to one of the highest offices in the legion. As he mused, he found himself beginning to feel something disturbingly akin to admiration for this barbarian people.

That is, until he recalled that all the contents of the well-stocked fortress storehouses – grain, wine, iron tools, and weapons had been burned to ashes. Virtually nothing of value was left. Not even on the bodies. Bodies which, had life remained in them, would have fetched handsome prices in the slave markets of Caesarea.

The baleful chill of agate-gray eyes alighted upon the smallest of the children hiding behind Miriam's robes. Without a word, Valerius grabbed the child by the hair and flung her against the low stone wall. Her wail lasted as long as the instant it took for her little body to fly though the air. Turning on his heel, he strode out of the tent, snapping an order to the sentries. Miriam bent down and picked up the little one gently. But it was a straw doll she cradled, its neck at an unnatural angle, and Miriam turned her face away. "Daughter," groaned Elisheva, trying to rise, "we will all die if we stay here, whether all at once or one by one. Their anger will not be quenched. You must take the children and get away when night falls. You must." Elisheva finished in a hoarse whisper.

The children's weeping was a heartsick dirge, glances darting anywhere in order not to rest on their tiny dead companion, or on the writhing old woman who had sheltered them. The slave Julius once more appeared from the shadows, and moved in the direction of the child. Stretching out his hand, he closed her eyes and mouth.

"What was the child's name?"

Miriam hesitated. She had understood the question, but realized that she did not know the answer. Her eyes met those of the oldest of this nameless band of orphans, a boy of about ten, and she repeated the question for him in Aramaic. "Yehohana," he sobbed "my sister." The slave began to repeat "Yehohana, my sister" over and over, obviously thinking all three words to be the child's name. He was offering his condolences to the strangers in the only way he knew, *extremum vale,* the mourning ritual.

He straightened up and looked into Miriam's eyes, his features now frozen as before. "You and the old woman are to be brought before the commander of the Legion, His Excellency Flavius Silva," he said. They will be coming for you in a few moments. The children will not be allowed to accompany you, I imagine they will be taken to the stockade." he finished, "for the meantime." His tone had the impassive quality of one whose life had taught him not to fear the future, merely to accept its inevitability.

Just as he finished speaking, the tent flap lifted again and a *pedes* stepped inside. The foot soldier's face was obscured by the helmet that covered his forehead almost to his eyes. He waited. "Go with him," urged Julius in a clenched whisper.

Miriam helped Elisheva to her feet. Shepherding the children ahead of them, they exited the tent. Three more armed men were waiting outside. Suddenly, the children were hauled off the main path by two of their guards, and disappeared into the darkness. The remaining two guards jabbed at Miriam with their short swords when she stopped to protest, and she had no choice but to continue. They walked past the tent-lined camp promenade to where a closed wooden gate in a rough stone wall blocked their way. The sentries at the gate stood aside with military precision. At their shouted command, the gate opened from the inside to admit them to the headquarters of Flavius Silva, supreme commander of the Tenth Legion Fretensis and governor of Judea.

Chapter 10

When the prisoners were brought into the legatus' tent, Silva was dictating to his secretary, who stopped the scratching of his stylus only long enough to occasionally dip it into the mixture of soot and gum in the inkpot. Without halting his stream of words, the commander's eyes flicked from the soldiers to the doorway. It was all the signal they needed. They saluted the *legatus* and bowed out of the tent.

Silva stood in front of a long table. It was of roughly planed field issue, but laden with delicacies. Beside golden brown bread of the best quality wheat, there were walnuts piled high in a wooden bowl. Dates stuffed with cinnamon and rolled in almonds swam in their own honey on a glass platter. On another glass dish stood a small pyramid of dried figs. Next to a silver amphora of Cypriot wine was a two-handled embossed silver goblet. The eyes of his prisoners moved uneasily between the dreaded "angry lion," as Silva was known, and the attractions of the table behind him. It did not escape his notice.

"Enough for now," said Silva to the scribe. "In any case we cannot proceed without the information that will be provided by the ladies who have now joined us. He turned to the prisoners.

"I believe you could do with some sustenance," he said with a flourish of his hand in the direction of the table. He nodded to the slave who stood poised next to the table, and the latter poured a small amount of wine into the silver goblet. Removing the lid from a large clay vessel standing on the floor next to the table, he filled the goblet to the brim and held it out to the older woman. Elisheva looked away.

"What are you thinking of, Mother?" Miriam whispered fiercely. "Take it!"

"The goblet holds the unclean wine of the stranger. We are forbidden to drink it." Elisheva drew the words up from somewhere deep within the wellspring of her past, before the war, before Masada, before the pain and the terrible thirst that now consumed her. For a moment she was back in Jerusalem, where life had rarely presented them with such temptations.

"Those days are gone," said Miriam, reading her mother's tortured thoughts. "Now, as you said, we must do everything possible to survive." She took the goblet from the proffered hand of the slave. A Nubian, he could not understand the meaning of the words that passed between them. He kept his eyes carefully lowered, to hide his wonder as to what possible objection the two disheveled, soot-covered, and obviously thirsty women could have to accepting the drink.

"I expected no less of you people," Silva said lightly, as if resuming a casual conversation instead of initiating an interrogation.

"I have made a close study of the events that led to the burning of your shrine." The streets around it were stained with the blood of your priests, who jumped to their deaths from its ramparts. Did you know that?" He paused to let the foreign words sink in.

"And there were rumors that some of your compatriots took the lives of their own children when our patrols rooted out the captives, dragging them even from your sewers. A very messy business indeed," said Silva with a slow, disdainful shake of his head. "Clearly, also an unprofitable one for whoever had hoped to augment his income by the sale of Jewish slaves. It is well known that your people, wherever they live in the world, pay high ransoms for their enslaved countrymen. My officers have been considerably displeased by the unprofitable end to our endeavor here."

Silva's tone had become far too icy for mere economics to be at issue. "However," he continued, "this wasteful siege is at an end. Might I include in my report that the last of Judea's insurgents now stand before me?" Silva seemed to be speaking to himself. "The question is, what is the true identity of the last of these insurgents, and how did they come to survive?" Silva looked over at a scroll that lay on his worktable and Miriam saw that it was her *get*. He stepped over to it, picked it up and unrolled it. "Divorce is, I believe, unusual among your people," he said. Then, almost warmly, "Tell me about the circumstances of your own divorce," glancing down at the parchment again and raising his head, "Miriam."

Miriam knew instinctively that unlike Valerius, Flavius Silva would have no trouble deciphering the Hebrew of her *get*. She also knew that if Silva were to discover the identities of her husband and of Elisheva, and their relationship to Elazar, their fate would be sealed. Death would be a certainty but that death would be long in coming. Silva's torturers, she knew, would attempt to extract the information he would need to make sure they were indeed the last of the Sicarii left to threaten Rome's rule.

She thought rapidly. "There is nothing to tell. I was a mere child when my husband married me. By the seventh night after our wedding," she continued, adopting a coyness of tone completely foreign to her, "I had learned enough to realize that my husband could not satisfy my needs. I demanded a divorce. My people are very understanding when it comes to this matter, for as you might have heard, our unions are expected to produce as many children as possible."

Suddenly, a cry of pain escaped Elisheva and she sank to the ground, a froth of blood bubbling up from her mouth. A barked command brought a guard back into the tent and Elisheva was pulled back to her feet.

"Please," Miriam implored, another tone unfamiliar to her. "Allow my mother to sit. She knows nothing that can be of help to you."

"Whether your mother stands or sits depend entirely upon you. Tell me what took place in the fortress and she will rest."

Miriam glanced at the slave, staring straight ahead, with his reed quill poised in mid-air. Silva was trying to verify that all resistance had been shattered at Masada, she assumed. The success of his future career depended on reporting this, and on minimizing the news of the high price of the siege. Inspiration came to her.

"I did know something of what was being planned," she opened, with an urgency that implied sincerity.

She raced ahead, encouraged by the commander's silence. "Since my divorce, my mother and I are without protection, and so in return for our keep I served in the household of one of our leaders. I went in and out of rooms, of meetings, as if I were invisible. I overheard our leader discussing with his lieutenants a hideous plan for taking our lives. I knew I could not allow this thing to happen to me, or to my mother. So as soon as I could, I got away. I hid myself in a cave with my mother and some children whom we pulled inside with us." I saw nothing – but the screams and the smoke told me all I needed to know." Miriam lowered her eyes in what she hoped the seasoned commander would read as a gesture of helpless surrender.

Silva rested his chin between thumb and forefinger, never taking his eyes off her as he took the measure of her words. Not daring to raise her head again, Miriam could not gage the impact her story had had on the Roman. She could only wait.

"What is the name of this leader of yours?"

"He was called Elazar Ben Yair," she answered in a level tone.

"And his relationship to you was … ?"

"I was a servant of his household," Miriam answered immediately.

The general turned away from Miriam. Naturally, he already knew the name of the rebel leader and how he had come to take the fortress of Masada. Intelligence analysis was his forte, and a sixth sense propelled him to look back at her with a quizzical tilt of his head. The fine network of white creases in the sunburned skin around his eyes disappeared as he narrowed them, as if he could bore into the young woman's thoughts with his own.

"It would appear that there are plenty among you who regard the taking of one's own life as honorable an end as we do. Perhaps your leader and his companions learned a lesson from survivors, such as you are now, of the massacre in Jerusalem, where hundreds of your people took their own lives and the lives of others while your temple burned.

Perhaps, serving girl, if you are allowed to live, you might wish to go on mentoring and counseling your people to persist in such action."

For the first time in this exchange, Miriam spoke her heart. "I do not condone what was done in the fortress." She had to cast about for words, and she watched the commander for signs that her halting speech made him think her uncertain, or weak. And she was neither. "We are taught that our lives are to be lived to the fullest, and the longest, for the glory of the Creator. We fight the rule of foreigners over the land God gave us for as long as we can. But if we fail, and if we have no choice but to live under the rule of another, then in this too we must glorify God."

The woman's speech only served to increase Silva's sense of unease. Did she know the names of other rebels? If so, was she the key to ending this debacle once and for all, not only here, but throughout Judea? Even if she was merely a serving girl, she still had a servant's intimate knowledge of the goings on in her master's house. But her Latin, and her bearing, were not that of a servant. Who was she, then?

He needed to think. The execution of the captives could wait, he decided. With the economic losses he had incurred already, the deaths of two more insignificant women and a few children – if the woman was telling the truth – would make no difference. They were of value only if they possessed information that would allow him to explain to his superiors how a handful of these mountain-dwelling rodents had held off his entire legion and in the end eluded his grasp. Only then could this episode be laid to rest. It would have to be expunged entirely from the record that reached Rome if he were to gain the confidence of the Senate necessary to become consul. And consul he would be.

"Guard!" Called Silva. "Take the prisoners to the stockade. See that they are fed."

"We will speak tomorrow," he addressed Miriam again, forcing a courteous note into his voice. "Perhaps by then you will recall details that are more helpful to me. If these details are not helpful," he paused to choose words he was certain no language barrier would prevent the rebel woman from understanding, "you will be useless to me. You, your mother, and the brats will share the fate of your brethren from the fortress after all, despite what appears to be your... ideological dispute with them," he finished dryly. He tossed the *get* at her feet like a scrap. The leather pouch followed, the coins within it clinking dully.

The guard moved in behind Miriam, as she bent down to retrieve the scroll and the pouch, and tuck them hastily back in the folds of her belt. He nudged her forward, barely giving her enough time to put her arm around her mother so she could half-carry, half-drag her along. Night was deep around them now. The acrid smell of pitch from a hundred burning torches filled the air.

The stockade, set apart from the rest of the camp, was the only structure made entirely of stone. The burly guard at the wooden door lifted the heavy iron elbow key from its niche and inserted it through the square opening above the lock and into the lock itself, its four prongs clicking into position. The door swung open.

In the dark interior sat the four children. The guard barked out a few words to them, the language incomprehensible but gestures and tone unmistakable. They tumbled over each other to reach his side and disappeared out the door with the guard holding the eldest by the scruff of the neck. He pushed the two women in and slammed the slatted wooden door behind him, shutting out all but slivers of light from the torch he placed in a niche near the doorway. The guard inserted his hand with the elbow key once more on the inside of the door to lock it. Then he withdrew it, leaving them in the near dark.

Shortly afterward, the door opened again. A clay plate bearing two *bucellata* and a fat-bellied bronze pitcher of *acetum* was placed on the floor, along with two clay drinking bowls. Despite the dull ache in her empty belly, she ignored the two pieces of hardtack. She poured out some of the caustic military wine and held her mother's head up to wet her lips with it. This time, her mother did not protest. It was a bad sign. She eased Elisheva to a sitting position against the wall.

"Thank you, Daughter." Elisheva's face was taut with pain. "I am ashamed to be such a burden. Perhaps if I do have a small bite, I can regain my strength and be of some help to you. What have they brought us to eat?" Elisheva asked, her voice falsely bright.

Miriam reached over to pick up the plate and examine its contents. "It is the hard biscuits of the soldiers, Mother." The hard tack evoked memories. She had actually never seen it so close up – their family had baked fresh bread daily for as long as she could remember, even at the height of the siege. They had always mocked the teeth-cracking biscuits of the conqueror; it was said that these could be weapons of the last resort to bash in the heads of the Empire's most recalcitrant subjects.

Miriam was not even sure how to go about eating it. She finally decided to smash it against the wall with the palm of her hand. She was rewarded with a shower of smaller pieces that scattered on the beaten-earth floor. She patted the floor until she found a fragment, which she placed against her mother's lips. "Try just to suck on this," she urged her mother gently. Miriam poured some wine into the other cup, and gulped it down in a few mouthfuls. She sat back and put her head against the wall. Images flashed through her mind in the closest thing to sleep she had experienced for the last three days.

The next sound Miriam heard was a desperate gasping and gagging. She groped through the thick darkness to where her mother had been sitting. The place was empty. She waved her arms wildly as her eyes sought out movement to go with the sounds. Finally, her hands came in contact with Elisheva's contorting body. She wrapped her arms around her mother from behind. Elisheva was on all fours, attempting to dislodge the piece of hardtack that had imbedded itself in her throat. She fell to the floor, and was quiet, and Miriam toppled next to her, one arm pinned beneath Elisheva. "You will be alright now, Mother, just rest," Miriam crooned, working her arm loose and sitting up. She cradled her mother in her arms and smoothed back Elisheva's tangled hair from her forehead. She could not see her mother's eyes, was but she knew they were open, and lifeless. She felt a roaring in her ears and her blood ran cold. Her mother had not deserved the anguish through which she had lived since the sun last rose. Relief coursed through her, knowing that Elisheva had been spared the horrors that surely lay ahead. She rested her head across her mother's still breast, and closed her eyes.

Miriam could not tell how much time had passed when the lock rattled again, but the last of the warmth had drained from Elisheva's body. The door opened, letting in the chill of the desert night, and the children.

Before the torchlight disappeared, Miriam saw that the dusty faces of the little ones were streaked with tears but those of the eldest were brimming with confusion. She roused herself from her sorrow.

"What is it, boy? What did they ask you? What did you say?"

"There was a very tall man with shining silver armor and beautiful weavings on his floor and his walls. He gave us food. He told me that he was sorry about what happened to my sister, and that he would see to it that the man who did it was punished. He said that the Romans would take care of us now, that wealthy Jews who live in Rome would take us into their homes and we would have fine new lives. He said how much he admired our leader Elazar, even though he had been his enemy. When he asked me about you, I thought it would help you if he knew you were related to the greatest of our warriors, and so I told him I knew you to be Elazar's cousin."

Miriam remembered this boy only vaguely from their time in the fortress; it had not occurred to her that he would know exactly who she was, or that he of all people would be the source of the information that she had tried so hard to conceal from Flavius Silva.

Chapter 11

The children had collapsed into a dazed sleep around Miriam. She had not moved since the boy had spoken, and sat staring into the darkness. Voices broke the silence outside as once more the hand with the key appeared and inserted it into the lock. The door opened to admit Julius, the slave. At first, she did not recognize him – it seemed to have been days, not hours, since he had uttered the only kind words spoken to her in this place, back in the tent of Valerius Felix. With barely a glance at Elisheva's crumpled body, illuminated in the light of the smoking torch he carried, he began to speak with an urgency that aroused Miriam from her stupor. "I have only a moment," he whispered. "Silva is furious that you attempted to conceal your identity. He raves that he will ship you off to Rome to be shown in the streets as the last rebel of this province and then send you to your death in the arena."

"What can I do? I can hardly see my hands in front of my face, I cannot open a door locked from the outside," Miriam said blankly, attempting to decipher his Latin as quickly as he spoke the words.

Julius sought out her hand. "The guard is alone outside. After he has let me out, he will have to put his hand through the opening in the door to lock it again. That is the moment you must act. The camp has drunk itself to sleep. It will be some time before anyone notices anything amiss. I will bring you and the children two donkeys to take you into the wilderness, westward to your people."

Miriam did not have to see what Julius had placed in her hand. She knew the feel of the short handle and broad, deadly curve of the *sica,* the weapon of choice of Elazar and his band for killing Romans, as well as quite a few of the Sicarii's Jewish opponents. Julius could not even begin to imagine, Miriam thought, the reception she could expect to have at the villages of "her people." But she had vowed by the words of Ezekiel to live, and this was the way that led to life. She sprang up, startling the children awake.

"Children!" Her low but compelling tone made them realize she was the only mother they had now. "I need you to listen to me very carefully. We are going to leave this place very soon. We will be walking in the dark for a long time. I will be with you all the time, but you must promise to listen only to my voice and not to speak or cry no matter what you see. Can you do this?"

The children nodded, wide-eyed and solemn, down to the youngest, a boy of about four years of age. Miriam had no way of knowing whether they had fully understood or would carry out her instructions.

"Guard," called Julius. "I have seen all is well here, as my master ordered. I will report to him." The guard opened the door and closed it behind Julius without even a glance within. Miriam knew what she had to do. When the guard's hand, grasping the elbow key, reappeared in the aperture to lock it, she leaped into action. The raised dagger sliced silently through the air, then tore cleanly through flesh and bone. Hand and key fell away together into the cell, and a heavy thud on the other side of the door told her that the guard had collapsed from the shock of his injury, without even the ghost of a cry.

She disentangled the key from the gory mass at her feet and passed it back though the door, where Julius took it from her and opened the lock swiftly and silently. He pulled the five of them out of the room one by one, signaling them in tight, insistent gestures to hug the low stockade building that shielded them from discovery.

Not far from the stockade was a gate in the camp's perimeter wall. That night, the night the rebels had finally been defeated, no one thought it necessary to guard it. Julius led the prisoners directly to it and in an instant they found themselves outside of the camp.

Nearby stood two donkeys that the slave had spirited out of the stables. From a cloth ring fixed to the saddle, he pulled out a soldier's forked carrying pole. A sack containing food for their trek was attached to it. Water skins bulged atop the saddle. Miriam and Julius lifted two children onto the back of each donkey.

She could not find the words to part from this strange gentile slave. In his impassive eyes she sought in vain the reasons for his selfless acts, acts that, if discovered, would sentence him to death by crucifixion or exposure. As she turned back toward him and moved toward the desert night, Miriam saw Julius' silhouetted hand lifted in farewell, gesturing westward to the mountains.

She allowed herself only a moment to watch his retreating figure dissolve into the shadows. She checked to see that the children were mounted securely. Then, leading the animals, she turned in the direction of the highlands.

The moisture-laden, pre-dawn desert breeze had already begun to undulate around the little group. She increased her pace as much as the plodding animals would allow. She had to complete their ascent at least to where the gorges' twisted meanders would swallow them up.

Chapter 12

ALEXANDRIA, 73 CE

To Tiberius Julius Lupus, Greetings.

Our prefect in Judea has crushed the rebels. However, I have been informed that some of the insurgents have escaped that province. Many have infiltrated Alexandria and are now responsible for the decline of public order there. Immediate action must be taken so the inhabitants know that Rome will not tolerate these outlaws. Therefore, before conditions deteriorate any further, I hereby order you to destroy by fire the shrine of the Jews at Leontopolis, known as the Temple of Onias.

Titus Flavius Vespasian, Imperator

Lupus laid The papyrus from the emperor on the table before him. A servant had entered silently to light additional lamps in his study. It was not necessary. He had reread the missive until he knew its contents by heart.

Rome's highest official in Egypt lowered his head onto his crossed arms, willing himself to discover the answer to his predicament. He had lost count of the number of times he had met with Alexandria's Jews, to try to persuade them to find a solution to the disorder that now gripped their city, a solution that would not draw unwanted attention to it. But now it was too late.

Now Lupus' duty was clear – at least to those outside his prefecture. But things were more complicated than they seemed. He had worked long and hard to reach this position, and now, finally it was his; the priestesses in the Shrine of Fortuna had come to rely on his frequent offerings of thanksgiving to the goddess for granting his continued success. He knew he could excel in government, and he had. But was the Egyptian posting going to allow him finally to taste the fruits of his success? Or was his career to be destroyed by that infuriating people, who preferred to sacrifice themselves in the thousands rather than reap the benefits of Rome's rule? Lupus' shoulders quaked in a bitter, silent laugh. No. These Jews never forgot anything. Not in Judea and not here in Alexandria. They had regarded him with suspicion from the beginning. For that he had the senseless excesses of one of his predecessors, Flaccus, to thank. The Jews refused to forget the latter's brutal suppression, more than forty years before, of riots over the installation of Emperor Caligula's statues in their synagogues.

The Jews considered themselves blameless for the riots, pointing a finger at their gentile neighbors whom they insisted had manipulated Flaccus. Naturally. They were never to blame for anything, never. Stubborn as they were, they refused to participate in the public life of Alexandria, a city with manifold pleasures and advantages, a city to which they should be only too glad to contribute and to serve. Yet parading their ridiculous sectarianism, they had the audacity to rail against the "insult" of not being accorded full citizenship rights!

Still, Egypt needed its Jews. *He* needed them, to make his prefecture flourish. Half of the all the grain, the linen, and the spices that passed through Alexandria were the result of their trade connections, which reached every corner of the world. All of that had to continue coming and going smoothly so that the coffers of Rome, and his own coffers, would continue to overflow.

Lupus found that his interest in Egypt's Jews, which he had pragmatically developed in order to ensure the smooth running of the prefecture, had rapidly turned into something more. In spite of himself, he could not deny a grudging respect for these intractable people and their invisible god.

The Temple of Onias at Leontopolis was the pride of Egypt's Jews. He had learned that a high priest of theirs by that name had built it, back in the days when the Macedonians had oppressed them in their own country and they sought to worship elsewhere. Lupus had heard that the construction of the shrine was a fulfillment of some sort of prophecy of one of their seers who had lived about 700 years ago. The seer had supposedly foretold that Egypt would be home to a magnificent temple to their invisible god, and that a Jew would build it. It was indeed a splendid structure, presided over by a whole cadre of priests who were the descendants of immigrants from Judea. Except for its smaller dimensions, it bore a great resemblance to their shrine in Jerusalem.

That shrine was in ashes now; Lupus recalled hearing that the Jews had even cast themselves into the flames. In the wake of that debacle, most of the Empire's defeated Judean subjects were barely eking out a living, leaving nothing for the tax collectors, and the Empire's functionaries complaining of the hardship of a posting to that wasteland. He shuddered to think what the destruction of the shine at Leontopolis would do to the stability of his prefecture. It would devastate the trade connections passing through Leontopolis to cosmopolitan Memphis, to his own Alexandria, and points farther east. He had to find another solution.

A polite cough outside the door interrupted his musings. Lupus' manservant entered with his change of apparel for the evening, a toga of finely woven Egyptian linen chosen from the finest cloth available at the Horrea Agrippana market, the purple band of his office adorning one edge. The slave draped the toga delicately over Lupus' left shoulder, then moved around his back to bring the remainder of the cloth around the front of his body and over his left shoulder again. The cloth fell elegantly in broad crescents beneath his one free arm, but the Roman cursed the custom that wrapped him in this unwieldy garment, however impressive, on a humid Alexandrine evening. Finally, he slipped his feet into pliant leather boots, and was ready for his face-off with the leaders of the Jews.

He knew the reason they had asked for this audience: It was to petition him to lower export duties on goods they imported from Cyrene and exported to Hispania. Indeed, in return for appropriate remuneration, he had decided he was going to favorably consider their request. But the emperor's order would brook no delay. The agenda of this meeting would be very different from what the Jews expected.

Lupus had chosen the small audience hall for tonight's meeting. The wall decorations in this chamber depicted only delicately painted landscapes glimpsed through imaginary windows, designs that would not arouse the Jews' inexplicable revulsion for the depiction of the human form. Had it been any other delegation, he would have hosted them at a banquet in his magnificently appointed triclinium dining hall, its many elaborate courses and fine service designed to demonstrate that this representative of Rome's abundance knew how to appreciate the cooperation of the locals. But with the Jews... it was well known that no morsel of food or even the finest wine would pass their lips except at the homes of their own kind.

Conversation stopped as the prefect entered the audience chamber where his guests were waiting. Each of the men present was known to him: men from the Jews' ruling council, among the richest merchants in the community. "Welcome to my home, gentlemen," he said with more jocularity than he felt, if only to dispel the gloom that had enveloped him as soon as he crossed the threshold. They were here to discuss serious business issues, certainly. But why did these Jews have to bring such bottomless depth to their gravity? They were more than grave – they were as glum as priests examining the inauspicious entrails of a ritually slaughtered cock. Lupus folded his arms across his chest to hold back the instinct to grasp them in greeting, an act which he knew would be rebuffed. He mounted two steps to take his seat in his richly carved wooden chair, the only piece of furniture in the room. He predicted that the first to speak would be Aaron son of Joseph, the priest. And sure enough, the obsequious little man, a few wisps of white hair floating ridiculously up from his bald, sweating palate, waddled out of the little knot of men to face the prefect.

"Our community is in an uproar," the priest whined. "Against our wishes, several of the families have taken in relatives from Judea."

Relatives from Judea – Lupus translated to himself – meant rebels from Judea. He could only imagine what it took for the priest to admit this to him, the very incarnation of the power of Rome as far as they were concerned. In fact, it was a welcome admission, he quickly calculated, for it brought with it the immediate solution to his problem regarding the Temple of Onias.

Lupus chose his words carefully, his tone revealing nothing but his usual diplomatic dispassion. "I am sure you realize that these people are bringing the Judean disaster to our shores, no more and no less. Emperor Vespasian will not brook unrest exported from one quarter of his empire to another. And we all know that the Jews of Alexandria already have less than an unblemished record when it comes to carrying out their duty to their emperor."

Uneasiness rippled through the little group. Every Jew in the room had a father, uncle, or grandfather who had been arrested, tortured, or murdered by Flaccus during the riots. And then, twenty years ago, Alexandria's Jews rose up again when news reached them of Rome's failure to prevent a murderous attack by Greeks on their coreligionists in Caesarea. Suspicions, real or imagined, on the part of Rome's secret agents had landed some of the men in this very room in the dank cells of Alexandria's praetorium.

"We understand Your Excellency's concerns. We would like to avoid further disruption and are willing to do what is necessary to preserve the peace, " wheezed Aaron, bowing as he spoke, his little white tufts rippling like wisps of smoke. Lupus hoped his diplomatic mien would conceal the satisfaction he felt at having so precisely gauged and induced this very reaction. He needed to preserve tranquility in the land, to ensure that commerce would continue unhindered. At this rate, the Jews would do the job for him.

Still, everyone knew that words were what the Jews excelled at. It would not do to be too taken by them. So Lupus pressed the issue. What could keep these Jews quiet? Over the past forty years, 50,000 of them had been killed in Egypt alone, and yet still they fanned the embers of revolt on the slightest pretext. He continued to play the game.

"Your brother priests are very busy, I understand, acquainting some of your refugees with their options for sacrifice to your god down in Leontopolis. I am told that the number of Jews visiting the Temple of Onias is rising daily. The same news has reached the emperor. Yet we cannot help but deduce from your actions that the privilege you Jews enjoy – of worshipping your own god in a shrine as magnificent as any to the gods of Rome – goes unappreciated. Your people still disturb the peace, still agitate, still plot against the empire at every turn. Our emperor now requires me to take action. My orders are to burn your temple to the ground."

The faces of the priests in the group went as gray as their bushy beards. But the businessmen understood this as merely an opening ploy. The bargaining began in earnest with the governor's next pronouncement.

"I am willing – at great risk to myself and to my office, mind you – to entertain an alternative: A pledge, accompanied by immediate and visible action of any type you see fit, that calm will prevail in the community. This will allow me to consider abstaining from issuing the order." Lupus waited for his words to sink in. He wanted them to think they had won. He wanted them off-balance.

Then he continued. "Naturally, I will not be able to ignore the emperor's wishes. And so my decision, pending your agreement to my conditions, is to close, rather than burn, the Temple of Onias, until such time as you have assured the cooperation of the Jews throughout Egypt. When peace and quiet are restored, you may petition me to re-open the shrine. Your sacred vessels, which I will order safeguarded in the praetorium for the meantime, will then be returned to you."

Aaron the priest was about to respond, when another of the party stepped forward. It was Lucias Jacobides. He was a frequent visitor to the praetorium's offices, whenever a particularly valuable shipment of the fine linen that had made his fortune needed to be eased through the rigors of Roman bureaucracy. Unlike the priests, he had spent many hours in the company of the governor.

"We appreciate your generous offer, Excellency, and we thank you for preventing the burning of our temple. We will see to it that order is restored. Everyone will know that Rome protects all her citizens, and allows them the freedom to pursue both their cult and their livelihood."

Being thus preempted by the merchant, the priest's complexion now turned the same shade as the stylishly painted russet wall behind him. Jacobides, at his aristocratic best, was careful to avoid Aaron's baleful eye. He kept his own gaze fixed on a point just below the Roman's chin, awaiting the next stage of negotiation.

By now the priest had begun to sputter. But Lupus had stood up, the signal for the slave to open the door of the chamber. The audience was over. Each man in turn inclined his head slightly in the direction of the prefect before exiting. Before taking his leave, Jacobides could not resist locking eyes with the governor for a moment so short that Lupus thought he imagined the discourtesy.

He watched the door close behind them. Lupus was sure that the knowledge that Rome could turn their shrine into a pile of ashes would ensure the Jews' cooperation. That would make it all the easier for his agents – wise for weeks now to the presence of the newly arrived rebels – to root them out. Lupus gave no more thought to the matter, and he exited the audience chamber on his way to a very satisfying evening meal.

The Jews navigated the corridor to the courtyard of the governor's villa. Tiny jets of water spurted from the mouths of the cavorting stone nymphs and other mythical creatures that decorated the fountain in the center and from which the men dutifully averted their eyes. The pulsating water sounded as loud as a Nile cascade in the silence that gripped the little group as they hurried past it. They maintained their silence until they were out the main door of Lupus' villa and in the street. Aaron the priest fixed a spiteful gaze on Lucias Jacobides. The merchant kept his own eyes straight ahead as he always did when he walked through the crowded streets, with the practiced elegance he thought befitted his lofty station. Although a large man, Jacobides sailed gracefully through crowds like a richly laden ship on the open seas. People made way for him without even realizing they were doing so.

"How can you assure the governor of our cooperation with such certitude, Ben Ya'akov?" the priest hissed through clenched teeth, scurrying to keep up. To have so readily agreed to the closing of the Temple, Aaron decided, the merchant must have forgotten his origins, as he was prone to do; using Jacobides' Hebrew name was the priest's way of reminding him of those origins.

Jacobides finally looked over at the priest, with a smile that stopped before it reached his eyes. "You are no doubt considering your priestly colleagues from Jerusalem who have joined us of late. They will seek to renew their sacred calling here, at your discretion and under your leadership. They are your responsibility, one might say. Does it not concern you that they may have been fleeing one burned-down temple for another?"

"I think not of the priesthood," Aaron lied smoothly, "but of others who have come from Jerusalem, those who refuse to stay their hand from bloodshed. These are the men who put the entire community at risk. Because of those rabble-rousers, our holy Temple in Jerusalem is now defiled by the likes of him," he said, emphasizing the last word with an imperceptible jerk of his head in the direction of the governor's mansion. Better a live priest with a locked temple, than a dead one because of a few fanatics, Aaron thought. To Jacobides he said only, "If we do not take care of our troublemakers, the Romans will do it for us, and you and I will both be the losers."

The two walked on together with the other men trailing, their heads inclined toward their leaders to catch their words. They had reached the Temple of Serapis where crowds were waiting to present their offerings to the priests stationed at small altars on the street. Many cradled tapestries in which lay effigies in clay, gold, silver, of arms, legs, and even internal organs, all symbols of healings that Serapis had granted them. With practiced self-control, the Jews restrained their tendency to speed up their pace through the crowd of Alexandrian idolaters so as not to offend the gentiles. In any case, the crowd surged along at its own inexorable tempo, as every Alexandrian knew. It was part of the city's magical effect: To join the river of people was to feel the pulse of one of the greatest cities on earth. No one in their right mind would rush, even if they could.

The human stream finally ebbed as they left the market area behind. They continued east down the main boulevard of the Neapolis Quarter. Jacobides was proud of the home he had built for his family in Alexandria's Jewish quarter, the last word in urban opulence, outdoing even the most ostentatious of the other Neapolis mansions. The intricate alabaster latticework of their windows revealed, rather than concealed, hints of the wealth behind them, and the marble walls gleamed in the late afternoon sun right up to their third story balustrades. To put off further discussion with the whiny old priest, Jacobides looked the buildings up and down, as if he were deeply absorbed in an architectural analysis of the new quarter. One after another, the men peeled off from the group and headed for home. There was no more time for discussion. It was past time to make preparations for the Sabbath.

Alone, Jacobides' thoughts turned to his son, Menahem, and the role he planned for the young man in the task that lay ahead.

Chapter 13

By the time first light was bathing the tops of the mountains, turning the ridges and valleys into soft, cinnamon folds, Miriam and her charges had disappeared from the view of the watchers at Masada's walls. Valerius had been able to convince Silva that it would be worthless to pursue a woman and children who would soon enough succumb to the vicious desert sun. And so, as the mammoth army surrounding the mountain made preparations to break camp, the tiny convoy of fugitives was forgotten.

Their water skins were nearly empty and so Miriam led the children along a well-worn shepherd's path she had spied through the desiccated, dun-colored brush to where it spiraled downward to the nearest spring.

"Where are we going?" the ten-year-old boy asked, as Miriam lifted the two younger children off the donkey and began to lead them down to the trickle of water. Until now, Miriam had avoided even asking their names. She thought of them as no more than a burden she had to bear for the time being. But her mother would want her to treat them with care and as much affection as she could muster, and so before answering she asked him a question, as gently as she could.

"What is your name, boy?"

"I am Samuel, son of…son of Solomon the sandal maker," the boy finished faintly. Uttering his father's name brought with it the realization that his parents were gone forever. How did it happen? The boy still was not certain he understood.

"Solomon was your father?" Of course, Miriam knew the nimble-fingered man who had repaired their sandals ever since she had first come to the fortress. He, too, had followed Elazar to Masada. He, too, had believed that God would help their leader and bring them victory against all odds. But unlike Miriam's Joseph, Solomon had been satisfied to serve the community in the simplest of ways.

Had Solomon the sandal maker even dreamed of the end to which they would come? Did he awaken to the terrible truth a moment before he died? Would he not be glad to know that through a turn of fate, his son had survived? Miriam stopped the whirlwind of thoughts and focused on the lad with the question in his tired, old man's eyes.

"I can't say for sure where we will end up, Samuel," she said, leaning toward the boy. "I myself have not left the fortress for two years. But from the tales our raiders told, northwest is the direction to go. We will follow the shepherds' paths upward to the highlands, and when we reach the first village at the edge of the wilderness, we will be able to rest and seek shelter. From there we will continue to Jerusalem."

Miriam kept to herself the kind of welcome they could expect from the villagers. It was not only that her fellow fortress-dwellers had regularly raided the highlanders' sheep pens and wheat fields, their olive groves and vineyards. It was the fact that those villagers had borne the brunt of Roman vengeance every time the Sicarii warriors had returned jubilant to Masada, heavily laden with enemy weapons. She would be greeted by people who had seen their neighbors snatched from their homes by the conqueror's soldiers and agents – who did not care to tell one Jew apart from another. She would be confronted by men and women who had seen their loved ones tortured and killed on the merest suspicion of granting aid and comfort to the Sicarii.

After watering the animals, filling the skins, and taking a long drink herself, Miriam allowed herself the closest she could come to relaxing. She sank to the stony ground, folded her long legs to one side, and leaned back on her elbows. She watched the three younger children as the shade and the water brought them to life again. In the way of children, they put horror away and frolicked in the shallow stream, swinging their arms in wide arcs as they bent down to splash one another. She tried halfheartedly to discern in their faces a likeness to anyone she had known at the fortress, but she could not.

Languidness began to settle over her like a fine silk coverlet. She rose, splashed her face and hair with the cool water to shake off her fatigue and tried to focus on their journey to the highlands. She probed the corners of her mind for whatever she could remember overhearing when Elazar debriefed returning raiding parties.

What was it they had said of the roads to the western highlands? Their first expeditions had been to Carmel, Maon, and other Judean villages that they had said were less than a day's march northwest of the fortress. But when the villagers had taken to hiding everything they could from the Sicarii, eventually they had had no choice but to range farther and farther west, then north across the wilderness of Judea, all the way up to the village of Carmel.

The hapless traveler unfamiliar with the trails, she had gleaned from Elazar's strategy sessions, would soon find himself at the edge of one of the great canyons that sliced the desert, dry as death in summer and raging with sudden, murderous floods in winter. Scaling the huge rock terraces would be impossible. She would have to climb carefully westward to Carmel, close enough to the main trail to avoid the canyon, but far enough to avoid a chance Roman patrol.

She called to the children and offered them one last drink from her cupped hand before lifting them up onto the backs of the placid donkeys. Samuel struggled alone to mount behind his youngest sibling.

"I want it to be night. I'm sleepy," protested the little one in a thin voice.

"Hush now, Matya," Samuel chided him gently. We have a long journey ahead of us. But we will be riding, and there will be plenty of little animals and plants to see along the way. Look there!"

The sight of a fat brown hyrax and its family scurrying into the shelter of nearby pale green saltwort bushes distracted the child. He began to chatter away about the little mice with the black, bulging eyes that lived in the courtyard at home and forgot his complaints for the moment. Samuel exchanged a knowing glance with Miriam. The ten-year-old had become her full partner in their expedition of survival.

The hours melted away as the little party trekked upward and westward. Finally, around midday, they collapsed in the generous shadow cast by an acacia tree's flat, spreading crown. It was clear to Miriam that if they dared to travel by day again, the relentless, scorching wilderness would be the conqueror's ally in their annihilation.

Miriam plunged her hands into the saddlebags hoping to find food. Her fingers closed around sticky dates and fuzzy-cheeked fresh almonds and she silently thanked Julius, their slave-protector, once again. "Come children, we'll eat, then we'll rest while we wait for the sun to leave us be." Her tone was as light as their prospects were dark. "And look what I found – I see I will be able to prepare a very special meal for you!"

A short distance from their tree, a ubiquitous saltwort bush spread low on the ground. Miriam picked a few of the biggest, darkest green leaves she could find. "This is the way I love to eat almonds, children." She wrapped the leaf around the velvety rind of an almond and bit into it. "Delicious," she cooed, tempting the children. The salt, and the much-needed moisture from the almond would tide them over and the tangy flavor would distract them, if only for a while. The little ones each followed Miriam's example, meticulously wrapping their almonds and comparing each other's skills before biting into the finished product. They each ended their meal with a sticky sweet date.

Miriam searched through the bag to see what else Julius had managed to pack. There was a whole *qav* of barley flour, enough for three days' supply of bread baked beneath the ashes of the fire she would make. There was also a cake of pressed figs that she decided she would save for later.

When the sun finally unlocked itself from its zenith and began its journey westward, she roused them. Gambling that they would reach another spring before nightfall, she decided she could afford to ease their discomfort a little. She poured some of their precious water from the goatskin bag into her palm, and washed each child's face, hands, and wrists again to revive them from their sluggishness.

They plodded along in silence. The children dozed most of the time. Miriam felt herself nodding off as she walked. But even at this pace, they had covered quite a distance, she calculated, when the acacia grove became a tiny dark spot in the distance and finally disappeared behind the hills. She continued along the lip of the craggy canyon that began at the shores of the Asphalt Sea north of Masada, following its winding way westward, just as she heard the warriors had done on their forays. They had covered over a parasang since their last stop. Just one more would put them in Carmel by midday tomorrow.

With nightfall almost upon them, the desert sky was the deep and flawless purple of fine Tyrian cloth. The smaller children, oblivious to anything but their growling stomachs and sore muscles, began to whimper. Samuel looked at Miriam expectantly.

"We will stay right here until morning," she decreed. Soon she had Samuel busy with the task of breaking off branches from the nearest acacias and searching the area for additional dead wood that would serve as fuel for a cooking fire.

She cast about for a digging tool, finally settling for a flat rock that lay nearby. "Come children, help make our oven and we will have bread before long!" she called out to the little ones. By the time they had a made a hole in the dry earth deep enough to start a fire, infinite stars winked and glimmered from the depths of the pitch-black sky.

Miriam opened up their bag of provisions once again, emptying it of the last of its meager contents. Laying the bag on the ground, she smoothed the skin out as best she could, then formed it into a concave that would be her mixing bowl. Into this shallow basin she carefully laid a measure of flour in a small mound. She poured a palm full of water from the water skin into a little hollow in the mound and began to knead in practiced strokes until she had a smooth little ball. This she worked with her fingers into a disk-shaped loaf and set it aside on the bag.

"Alright now everyone, while we wait for the fire to die down to embers we'll have our meal of date cakes. And then we'll have hot fresh bread to tide us over."

"When will we come to our new home?" asked seven-year-old Salome, as they gnawed gratefully on the compressed dates.

"I hope that by tomorrow evening we will be in the highlands, and we'll meet good people who will help you find new homes." Miriam knew better than to use the word "us" in regard any future home for herself. *That* was much further away than the distance she could cover in one cold night and a half a day's walk.

"See, our fire is ready already," Miriam pointed to the pit where the acacia wood had burned down to a bed of glowing embers. She turned away from the children and laid the bread on the coals, covering it with earth. By the time she turned back, all three children were in a disorderly, sleeping heap, their faces still smudged with the remains of the date cakes that had filled their stomachs. The bread would wait until morning, Miriam thought, as she covered up her little band of fellow-travelers with the rough blankets that also served as their saddles. Finally, she lay down on the stony ground, pulling her robe tightly around her.

She was at the place beyond exhaustion where sleep is a stranger and worry an uninvited guest who refuses to leave. Had she correctly estimated the point at which to turn northward? If not, they would find themselves at the edge of an impassible abyss, too far from the next water source to survive.

Years later, Miriam could never think back on the events of the next day without recalling her mother's favorite story from the Writings, the story of Ruth. The Moabite woman must have felt much as Miriam did now as she plied the wilderness trails – perhaps these very same ones as Ruth had trod with her mother-in-law. As it had been for Ruth the Moabite, so it was for Miriam, daughter of Jonathan: A great unknown yawned at the far end of the trail. But if she trod carefully, she dared to believe, a new life would be her reward.

Chapter 14

Miriam roused the children as dawn was breaking, and the little group began its second day's journey. She scanned the northern horizon constantly, seeking a passageway across the canyons. At times she felt they were moving so slowly that they were not moving at all. Finally, the crumpled canyon stretched out to a negotiable valley and they were able to turn northward.

"Look! Over here!" Trail-savvy Samuel, whose playground had been the Judean wilderness from the time he could take his first steps and until his fortress-home was besieged, had been the first to spot the sign that their journey to Carmel was nearing its end: Pungent oregano plants now studded the rocky hillsides. Miriam picked a sprig and crushed it between thumb and forefinger. A familiar aroma exploded from the tiny crumbled leaves. It conjured up visions of family meals: dipping their bread in a common bowl where the fresh-picked herb floated generously in warm, golden olive oil. The aroma lifted their spirits and quickened their steps. It was not long before another smell dominated – the acrid air of the goat pen. Sure enough – the corrals of Carmel were around the next curve.

They were on the path that led to the village, trailing behind the shepherds leading their sheep and goats home after a day's foraging in the east. The children's incessant chatter finally drew the attention of the shepherdess ahead of them on the path.

She turned around. Her mouth dropped open as she fixed a tiger-eye gaze on the disheveled, dusty band. But she remembered her manners at the last moment, and the most natural of all questions died on her lips – travelers were not to be asked either their origin or their full name. It was said that the patriarch Abraham himself practiced this custom; it was the only proper way to treat a shelter-seeking stranger whose ties to a rival tribe might otherwise make them unwelcome.

"Blessed be your coming," the shepherdess called out to them. The ancient greeting floated melodiously over the evening breeze. She waited for Miriam and the children to come closer, focusing all her attention on the newcomers while her flock headed confidently toward the pen, single-file up the slope in long lines along the ancient paths.

As they came closer, she took note of the condition of their clothing and their gritty faces. "You have come a long way," she offered. This was the first round of what was understood by both parties to be an interrogation, albeit a gentle one. "Indeed," Miriam responded formally, "the sight of the houses of Carmel and its vineyards is a welcome one."

"After I have taken care of the animals, I hope I may extend to you the hospitality of my household. I am Leah, daughter of Joseph."

"I am Miriam, daughter of Jonathan of Hanablata." Miriam hoped that her willingness to identify herself so forthrightly would go a long way toward assuaging suspicion of the newcomers. She was taking a big risk in doing so. She would suffer if anyone in the village recognized her father's name and recalled his allegiance to the most extreme of the rebel sects.

They continued, led by the shepherdess, along the path. The children dismounted from the donkeys and ran ahead willingly, but Miriam's steps were weighted down by far more than the fatigue of the road.

At the corral, the travelers' donkeys made straight for the water troughs. With low-throated huffs, the ancient language of a shepherd to the flock, Leah shooed the last of the sheep and goats into their pens. Then she entered it herself and closed the gate behind her. She plunged into the center of the shuffling mass of wiry-haired goats and stood quietly among them. Slowly but surely, they responded to her reassuring presence and their restlessness dissipated. When she emerged, the stall was still. She motioned Miriam and the children to follow her.

The narrow path followed the low stone terraces, beyond which Carmel's sturdy stone structures huddled like long-time companions. Hardly any space was left between one house and another; as families grew, rooms proliferated until the village lanes had become a maze no wider than a laden donkey could traverse. Here and there, courtyards forced open spaces between the houses, and even at this hour, with the evening meal in full sway, they echoed with the play of children too restless to remain in the small, dim chambers. From every courtyard doorway, curious eyes followed Miriam and the children in the wake of their shepherdess. In that mysterious way of the village, word of their presence preceded them as they went.

Leah stopped, and with a slight motion of her hand indicated that they had arrived at their destination. She stepped over the threshold into the courtyard, and then into her family's home, standing aside so that Miriam and the children could enter. All conversation came to a halt around the mat on which the evening meal was spread. A rustle of cloth and a shifting of weight upon the beaten earth floor was all Miriam could make out at first as the diners, half-hidden in the shadows cast by the flickering light of small olive oil lamps, turned to look at her. The silence lasted a split-second longer, and then a man's deep voice broke it.

"Blessed be your coming. Sit."

The group moved closer to each other to make room nearest the door for the newcomers. The children stared wide-eyed at the array of food on the mat. As Miriam's eyes adjusted to the flickering lamplight, she made out a man sitting against the wall on the far side of the mat. The gleaming whiteness of his hair and beard and the deep furrows around his eyes, as well as the deferential way the family looked at him – or away from him – told her that he was the patriarch of this clan. Rising slightly, as if to adjust his robes, he nudged his wife. She initiated her own system of signals, and a stir ensued around the table. Leah, still standing by the door, stooped to push plates and bowls over to the children. Another young woman exited the room and returned a few moments later with steaming hot, flat bread, which she laid in front of them. A clay pitcher of wine was passed around the mat from hand to hand until it reached the visitors.

With a practiced motion, the children tore a piece of bread from the loaf, and used it to scoop up a mouthful of spiced nettle paste. A bowl of hard-cooked eggs was rapidly emptied of its contents, several squares of rehydrated, salty cheese disappeared and another plate was picked clean of its slices of sea squill floating in vinegar. Miriam nibbled nervously at whatever was passed to her, tasting nothing.

The adults resumed eating. No one spoke. Eyes shifted toward and away from Miriam, watching, waiting. Finally, the meal was concluded and grace was said hastily. Heavily, the patriarch got to his feet. It was a signal for everyone else to rise. The men and older women followed him out of the room. Waiting impatiently for the elders to disperse, the children finally scampered out, eager for a few more moments of play before their mothers, who had remained behind to store away the remnants of the meal, would put them to bed. Miriam caught Samuel's eye, then glanced at the two children in their charge. Obedient to her wordless command, he shepherded the little ones outside. Leah stayed to work with her sisters and sisters-in-law, but indicated with a gentle motion of her head for Miriam to follow her grandfather outside.

The older people took their customary places on the ground, resting their backs against the courtyard wall. The patriarch motioned Miriam to sit next to him. The air was cool and fresh, innumerable stars piercing the black firmament. The previous night, that sky had been the last thing Miriam had seen before closing her eyes on the rocky ground. Of the nights before that, she did not permit herself to think. Tonight, she allowed herself to hope, would be different.

"I am Mordecai," was all he said. When Miriam volunteered her name, the response was as she had feared. The others began murmuring. Too many Sicarii victims from Hanablata hung from Roman crucifixes, and too many such victims, living and dead, had been natives of Carmel, for the name of her father and of his town not to be recognized. Only Mordecai remained impassive. Eying their elder, the murmurers finally fell silent.

"You have had an ordeal. You and your children will go to bed now. In the morning we will talk." He turned away from her to address the man next to him and appeared to forget her presence. A short while later the younger women came out of the house to call their children to sleep, and the group broke up. The various family groups gradually made for home, each through its own doorway off the courtyard.

Leah came to call Miriam who in turn sought out her brood. She found the little ones standing shyly on the edge of a group of children playing with puppets. Samuel had moved off to watch the older boys cast pebbles against the wall. They looked up at the now-familiar sound of her voice, and moved toward it gratefully.

Inside, all evidence of the meal had been removed. The mat on which they had eaten had been rolled away, replaced by smaller sleeping mats and blankets.

"You look as if you cannot stay awake for even one minute longer," Leah said, and for the first time something akin to sympathy crept into her voice. "You and the children can sleep next to me." Another woman, whom Miriam assumed to be Leah's older sister, lay down in the opposite corner of the room. Her elbow under her head, Leah watched Miriam's every move as, with the boy's help, she covered the younger children. Miriam removed her outer robe. She caught Leah eyeing the leather pouch quizzically when she saw that Miriam was not going to remove it from her waistband. Finally, Miriam lay down and turned away, facing the children. She could still sense Leah's eyes upon her as her heavy lids dropped and she floated into an exhausted, dreamless sleep.

Chapter 15

It took Miriam a moment to identify the aroma that woke her – was it roasted grain? Odd for an early morning meal, she thought. Agitated voices emanated from the courtyard. She shook off the last vestiges of sleep, hurriedly drew her robe around her and went to the doorway. A knot of people was passing the courtyard door. They paid no attention to her when, without thinking, she stepped in among them. She moved along with the people until they arrived at the main square of the village.

Miriam raised her hand to her brow, against the glare of the morning light, trying to make sense of the scene before her. She had never seen anything like it. Two great clay jars stood in the square, of the type that had once stood row upon row in the fortress storehouses. They were filled to the brim with freshly roasted grain, mixed with nuts. What holiday was this, she thought blankly. A family celebration, perhaps the birth of a daughter, to which the whole village had been invited?

A man was scooping out grain from one of the jars, handing it out to other men and women standing nearby. They were cracking the shells, but instead of placing the tiny, tasty meats into a dish, they were throwing them onto the ground! A pack of children scrambled at their feet, pushing and pulling at each other to get a hold of the tasty granules that had wedged themselves between the plaza's broad, smooth paving stones.

It was more than the act of throwing good food on the ground that confused Miriam. It was the face of the man doling out the grain – a frozen mask of anguish. It was like some sort of disturbing dream. The children were singing as they picked at the pieces of fallen grain, with the women egging them on, adding their own voices to the chant. Miriam strained to catch the unfamiliar words. "We have eaten the *kesisa* of Jacob of Carmel, Jacob of Carmel is *niksas*." And again, "We have eaten the *kesisa* of Jacob of Carmel. Jacob of Carmel is *niksas*..."

Suddenly it dawned upon her.

It was a pun. There were many in the Aramaic they spoke, and in the holy tongue of Hebrew as well. With such word play they were taught to turn symbolism into actions, making both the words and deeds unforgettable. This pun, though, was a cruel one: *Kesisa* normally meant simply food that had been chewed. But in its root was also the word for a man cut off, a man destroyed. As the bizarre singsong continued unabated, its subject became clear to Miriam. The man standing next to the jar was Jacob of Carmel. He finished handing out the grain and stood off to one side, his arms around his wife and children, tears of shame streaking their faces.

"Why do you look so confused?" came a voice from behind her. Miriam turned and saw one of the women who had sat across the mat for her at last night's dinner. Then, the woman's eyes had betrayed only the mildest curiosity. Now they blazed with hostility. "You and your kind are the root of the evil that has befallen our neighbor Jacob."

Miriam opened her mouth to protest, but the woman's anger continued to flow in a raging stream of invective. "We know who you are. While we struggled to find a way to live a life that gave both praise to God and no offense to our Roman overlords, your father and his kind struck out against the rulers. You have brought nothing but evil upon us all. And what are you doing among us now? Have you come to stir us up again for the sake of your accursed cause? Or do you want merely to gloat over what has become of us?"

The woman placed her hands on Miriam's shoulders and spun her roughly back toward the scene in the square. "See, then," she snarled, her mouth next to Miriam's ear. "Take a good look at Jacob. Our Roman masters have doubled and tripled our taxes. Jacob cannot pay, and so his land has been taken from him. He will be fortunate to salvage a few head from his flock – to become a herder of sheep and goats in the wilderness."

A knot of people had formed around Miriam and the woman. The singsong died out, replaced with angry shouts. "Yes, it is the fault of your people!"

"The Sicarii are our misfortune!"

"If it were not for you, Jacob would not have lost his land!"

"Why have you come into our midst?"

"Go back to the desert where you belong!"

A throng now closed in around her, hurling abuse like stones at an execution.

Miriam, who had not taken a breath since the first gasp of shock at the woman's attack on her, felt her surroundings fade and grow dark around the edges of her eyes. Suddenly, something silenced the screams of the mob. Just before she lost consciousness she saw the crowd part. Mordecai was moving toward her.

When next she opened her eyes, she was looking straight up into the old man's pallid ones, sunken deep between the creased parchment of his cheeks and his thick white brows. She lay on a thin, reed-stuffed mattress, back in the room where dinner had been served the night before. Leah sat at her side and wordlessly offered her a cup of water. Miriam struggled to sit up to drink it. Self-consciously, she smoothed out her robe, and as she always did, felt to make sure the leather pouch still rested securely in her belt.

The old man answered the question he saw in the young woman's eyes. "Where should I begin, my daughter? When your leader Menahem pranced around the Temple Mount in the high priest's robes? Mordecai raised spotted hands and fluttered his fingers in mocking imitation of a dancer. "Yes, that would be the place to start," he said, as if to himself. Miriam was confused. No one she had ever known had ever spoken of Menahem with anything but grief-filled reverence.

"Of course, they had no choice but to kill him for his blasphemy. But it was too late to mollify the conqueror, the only thing most of us desired. To return to the way things were… But who was left to go back to the old life, even if we could have? The dead, who filled the streets of the cities as far away as Damascus? The patriarch licked his cracked lips and stroked his beard nervously. Leah glanced at her grandfather, concern knitting her brow. His voice had begun to tremble with the burden of telling things that by tacit agreement the community never mentioned any more. When the headman spoke again, he had forced the calm back into his voice.

"But that, as it turned out was not enough death for your Sicarii," he continued evenly. Did it escape your attention that it was your own who slaughtered so many at Ein Gedi – some say as many as 700 people? Did no one tell you what every little child here in the highlands knew? How the people of Ein Gedi were forced to their knees – ten, then twenty at a time, the young with the old, forced to bow their heads, bludgeoned to death by the blows of your clubs. Then your people stole everything a pack animal could carry.

"Oh yes, yes, we know it to be true," Mordecai persisted in a quiet, terrible, measured tone, when Miriam began to shake her head convulsively. "We have a survivor from Ein Gedi living among us." Mordecai put a hand on her arm to stop her attempt to cover her ears.

He kept his gaze fixed on the young woman's eyes, which now moved back and forth like caged leopards. Had Mordecai been able to see behind her eyes, he would have glimpsed the tall balsam jars that the men had brought back to the fortress, jubilantly presenting them to Elazar before bearing them off to lock in the storehouse. "Taxes of the revolt," she recalled them saying grimly.

Miriam wrung her hands until her knuckles were bone-white. She wanted to escape the truth, but she was chained to it by memories she had not even realized she possessed. "I did not know," was all she could say, over and over again.

"The people of the Holy City spent their last days snatching food from secret hiding places," Mordecai pressed on, "and from each other, mothers from the mouths of their own babies, children from within the robes of their dead fathers. Any who tried to escape the city were caught and crucified. Hundreds were hanged each day from the trees, blessing this fate rather than one that forced them to remain alive in a city where a mother, crazed with hunger, could kill, roast, and eat her own baby son."

"I can see that your leaders have kept the knowledge from you of what has happened in our villages since the destruction of our beloved Temple. If you had known, you would understand the rage against the Sicarii of the people of this village, and every village of Judea and far beyond. People like Jacob are everywhere. Not only are they forced to sell off their lands to the conqueror, they often see it awarded to those of our own people who now serve the wicked kingdom."

Now the old man headed for firmer ground, repeating words he had uttered countless times to encourage the villagers, to remind them of their rightful place in God's eyes. "You and we belong to two different peoples. We do not insist, like you, that God redeem us at the time of *our* choosing. We will wait to the time of His choosing.

"This is not a sign of weakness, a crime punishable by death, as your leaders taught. We have not forgotten or ignored the indignities and cruelties of the last seven years. What you witnessed out there today is a part of the remembering. *Our* way of remembering. Our children will always remember that this day they have eaten the last harvest of Jacob, one of the most skilled farmers of Carmel. As they grow up, they will pray to be worthy, and work to be worthy, for God to bring us our freedom."

Miriam tried one last time to flee to the only truth she had ever known. "Our leaders taught us that God had come to despise us, and that our suffering was deserved," she said to Mordecai. But her words suddenly sounded hollow to her. Especially that one, "suffering," which, despite what she had seen just days ago at Masada, and the loss of her young husband, almost paled in the face of the things she had heard here.

"You have been led astray, my daughter. In the eyes of the Holy One, blessed by He, there is no meaning at all to suffering brought on by our own attempts to free ourselves from the yoke of the wicked kingdom. God has greater plans for us. A few months ago, during the last days of Kislev, a man came to our village, a learned man, nephew of the great Rabbi Yohanan ben Zakkai, and marked the Feast of Dedication with us." The old man's voice faded as he relived that day in his mind. "Abba Sirka is his name. One of your own band, I believe."

The headman's diffident musings were a pretense – he knew very well that Abba Sirka's beliefs were moderate compared with those of the Sicarii. Miriam sensed that the pretense was kept up out of compassion to her, of the kind sometimes shown to children and wounded creatures, and so she said nothing, waiting for him to continue.

"Abba Sirka had abandoned the path of violence. He taught that the Kingdom of Heaven depends not on the presence, however odious, or the removal, however wondrous, of our conquerors. The Kingdom of Heaven is ours to achieve from within. It depends first and foremost on the compassion with which we treat each other."

Leah stood suddenly and began to move restlessly about the small room. It was clear she had had enough of what she considered her grandfather's pointless reminiscences. Mordecai glanced disapprovingly at her, then took another long look at Miriam.

Miriam took this as an invitation to speak. "At the fortress of Masada the fact that we continued to survive meant that we were fighting. But when we knew the end was near, we continued to fight, choosing to..."

Mordecai raised a gnarled hand to stop her.

"I do not wish to know any more about your fortress, or how you came to arrive here from the wilderness, alone with these children," he said. "What I do wish is for you to leave here immediately. We will take the children in. We will care for them as our own. Our people here are too angry to see you as I do, as the last remnant of those who have been wronged by their leaders. They may discover this someday. But you *must* discover it. Go to Jerusalem, see with your own eyes what has befallen our beloved city." He motioned to Leah to help him to his feet, turned away from Miriam and began to shuffle toward the door. Suddenly, he stopped and turned back to face her. "And you, of all people, must live. Because of all you have seen, and all that you will learn."

Chapter 16

Mordecai walked out, leaning on Leah's arm. "See to it that our guest has a proper meal," he instructed her. "Pack her food for two days, prepare one of her donkeys for travel and make sure she is given three denarii for the other one.

Alone in the room, Miriam sank back down as if felled by a blow. The last image of her husband Joseph, the vision in which she had taken refuge so often, was swept away forever by the realization that he, too, had been a part of the unspeakable acts she had heard about here for the first time.

For the first time? The image of the balsam jars in the storehouse, their squat ordinariness belying the treasure they held, again came to mind. In the days of the fortress, as she sat and waited to hand out food to her neighbors, had she not glanced over at them, wondered about them? It was one thing to take a portion of the highland people's harvest to feed the community at Masada. The rebels were fighting everyone's battle, she had been taught. They could not win the war against Rome if they were starving. But how had the inhabitants of Ein Gedi been parted from the balsam, their most valuable asset? And why? Had she, all these years, been a refugee from the truth as much as from the conqueror?

The meaning of the message that she had been selected to bear, first by Elazar and her mother, and then by Mordecai, had changed beyond recognition in the space of two Sabbaths.

The headman had given her no choice – she was no longer welcome in Carmel. To Jerusalem, Mordecai had directed her. A city in despair. That would suit her mood, she thought. Living among those without hope was where she belonged.

Still, word of Joseph might reach her there. At that moment, the document he had given her out of love burned like a leech burrowing into her skin. She saw herself tearing at her clothes to rid herself of this testament to her past. But it had carried her through so much. Her hands remained at her sides. The love she felt for Joseph still seemed a thing apart from the grisly secrets of his life.

When she stepped out into the courtyard again, the village had returned to normal. The first of the day's loaves were already rising in the mud brick oven, and the older women had taken their places at the loom. She saw people passing the courtyard doorway on their way to their daily tasks. The same people who, moments before, if not for the patriarch's intervention, would have run her out of town, or worse.

Leah reappeared. She bore a wooden tray with a plate of white, watery cheese, and small bowls of olives, radishes, and cucumbers, as well as a clay drinking cup and pitcher. Leah held the food in front of herself, more like a shield than an offering.

"Your children are playing with the others that they met during the…this morning," she finished lamely. "Mordecai has already spoken to two families who are willing to take them in. He feels it best that you leave right away. The children will be told later that you have gone."

Leah kept silent, but her gold-flecked eyes flashed with accusations. This mysterious woman, she understood all too well, was from the same band that had raided their village more times than anyone cared to remember, making off with what little the Romans had left them. All through the years that Leah had gone to her sleeping mat hungry every night, this woman had been eating the food raised by *her* father, harvested by *her* family's labor, she thought.

"When you have finished your meal, find your way back to the corral where I brought the herds last night." Your donkey is there. It should take you two or three days to cover the three parasangs between here and Jerusalem. There is enough food in the saddlebags until you reach the city, and the water skins are full. Go in peace." The formal words of farewell were as brittle as dried reeds. Let her try to buy food in a city in which a trifling quantity of grass sold for four denarii, Leah thought. It would be the rebel woman's turn to go to bed hungry.

Miriam felt the younger woman's loathing like a hot wind from the east. Without another word, Miriam reached for her cloak, leaving the meal untouched.

She kept her heart sealed against the thought that she was abandoning the two little ones – they would blend into their new families soon enough. But she was sorry to leave without saying goodbye to young Samuel. She did not know that the boy was watching her from behind the curtain in the doorway of the home he had been taken to. "Miriam of Masada, Miriam of Masada," he whispered. He would never forget her name, he told himself. He was old enough to remember, and – somewhere in the depths of the sorrows such a young heart should never know – to understand.

Carmel was less than half a day's walk from the Hebron–Jerusalem road and she covered the distance quickly. Miriam was alone on the track and she let the plodding donkey carry her forward without thinking about anything beyond the next turn. Even after she reached the main road, she had little company. A few peddlers slept in the dappled shade of an olive grove, waiting for the cooler hours to continue their journey north to Tekoa, Bethlehem or Jerusalem or south to Hebron. By evening, Miriam had made enough headway to see the houses of Bethlehem in the distance. She knew she would not reach the town before darkness set in and the gates closed. Now it was her turn to take shelter in an olive grove. She spied a patch of exposed bedrock and a shallow trough hewn by some ancient farmer in the rock. After unsaddling the donkey, she pulled off the rough blanket that had cushioned the wooden saddle frame, and poured water from the skin into the depression for the donkey to drink. A quick survey of the little patch of ground she had selected satisfied her that it was devoid of any rocks from under which a deadly yellow scorpion or stippled snake might crawl when the sun rose. She unfolded the blanket with a shake, laid it on the ground, and herself upon it. One arm curled up beneath her head, she fell asleep instantly.

The next thing she heard was the agitated snorting of the donkey and the scurrying sounds of an animal, probably a fox, attracted by the food in the saddlebags. A pale dawn was already staining the blackness of the night. Miriam stood up with a start and gave a hoarse cry, frightening away whatever intruder had been sniffing around. Untying one of the water skins from its loop on the saddlebag, she raised it to her lips and took a long drink. She rubbed a few more drops on her eyes to wash the last vestiges of sleep away, untied the donkey and led it to the road.

By the time the sun was up, the outskirts of Bethlehem lay before her. Tiny compared to Jerusalem, but still an important hub on the mountaintop highway, which was the most important road in the country since the days of Abraham.

Some Bethlehemites, her father used to tell her, considered their city as just as important as Jerusalem, if not more so. It was, after all, where King David had been born. King David, he had taught her, was the ancestor of the liberating king-messiah who would also come from Bethlehem; as the darkness deepened around their lives, everyone said he would soon appear to ensure their victory over the conqueror.

When she was a child, everyone she knew hoped for the coming of the Messiah. Especially after Menahem had been killed, when many had begun to shun her family for their links to the Sicarii. Then came the times when playmates from her courtyard began to vanish without a trace. She could not know that neighbors had informed on their parents to the authorities and that some of these children had become orphans by the time they were put aboard the slave ships bound for Rhodes or Rome.

These were the times when Miriam's mother would lay a hand absently on daughter's curls and sigh, "Now would be a good time for the Messiah son of David to come to us. Now would be a good time. It's less than a day, such a short trip, from Bethlehem to Jerusalem..."

Immersed in thought as she plodded along, Miriam discovered she had become wedged into a crowd of travelers trudging the last mile to the gates of Bethlehem. There were more people here than she had seen in one place for years. She squeezed in ahead of the donkey to lead it through the dusty throng. In normal times it would be considered strange for a woman to travel alone. But in such days as these she merited not even a passing glance, not even by the Roman soldiers standing diffident guard duty. Oddly, as close as the crowd pressed in around her, she could hardly feel their presence. A sense of invisibility had enveloped her. Like a veil, the truth she had learned at Carmel had floated down to separate her from the rest of the world.

She moved with the crowd down the paved main street toward the market, whose stalls were almost bare. She needed only one commodity from the town, and she would stay here no longer than it took to obtain it. She sought out the women and girls bearing empty water skins on donkey-back or jars atop their heads, and followed them to the village's main cistern.

Then, a demonic shriek penetrated her shroud of isolation. Before she could divine its source, she felt a vicious yank on her robe that threw her off balance, and sent her tumbling to the ground. She looked around dazed. No one else seemed to notice her predicament. Bracing herself against the low lip of the well she pulled herself up. She found herself staring into a pair of sooty eyes embedded in folds of leathery skin, burning with the fever of madness. Somewhere beneath the eyes, a thin, matted beard of indistinct color sprouted, the only covering of a pockmarked chest from which every rib protruded. The man wore only a filthy loincloth, and sores on his bare feet and legs oozed pus.

"Beware, beware!" the man screeched. "A stranger is among us. We must protect the well of David our king! His seed will be born here, in his beloved Bethlehem of Judah. As in the days when the Philistines surrounded our town, he may ask us to bring him water, to bring him water, to bring him waaaater," the man's screech became a piteous wail. "We must not let the well fall into the hands of the stranger!"

"Be quiet, you old fool," ordered one of the townswomen. Obediently, he crouched down on his haunches and his wail subsided into the unceasing murmur of the mad.

"Pay him no attention," the same woman now addressed Miriam curtly. Miriam noticed that the woman was careful not to meet her eyes – the economy of those who lived with loss after loss of those they loved. "There are many like him in these days. Get your water and leave us in peace."

Miriam did as she was asked, skirting the old man carefully this time. She lowered an empty skin into the cistern and pulled it up swollen with water. She poured some into the nearby trough for the donkey to drink. Refilling the skins, she secured them to either side of the saddle frame. Without a backward glance, she left the square and retraced her steps to the gate and began her walk northward to the Holy City. Her mind was filled with childhood memories of Jerusalem. She had loved the special days when her father would bring her to the Mount of Olives, where he would point out the Temple courts to her, pride and reverence honey-coating his tone. On very clear early mornings, they could see the sun glinting on the silver and gold threads in the brilliant white robes of the Levites as they played their harps and cymbals atop the semicircular steps leading to the Nicanor Gates.

And the Holy of Holies! That was a sight she would never forget, its marble walls and copper trim gleaming in the distance like gems in the diadem of the King of Kings. She liked the view from the Mount of Olives even better than the view she had close up, on the days she stood at the top of the steps leading to the gates, when she accompanied her mother, her aunts and the other well-to-do women bringing their lambs for offerings after childbirth. The veil that had settled on her at Carmel was back, but it was now a benevolent cloud of memories. It lulled the sting of Carmel's truth into a dull ache.

Chapter 17

By the time Miriam reached the edge of the Hinnom Valley, the walls of the city were undulating in the midday heat. With one corner of her once-white flaxen head scarf, she wiped away the sweat that dripped into her eyes as she strained to get a better look. She surveyed the city wall west to east, east to west. Something had changed. But what? The three lofty turrets still jabbed the sky as always, like admonishing fingers, warning of the unreachable heights of old King Herod's ambitions and power. Then she saw it: The great Psephinus Tower, that gigantus of blue-veined marble that had been the crowning glory of the northwestern corner of the wall – it was gone! Not until she felt the leather of the donkey's reins grow sticky, and she relaxed her grasp on them, did she realize that her fingernails had dug so deeply into the palms of her hands that four small moon-shaped cuts now oozed with her blood.

When she reached the gate nearest the palace, the pace of the crowd approaching the city with her slowed. Soon she saw why. Soldiers stood on either side of the huge, iron-studded wooden gate. They were stopping passers-by, pulling them aside to ask their names and place of origin. Some were allowed to proceed, Miriam noticed. Others stood helpless as their bundles were torn apart and searched. Still others, eyes round with panic, were marched off abruptly between two guards with short swords drawn, to disappear behind the barred inner doors of the palace.

There were no voices raised, either in anger or in protest. In fact, there were no voices at all. It seemed to Miriam that she was watching one of the mime performances the conqueror loved, which her friends used to laughingly imitate to pass the long winter nights in their early years at Masada.

In another moment, it would be her turn to pass through the gate and come under the scrutiny of the sentinels. If the guards found the scroll in the pouch at her waist, the first line of which bore the name of her most recent residence – feared and hated by Roman and Jew alike – her identity would be revealed. She would be the next Jew to be marched off to garrison headquarters.

Her eyes darted around her furtively. There! A group of people was making their way up the hill behind her. She hung back in a manner she hoped was unobtrusive, until they caught up to her. There were several young men and women her age, brothers, sisters, and their spouses. Some were carrying babies and painfully thin, road-weary children. A stooped grandmother shuffled alongside one of the younger women. Miriam slowed down long enough to entwine her arm with that of the old woman. The woman did not respond. If anyone in the group noticed, they too said nothing. These days, strangers never inquired into the business of other travelers. But they rarely turned anyone away, either. The family, with its temporary new member, proceeded past the guards with only the most cursory inspection.

After seven years, Miriam once again walked the streets of Jerusalem. She set off for the southeastern part of the city, following the vague plan she had made to head for her old home. The setting sun bathed the whitewashed houses of the Upper City's main thoroughfare in the rosy wash of her childhood evenings. It did not take long for her to realize that the cast of the light was the only thing about the Jerusalem she had once known that had not changed. Here she was, once again, beneath the long stretch of arcade, with the row of shops that once provided the commodities that filled their pantry and storerooms. In the old days, on spring evenings like this one, between Passover and the Feast of Weeks, the street would still be bustling. Some shopkeepers would be busy with the last of the day's customers, others already locking their wooden doors and placing the heavy key in their girdle before making for home.

Miriam's glance swept the open shop doors, searching for a familiar face. But only darkness greeted her, and an unaccustomed silence. Uneasily, she approached a doorway and looked inside. Wooden shelves, splintered like fractured limbs, still managed to support a few orphaned pots and jars. A moldy odor hung heavy in the air, revealing that the room's occupants had long ago abandoned the place. Backing out, she reached instinctively to close the door and realized that there was none. A glance at the neighboring premises, and to the row of shops on the other side of the broad boulevard, was enough to understand. Every single doorway yawned open and dark like a silent scream.

"Filling your larder, Jewess?" An unruly voice in broken Aramaic came from behind her. Miriam jumped, and spun around to face a grinning *eques*. The smell of the stable clung to the young cavalryman. Behind him was a cart bearing a dozen woven-straw training shields and wooden swords. With the trooper stood three other soldiers, who glanced at each other with anticipation. Finally! A chance to break the tediousness of their thousandth errand of the day. Breastplate and javelin made these men a fearsome sight on horseback, but with the shadows deepening around them in a city which – despite everything – was not their own, they looked pitifully inadequate. And, Miriam recognized immediately, they were steeped in varying degrees of drunkenness.

It seemed like a lifetime ago that she had last stared into the eyes of the conqueror, back in the tent of Flavius Silva. Differences in social class and education were an ocean separating this simpleton, carrying out his military make-work, from the supreme commander of the Tenth Legion Fretensis. Yet they had at least one thing in common. It was the look in the eyes – the eyes of Flavius Silva, whose color she could not remember, and those of this trooper, the color of a worn, soil-encrusted hoe.

She saw neither coldness nor cruelty in those eyes. It was the vacant place behind them, the place where understanding should reside, which both men shared. Neither Rome's supreme commander nor this churlish horseman had the slightest idea what they were up against in this war of theirs against the Jews, she thought as she unwillingly locked eyes with the man. They even believed that they were the victors.

The five men left their equipment behind in the street and advanced on Miriam. In vain, she sought a retreat before they closed in around her. "Dear little Jewess, do you scorn the hot meal and warm pallet that awaits you in the company of our ragged little band?" They taunted her in their native tongue, showing off to one another. Her arm jerked nearly out of its socket as the carousing troopers yanked her to their side.

"Come away with us!" sang one in sickening falsetto parody of a song. "A glooorrrrrious future awaits you!" added another, to a chorus of snickers. Miriam could not prevent the men from dragging her along with them. Finally, she stopped struggling, hoping to avoid turning drunken mirth into rage. Two of the men resumed pushing the heavily laden cart. The others marched Miriam between them.

One of them pulled Miriam's robes tightly from the back, revealing the lines of her young woman's body. "Well, look what we have here, Cerficius," he called to his companion. "This is a *rara avis*. Still plenty of fat on those bones, eh?" He pushed his face close to hers, until she could see every one of his few remaining stinking, blackened teeth. "I think that's what we'll call you ... *Rara,* our rare bird. Not a hint of disease either. I wonder where this one's been for the last couple of years."

"Not in this town, Aio, you can be sure," replied the one called Cerficius.

The streets were darkening fast. An occasional hooded figure stole by, head bowed, avoiding Miriam's attempt to make eye contact. A matter of survival. Soon the soldiers and their captive were alone in the street. The only sounds were the creaking wheels of the cart groaning under its load, the labored breathing of the soldiers pushing it, and the scuff of their hobnailed shoes on the broad smooth paving stones. Unable to bring herself to contemplate what lay ahead, Miriam tried to seek familiar landmarks as Aio and Cerficius pulled her along. They had now left the broad main market street for one of the east-west cross streets that would take them straight back to the garrison and the gate Miriam had entered not two hours ago.

Desolation had greeted her openly on the main thoroughfare. On these less frequented side streets, it lurked viciously in doorways. The odor of death wafted toward her from the bloated bodies of rats and dogs that lay atop heaps of garbage. Lumps of rags lay at the entrances to some of the houses. Miriam gasped the first time she saw one of them shift position, exposing the face of a hollow-eyed beggar, spending this night, like every night since the conquest almost three years before, outside a home no longer his own.

Hearing the sharp intake of breath at his side, Aio spoke without looking at her. "Haven't been to Jerusalem for a while, my sweet Rara? Must have been passing time at your country estate."

Miriam tightened her lips, vowing inwardly not to reveal that each new sight of her once vibrant, shining city was like a physical blow, giving her captors another chance to mock her.

The massive, iron-studded wooden gates of the fortress were already closed for the night. When the two sentries flanking the gateway caught sight of the little group, they crossed their six-foot long *pila* in front of the huge doors. The clang of the iron shafts sounded a warning of the strangers' approach to the guards on the other side of the gate.

Aio and Cerficius shouted greetings to the sentries, who recognized their comrades by uncrossing their spears with a military flourish and stepping aside simultaneously. One of them pounded on the small, low door that could be opened more easily than the huge gate within which it was installed. If the sentries noticed the young woman the troopers had with them their eyes, half hidden beneath the brow of their globular metal helmets, revealed nothing, and the little party passed through.

The smoky torchlight failed to challenge the darkness as unfamiliar odors and sounds assailed upon Miriam's senses. A group of soldiers were dropping pebbles of incense over glowing coals on a small, square altar in front of a niche occupied by one of their idols. Others worked on their weapons in the desultory manner of exhausted conscripts whose commanders were out of sight. But most of the activity revolved around consuming as much meat and drink as possible. Miriam felt her mouth water at the aroma of sizzling meat, unclean though it was, turning on a spit over an open fire.

Conscious of the eyes of comrades greedily evaluating his find, Aio hastily propelled Miriam across the courtyard.

Cerficius and the others began to grumble to each other as they saw the way things were working out.

"Aio," Cerficius finally called out when he saw his friend was going to ignore the disgruntled mumblings of the others, "where are you off to so quickly? Are we not all to share the joy of this evening's little acquisition?" His words were light, but there was no mistaking his menacing tone.

Aio turned to his them. "What are you complaining about? If I had not been there, you three virgins would have been too shy to approach our lady friend," he countered. "Therefore, she's mine. If I choose, tomorrow, I will allow you to visit her. For tonight, find yourselves another billet."

In the time it had taken to cross the small expanse of courtyard, moods had changed. Hands hovered dangerously close to the daggers that hung from each belt. Cerficius gauged his chances against the determined glint in Aio's eye. He retreated, glancing here and there to see if anyone in the courtyard had witnessed his humiliation.

Once inside of the quarters he shared with the other men, Aio finally let go of Miriam's arm. She backed away from him, gingerly rubbing the bruise that had begun to form there. "You probably don't understand me, but you should be happy that I chased those clods away. You are too fine for them, anyone can see that. And if you please me, those easily bruised arms of yours will never turn meat over the fire pit like those sickly courtyard slave women I saw you looking at. I will enjoy the feel of those arms too much around me for you to work at anything else but pleasing me."

The horseman's porcine eyes widened when Miriam answered him in his own tongue. "I am not who you think me to be, sir." Once again, as she had tried to do at Silva's camp, Miriam began to fabricate a life she hoped would save her from what she saw coming. "It is true. I have not been in the city for many months. My robust appearance, of which you so kindly take note, is thanks to the many gifts of the legionaries in the countryside camps. Unfortunately, as you have no doubt heard, many of them have fallen ill because of their unrequited taste for our charms."

Aio's eyes rolled as he struggled to consider the meaning of the woman's words. She could easily be lying. But what if she were telling the truth? One night's pleasure could land him in the garrison infirmary with suppurating sores, then shivering with endless fevers, with madness waiting to overtake him. He would be rousted out of service, and his commanding officers would have the best excuse not to recommend him for pensioning – as if they did not avail themselves of the same pleasures. His lust-clouded mind had begun to clear. He would have to find another use for her.

Chapter 18

Every nerve was as taut as a crossbow. Her ruse seemed to have worked, but although Aio had departed hastily, her flesh crept at the thought that he, or one of his band, might reappear at any moment. But when dawn came and she was still alone, she allowed herself a small smile of satisfaction. The Romans should try some of her brand of acting in their theaters, she thought wryly. Transforming herself into a different person without the benefit of their huge masks was easier than she thought it could be.

Now, a mutter of voices. The wooden door was pushed inward. Aio stepped over the threshold, followed by another man.

Aio bared his filthy teeth in a leer. "Look at what I have for you, Sossius, what a beauty! When I first saw her yesterday, I thought, now here's a charmer, no less than a treasure for my good friend Sossius to enjoy. I could get at least 300 denarii from any of the traders, but I came to you first."

Hair of the color of fetid straw barely covered the long, narrow skull of the man called Sossius. He wore it unshorn and pulled back from his face with a piece of leather, where it fell down his back in a thin oily stream. His tiny eyes darted here and there, never resting. His spike of a nose started high on his forehead and protruded so far from his face that it would have been comical if not for the aggression of its flaring nostrils. His foxlike head rested atop a neck that blended into the narrow body below. As Aio knew well, those ridiculous hands only seemed too tiny to be cruel. They could tighten like the catapult bands around the neck of anyone who crossed him.

"I thank you for your generosity," Sossius replied, a sardonic tone in his reedy voice. "But I cannot imagine that you have not tasted the sweetness of this honey cake. You and likely half the garrison since last night." Turning partly away from Aio, but continuing to eye him slyly, he added, "You might want to consider something... think of it merely as friendly advice," said Sossius with a flourish of his little hand. "If you keep her you'll have to feed her, together with all the rest of the slave women who warm the men at night. And what will you get for your pains? Soon enough you'll be denied such a fine one as she, that's what, when the praefectus castorum sees her. And don't forget what awaits you then – you will no longer know the pleasure of her but you will still have to pay for her keep. And even if you only stuff her face with donkey meat, you know better than I that it will cost you one hundred denarii just to buy a sickly ass."

At the mention of the praefectus castorum, Aio saw his advantage slipping away. The wily trader was right. It would not be long before the garrison's grasping third-in-command caught sight of the Jewess on one of his daily rounds. He reviewed his options quickly.

"I swear to you," Aio said trying to keep the anger out of his voice, "no one has laid a hand on her. I'll take a hundred denarii for her. You'll soon have some rich Jew at your door, begging to ransom her for double. The ones from Egypt are always sniffing around waiting to get their women back for themselves. You'll unload her in no time, and have her for pleasure in the meanwhile."

"You know my business, Aio," said Sossius, bored by now with the proceedings. "I purchase slaves for the arena. I've been holding games and matches almost every day to keep the soldiers from each other's throats in this tiresome cesspool of a city. We're running out of captives. I have money to buy slaves so we can get on with the spectacles. That is the only reason we are conducting this irritating little meeting. But I see the likes of what you have to offer every day, so don't try my patience."

"Don't try mine." Aio had suddenly decided to push Lady Fortuna to the brink. "You're not exactly the agonothetes of Rome, organizing games for the emperor, now are you? So what if she is intended only for the arena? A beautiful woman like this for the crowd to drool over before she is shredded limb from limb in the jaws of a bear or a lion? It would be the spectacle of the week! Why, I'd pay you myself to see it! One hundred denarii is nothing to ask for such a treasure."

"Keep your hundred denarii and ransom her yourself," Sossius spat, knowing very well that the cavalryman could not. "I'll give you twenty for her. That's enough to buy yourself a fatted calf, if you can find one, to eat, or take her place in your bed." The man's ugly titter cut the air.

Aio's face reddened, but he did not answer. His silence told the master of the games that he had struck a bargain. Sossius loosened the leather thong of the money pouch at his waist and counted twenty silver coins into the cavalryman's grimy palm.

Miriam had not caught the meaning of all the coarse utterances that passed between the two men, but it was clear that her fate was being decided here and now. Her exhausted, aching body had no strength to resist as Sossius pulled her to her feet.

Once more in the captor's rough grasp, she was made to cross the city.

In the glare of the cloudless morning, the misery masked by last evening's shadows had no place to hide. People scurried by, their sunken eyes avoiding her own as they had the day before. Tattered garments hung from starving frames, their colors now an indistinct monochrome memory.

Miriam had hardly ever set foot in the market, but from the rooftop of her home she could watch the hustle-bustle of the Cheesemakers Valley that she now traversed with Sossius. Her family had had servants to do their shopping, and when they went to the Temple, like other Upper City aristocrats, they favored the holy precinct's more exclusive entrance along the old bridge to the north, which carried water as well as people to the sacred courtyards. They avoided the thick of the market, the poorer neighborhoods, and the Hulda Gates. It always seemed exciting though, and she used to wonder what it would be like to be part of that throng. The feeling of strangeness that had nested within her from the first moment she entered the city now closed its sharp talons around her heart. Despite the harsh urgings of her captor, she stopped in her tracks as her eyes rose to the Grand Staircase over the Cheesemakers' market. The last time she had been here, she had watched from above as a river of pilgrims had flowed along these stairs into the Temple, alive with anticipation so palpable that it seemed to wrap each person in its embrace. Even the people who called this city home never tired of the excitement of the ascension toward the sacred place.

The shafts of molten-gold light that had burst over the Mount of Olives from the east and bathed the Holy of Holies every morning of her childhood now mercilessly illuminated the scene before her: The Temple's ramparts now staggered unevenly across her field of vision. The once-proud pilasters of the western wall lay heaped on the pavement, drowning in their own blackened rubble.

Sossius followed Miriam's gaze and his lips curled derisively. "Where is your beloved shrine, then, you are wondering," he slurred. "Why, you've been away so long you've even lost the chance to pick through the ruins. It's all gone now. Such beautiful gold and silver we found there, even your own Jews didn't shrink from that garbage picking!"

Another serrated snicker scraped her already raw senses. Her eyes burned beneath lowered lids as they continued downward toward the valley and out the Dung Gate into the Kidron Valley. Sluggish and foul-smelling, a trickle of water coursed beneath the makeshift wooden bridge that spanned the Kidron. They made a mockery of the magnificent stone arches of the overpass that once linked the eastern entrance of the Temple Mount to the Mount of Olives.

On the far side of the Kidron stood the city's amphitheater. Some of Jerusalem's Jews were repulsed, some could not stay away from its spectacles – often the two urges coexisted in the same breast. None could ignore its presence, a fact of which Herod had made sure when he ordered its construction. In Miriam's family no one had ever been to the races or the games held there. But she knew of them, of course; often enough she, like anyone living in Jerusalem, had heard the cheers and jeers of the crowds wafting up from the valley.

Now, for the first time, she found herself passing beneath the massive arched corridor that led into the amphitheater. Her captor pulled her toward a doorway near the entrance. He shoved her against the wall and began to pound on the locked door, whining to be admitted. Miriam's eyes roamed across rows of seats that seemed to stretch into an infinite distance around the empty arena. On the wall behind her, a creeping mold had now spread itself across peeling plaster, difficult to tell apart from the hues of green with which the wall had once been artfully painted to resemble a forest.

When King Herod was alive, spectacles pitting humans against animals were not permitted. Not that the old king or his monster of a son Archelaeus would have minded if they had gone on. It was the priests that were the problem. To Herod, they were like serpents among the rocks. They lay in wait for the opportunity to inject their poison among the masses. Then they would sit back and watch as the people lashed out against the Jewish king they despised. Herod did not want to give the priests the chance to gain from the unrest they fomented so maliciously. And so he limited his spectacles to athletic events.

But since the destruction of the Holy Temple, things had changed. A few unlucky souls among the tiny number of Jews that remained in the city were brought to the amphitheater to witness gruesome spectacles that now took place there on a regular basis. As the soldiers cheered, wild beasts, starved into madness, charged into the arena. And the Jews, forced to watch, sat frozen-faced as one of their number, everyone's neighbor, stood helpless below them in sand so clotted with blood that no one bothered even to clean it. The animals pounced on their prey; in the evil conceit of the spectacle, the victim was meant to play the part of the hunter against the painted woodland backdrop.

At Masada, Miriam had caught scraps of whispered exchanges about these outrages between Elazar and his lieutenants, who had been to Jerusalem after the fall of the Temple. But Elazar had instructed his men to keep this information from the rest of the community at all costs, and in the days when her elder cousin ruled unconditionally it had never occurred to her to do otherwise.

The door creaked open, and Sossius pushed himself inside, pulling Miriam in after him. "We'll use this one tomorrow," Miriam heard

Sossius say to someone she could not see. Another pair of hands now seized her and tossed her onto a floor littered with stinking straw.

She lay unmoving. Images of devastation and decay crowded behind her closed eyes. Her ears roared as she willed herself to hold back the tears that threatened to engulf her. If she did not allow herself to weep, she told herself, she could remain strong.

She was not alone. "Would you have some water?" came a respectful voice from the other side of the cell. A scraping sound followed and Miriam opened her eyes to see a bowl of water before her.

"Thank you," she acknowledged, in the same Aramaic in which she had been addressed.

"I was sleeping until you got here," the voice offered. "Since it won't be long before they come for us, we may as well begin our soon-to-be eternal sleep a day ahead of time." The grim words floated over to Miriam in a fog of confusion. Unlike the owner of the voice across the room, she had no idea what awaited her, even in the coming hour.

"Who speaks?"

"I am Immanuel."

"I am Miriam."

The shy timber of Immanuel's voice gave him away as a young man. Miriam peered into the gloom in an attempt to further identify him. "Are you from Jerusalem?" she asked, pushing all other thoughts aside and hoping to discover if her fellow prisoner could provide clues as to Joseph's whereabouts.

"I am. But my origins are the last thing that should concern you," the soft, steady voice replied. "The soldiers will soon be arriving for the spectacle. You and I, Madam, are this day's entertainment. We may have no more than an hour or two before they come for us."

Miriam opened her mouth, but no words came out. Dread took hold of her as Immanuel's prediction brought meaning to the half-understood words that had passed between Aio and the "master of the games" to whom she had been sold, and to the whispers she had half-heard at the fortress.

The door creaked open again to admit their keeper. "Here, you – you want to use the chapel?" he said, addressing Immanuel in broken Aramaic. "We've had lots of you sun-worshippers in here. All the others wanted a last chance with their god. We've got the chapel for that sort of thing."

Miriam was confused. The most boorish of their conquerors knew that Jews, even condemned ones, would not pray to false gods. She glanced sharply in the direction of her cell-mate. So Immanuel was a pagan? But with such a name? Immanuel, staring straight ahead, shook his head slowly from side to side.

"Suit yourself, boy." The door slammed shut once more.

"Why does he believe you to be a sun-worshipper?" Miriam's addressed the stranger with a directness that had gotten the better of her.

"Our spiritual leaders have directed us to abandon the dress of Jews, and so you cannot tell that I am… I am an Ebionite, a member of the congregation that has taken gentiles into our midst. We are waiting for the appearance of our master, Yeshua of Nazareth. Most of our community escaped Jerusalem and are gathering in Pella. I delayed my own departure, waiting for others of my family to join me from Galilee. They never came so I finally left without them and on my way to Pella I was captured by a Roman patrol. Some of our conquerors think me a Jew, others a gentile. But I am merely one who waits. Except for the sadness it will bring my family, who will never know my fate, it is no special sorrow for me to leave this earthly life," he finished quietly.

Miriam recalled the persistent tales of a man who had lived some years before she was born. Some had hoped he was the messiah. But then he had been crucified by the Romans for disturbing the peace. That was the end of that – to her and everyone she knew, the idea that the messiah son of David had lived among them and then departed this earth without fulfilling the promises of the prophets was unfathomable. Still, when they taught in the Temple courts, the disciples of this Yeshua never failed to draw an intrigued cluster of listeners, and there had been tales of numerous miraculous healings. Once, Miriam had tried asking her father about these people. He had responded with the same scornful raising of his bushy brows, eyes rolled heavenward, that he reserved for those clusters of gesticulating sages he whisked her past as they walked beneath the Temple colonnades. She certainly never expected to sit face-to-face with one of these believers.

Both prisoners turned their eyes warily toward the rough-hewn door. Through the slats now came the raucous singing of arriving soldiers, who had started downing their diluted wine well before the end of their watch. The door opened to admit their keeper again. Grabbing a captive's arm in each of his meaty hands, he pulled them into the short, arched corridor leading into the arena. He thrust a rapier into Immanuel's hand, a weapon intentionally inadequate for the task that lay ahead. Over the noise of the crowd, the keeper put his mouth close to Immanuel's ear and bellowed, "Do as I say, when I say, and you may even survive."

As they entered the arena, Miriam could not believe her eyes. The seats in the curved northern end where she stood were partly filled with a motley crowd of foot soldiers. A makeshift podium had been set up. The original podium, from which Herod himself had watched the games, was much further down. But that section lay toppled on itself, like so much of the rest of the structure.

The afternoon sun cast a bronze light on the victims, blinding them to the faces of their tormentors. But the shouted taunts from the sparse audience were perfectly audible to the two. "Let's see if they have any fight left in them," came a voice from the glare, "Oh, they do, they do," came another. "On your watch they sleep, so that on mine they have more strength to make life miserable. Today they'll entertain us instead of plaguing us!" came another voice, rewarded with a few half-hearted guffaws.

From across the arena a deep growl drew the attention of the audience. The bear's head was lowered, but its beady eyes moved from side to side taking in the unfamiliar brightness of its new surroundings after the darkness of its confinement. Bewilderment turned into rage as the commotion from the bleachers caught the beast's attention. It rose up on hind legs and let out a howl. As the animal turned to face the men in the lower rows, they stood, caught in the seductive mixture of fright and amusement that was at the heart of this diversion.

"Don't let that little brown thing scare you so, ladies!" came a taunt from the upper rows. "Last bear I saw that could jump the wall and the barrier into the first row of the arena was performing for the emperor in the carnival in Rome in honor of Bacchus. It was not one of these little Syrian fur balls, but a gigantus straight from the forests of

Germania. What do you say, men? Has that very beast been shipped to Jerusalem especially for the enjoyment of us heroes of the Tenth Legion Fretensis?" The men roared at the discomfiture of their friends in the lower tiers, who sat back down self-consciously.

The animal had finally spied the two prisoners, now barely four cubits away from it. With a huff it thudded back down on all fours and lumbered toward them. It took only a moment for the beast to mount its first attack, the sooner to break the fast its keepers had forced on it. Immanuel crouched and drew the rapier back over his shoulder. The crowd jeered at his unskilled move. Miriam, standing behind Immanuel, could smell the animal's fetid breath. It raised one paw, claws outstretched, and swatted at the young prisoner.

Immanuel dodged the blow. Miriam, too, crouched instinctively and moved with him. Circling around behind the beast, Immanuel thrust the rapier into the spot where the bear's solid torso met its foreleg. The weapon disappeared up to the hilt and Immanuel immediately heaved it out. Blood, pieces of flesh and fur flew into the air. The wounded animal bellowed, and the crowed howled its approval at the move.

The beast rose up on its hind legs in front of Immanuel and enveloped him in a deadly embrace. When it released him, he crumpled to the churned-up sand. A wet cough welled up in his throat before he drowned in his own blood.

The animal sank its fangs into the dead man's shoulder, shaking its head back and forth. It was Miriam's chance. She forgot the crowd, forgot everything but the fact that her life had been spared. She intended to protect herself now. She edged away along the wall, broke into a run, and headed for the far side of the ring beyond the animal's field of vision. The crowd shouted to the master of the games to distract the animal from gnawing at the bloody torso of its now-dead prey to its still living one.

But Miriam's struggle to live had found an unexpected ally. From the group of Jews whom Sossius had brought to witness the spectacle, a figure detached itself and strode across the arena toward Sossius. The Jew leaned coolly toward the Roman's ear and began to speak.

Hooded eyes sidled in the direction of a profit about to be easily made. This foolish Jew, Sossius thought, had just committed what could only have been a huge portion of their meager community resources in seeking to "redeem," as these people called it, a condemned co-religionist.

But usually the offer came before the spectacle began, and was accompanied by lively negotiation. Never had one come virtually at the moment of the kill. This will turn a tidy profit, not to mention make a good tale to tell over a jug of barley beer. On the other hand, Sossius debated with himself, if he let the woman go, he would have the unconsummated blood lust of his unruly audience to deal with. Bah, let them complain, he concluded. In any case, the girl's death would have been an anticlimax after the thrill of the "hunt."

Sossius stood. An imperiously raised arm brought the prisoner's keeper, bearing a bright cloth, from the side entrance to the ring leading to the animal's cage. He waved the fabric in front of the bear, which swung its heavy head to and fro, finally charging it blindly. The keeper ran for his life ahead of the animal, at the last moment jumping behind the cage door to slam it as the beast ran straight in.

Catcalls echoed through the arena at the unexpected end to their afternoon's show. As he had suspected, Sossius saw that his reputation as this city's entertainment master was about to be compromised. A nod of his head opened another door in the arena and a gaily clad trio of jugglers emerged. Sossius noticed with satisfaction that the audience was grumpily refocusing its attention. He motioned with his head to the keeper and then to Miriam.

The keeper strode forward, grabbed Miriam by the hand and hurried her back to the same holding cell that she had only moments before occupied with Immanuel. The keeper had never seen a life saved in the arena without the master of the games initiating it. It could only mean that money, and plenty of it, was changing hands probably at this very moment. As for him, at least a few bronze issars, perhaps even half a denarius, would be thrown his way if he knew how to earn it and ask for it. He grabbed a water jug from his table and thrust it into Miriam's hands. "Drink," he ordered her, "and wash yourself." They'll be coming to fetch you soon."

Before he had finished speaking, a tall man stood framed in the doorway. His black beard, flecked with grey, was as heavy as a breastplate and groomed to perfection. As for his garb, Miriam had not seen such finery in the decade separating her from her home in Jerusalem. In the manner of the gentry, his immaculately white, wide linen *tallit* nearly covered the saffron robe beneath. Discreetly, the man raised a corner of his sleeve to cover his nose and mouth – the only indication that he had not come upon a lady in her reception room instead of a captive in a stinking cell.

"I am Jacobides of Alexandria," the stranger announced. "You have been redeemed with funds entrusted to me by the Jews of my city for that purpose. I am required to take you with me and leave the city by tomorrow. I trust you have no objections," he finished.

Neither the gentle derision of his last comment, his elegant clothing, nor the neatly laced, soft leather boots could hide the flint-hard core of the character that Miriam sensed in the man. Here was a man to be reckoned with.

She stepped out of the shadows, unconsciously straightening her back. At the fortress Miriam had held her own fate in her hands. She had continued to do so in the desert, too, and even when she first entered Carmel with the children. But once she walked through the gates of Jerusalem, she felt buffeted like the leaves torn by the wind from last summer's grape vines. Her heels rose imperceptibly off the floor, her hands clenched at her sides. Here was her chance, she sensed, to take back her life.

"Come," Jacobides commanded. "Every moment in these streets might be our last. We will spend the night in the Hulda Gate hostel and be on our way to the port in the morning."

It was dark now. The deserted, stepped alleyways were bereft of witnesses to their climb to where a vast staircase led to the Hulda Gates and once, to the Temple. Unlike the first time Miriam had made this walk, dragged by Sossius to the arena, this time she gave no thought to the now-devastated sacred space. Her search for the familiar was over.

Chapter 19

On their three-day journey to the port at Caesarea, Miriam became reacquainted with a life she had nearly forgotten existed. Servants accompanied them and prepared their meals. Tents were put up for them at night and water was brought for her to wash away the dust of the road. On their first night out of Jerusalem, they reclined at a low table set under a vermilion evening sky. Miriam had difficulty concealing her shock at the smoked turtledove, pickled fish, carrots, cauliflower, and parsnips that were set before them. "Did you think," Jacobides had said drily in response to her open-mouthed gaze at the food, "that all of us were willing to live like the renegades at your fortress?"

Miriam had pledged to herself not to share her story, but by the end of the first day, she found she could not keep the truth from this imposing elder the way she had from Silva. She spoke of the longing for her Joseph. "Perhaps the rumors are true. Perhaps he escaped the destruction of our Holy City and is still in Alexandria. Perhaps I am only days from being reunited with him." Jacobides stiffened at the mention of his home city, and from that moment, Miriam felt him grow even more distant. It did not take much for her to realize why; all her life she had been around men whose survival depended on hiding their actions and their emotions. So it was true, she thought: Joseph would be waiting for her in Alexandria. But she had begun to wonder whether the Alexandrian did not now regret intervening in her fate in the Jerusalem arena, and she told him so.

Jacobides looked up at the starry firmament. “It is true, young woman, that I did not know who you were when I saw you in the arena,” the merchant replied. “But, like Moses before Pharaoh’s taskmaster, no Jew should stand idly by the blood of another Jew. And so, whenever I travel, it is with a sum entrusted to me by our brothers at Alexandria. This time I exchanged it for one young woman’s life,” he finished, looking away. Other than curt instructions, these were the last words Jacobides spoke to Miriam for the rest of the journey.

Caesarea was another world, seemingly untouched by the events of the past decade. At the southern gate to the famed port city, the Roman sentries were giants who towered over the local population just as they did in Jerusalem, and with their beaten bronze breastplates glinting in the sun they were no less formidable. But these men seemed more at ease than Miriam had ever seen a conqueror’s sentinel, calling out a greeting to people they spotted here and there in the multitude squeezing its way in and out of the gate. With her attention attracted in a hundred different directions, Miriam could not keep her distance from a caravan of heavily laden donkeys. When they jostled her to one side, it was all she could do to avoid being trodden underfoot on the other by a line of camels, tethered nose to tail by the dozens. She tried to keep her eyes fixed on the appearing and disappearing turbaned head of Jacobides as he plunged into the throng. They soon left the crowded gate plaza behind and reached the entrance to the port.

Here the guards were more alert and there were no smiles. Looking them up and down, one addressed Jacobides. “What is your business, here, Jew?” It was only then that Miriam realized that so far she had seen no other Jews in the city.

The merchant ignored the guard’s insolent tone. His own was as imperious as always. “We have booked passage to Alexandria on that ship that sets sail in the morning,” Jacobides replied, gesturing toward one of the merchant vessels anchored at the quay.

The guard took stock of the situation. He raised his chin to check behind the man and the young woman. No cargo. That was strange. But one less Jew left making a nuisance of himself in the city suited him just fine. He waved them on. Accommodations for the night were arranged. The next morning, at first light, their ship set sail.

The three days of Miriam's first sea voyage were a blur in her mind. They paled to nothingness when the port of Alexandria sailed into view. The human stream into which they waded as they disembarked made Caesarea look like a sleepy fishing port. How would she ever find Joseph in this gigantic crush of buildings and rushing crowds? But Jacobides was in no mood for sightseeing. He hurried her to his home and placed her in the capable hands of Iscah, his wife. The Sabbath would soon be upon them.

Chapter 20

Menahem son of Jacobides walked alone to synagogue. This evening especially, he wanted to avoid his father's company for as long as he could. It was enough – too much – that like every other young man of Alexandria's merchant class, Jew or gentile, Menahem spent the entire workaday week in his father's company. But how else would he learn the business, his father hammered at him endlessly, which he would one day inherit? How better to discover the strengths and weaknesses, the negotiating tricks of the other merchants, and at the same time earn their trust and that of their sons, who would someday be his business adversaries or his partners, and sometimes both.

Opportunities for avoiding his father in their spacious home were never lacking, and so he was able to leave the house undetected. But once they arrived at the synagogue, tongues would wag if father and son sat separately.

Menahem entered the hall and stood at the central door, between the first pair of columns of the double colonnade lining the central nave. As always, the murmur of discussion rolled toward him like a wave. Acoustical tricks brought snippets of conversation to his ears from various parts of the hall. "I never thought I'd see the day... his entire shipment was stolen right in front of his eyes, he was lucky the rioters spared his life…"

"No, no! What you have deduced from the story of the Golden Calf has no bearing at all on whether we may enter the stadium during a contest… I have heard from one of the rabbis who has joined us from Jerusalem that he looks with favor…" Menahem's eyes swept the hall. Beyond the outer colonnade, benches extended the entire length of each wall. They were filling with men who had come together to read Psalms before the beginning of Sabbath. Some had already begun to chant the powerful opening words of the Psalm that hailed God's completion of creation – "*Lechu neranena*… Oh come, let us sing unto the Lord… let us come before His presence with thanksgiving…" Others seemed reluctant to let go of the workaday week and so the sounds of Scripture mingled with those of the affairs of the workaday world. In the section of benches occupied by ship owners, a man called down his row to where the merchants were sitting. "Don't bother to come down to the wharf on the first day of the week – there's no need, we have already finished loading your merchandise…"

Some of the other young men and their fathers were already seated in the upper tiers. One nodded politely at Menahem, as he took his place next to his father. Menahem turned slightly away so as not to let on that he had seen the other young man nudge his neighbor and lift his chin in Menahem's direction with a disparaging wink. But the acoustics in the hall carried the comment that accompanied the nudge effortlessly down to Menahem. "Couldn't he leave that look of his home, at least on the Sabbath?"

"He thinks he's Elijah the prophet."

The jibes had nothing to do with his appearance, Menahem knew. His hands were just as soft and his nails just as buffed, his long hair as well oiled as any of the other young men. But, as everyone said when they thought he was out of earshot, "Menahem had a look about him," which was his and his alone. No one could quite define it; some, who thought they could, were afraid of it. It was a heat, which burned like coals in the winter brazier. Some said it came from his eyes, but, in fact, just being near him was like sitting uncomfortably close to the brazier. Every other wealthy young Alexandrian took the life they lived for granted. Menahem had tried to do the same. He worked every muscle in his stocky body to cleanly defined proportions in the gymnasium in the afternoon. He followed his friends to the steam room, sweating with them as the slaves scraped the cleansing and softening oils and perfumes from his skin with gentle motions of the sharp, curved strigil. For as long as he could remember, when he went with his companions to the public spectacles, he would looked sideways at them, trying to imitate them as they reveled, applauding as loudly as they did at the antics of the jugglers. But none of his young acquaintances ever let on to him that they felt anything like the vague dissatisfaction that gave Menahem no rest, not even on this Sabbath eve. None had ever hinted that they had even the slightest desire to trade their lives for anyone else's.

But Menahem had considered just that possibility, and often. He considered it when he met the strong, scowling men their bodies scored with wounds just hardening into angry red scars, warriors from Jerusalem, who refused to sacrifice at the Temple of Onias. These men made him realize how Jerusalem's ruined and desolate shrine would always be more sacred to them than a thousand sacrifices at the magnificent Temple of Onias. For a time, he had tried to interest his friends in the tales these Judeans told, tales that had sent a chill though his body. "Menahem is off on one of his tirades," his friends would say, swatting the air between them with derisive hands before they turned their backs on him.

Menahem had never even tried to broach this subject with his father. Experience told him that if he did, Jacobides would stare back at him as if he was speaking the incoherent singsong that the silk traders from the East exchanged in the thick of negotiations. Then he would sniff and turn away, as if no words at all had been spoken. But the thoughts would not go away. Menahem would use his moments alone, like the walk to the synagogue, to imagine what it would be like to own the kind of passion that these men did, to have it to guide his every move and give meaning to his existence.

A woeful warbling made itself heard over the din in the synagogue and broke into Menahem's thoughts. "If you refrain from trampling the Sabbath, from pursuing your affairs on My holy day, then you may seek the favor of the Lord!" The voice came from across the hall, from within a group of older men, their *tallitot* pulled so far over their heads they looked like a flock of sheep huddled against the rain. The other members of the wailer's group, the Theraputae – who spent their days railing against the pursuit of pleasures that everyone else felt were no more than their due by dint of hard work – bobbed approvingly at these words from Isaiah, meant to silence the talk of business. These old men were a constant irritation, yet they were tolerated because of their undisputed healing skills. And in fact, the murmuring died down significantly.

Finally, the prayer leader could be heard reading Psalms, at least by those closest to the central platform. And then, as the three trumpet blasts announcing the beginning of the Sabbath sounded from the synagogue roof, a pair of cinnamon eyes stopped Menahem's bored sweep of the room. They belonged to a young woman seated down the row next to his mother. Menahem felt the small wings of something unfamiliar stir within him as those eyes locked onto his own. He made a mental note to find out from his mother who the newcomer was, and tore his gaze away, when he felt Jacobides' eyes on him. He met his father's gaze momentarily, but saw no more there than he always did, vague disappointment. Menahem looked aside again, and did not see that his father's eyes continued to rest on him, thoughtfully.

In the weeks since their meeting with Tiberius Lupus and the announcement of the ultimatum regarding the Temple of Onias, the older man had wrestled with a decision. He understood – even if the others did not – that this Sicari rebel leader, whose identity was a secret to all but Jacobides, could not continue to dwell among them. For the good of the community, that man would have to be sacrificed. Tonight he finally opened the door to the thought that had refused to stop lurking on the outer threshold of his mind.

The task could not be entrusted to anyone but his own son.

Jacobides did not hear a word of the homily delivered that evening, and barely moved his lips on cue when he heard the ringing communal refrain of the closing prayer, "May His great Name be blessed forever and ever!"

People began to file out of the synagogue, and hurried greetings were exchanged. Some made straight for home through the now-silent streets of the Jewish quarter, others waited for wives, mothers, or sisters to come down from the gallery. In a few moments, the synagogue was deserted. The *gabbai* closed and locked the door, placed the key in the Sabbath niche, and disappeared into the gathering dusk.

Jacobides' prominence in the community meant that his Sabbath-eve meal was always attended by newcomers to the city, and tonight was no exception. As servants brought around the bowls of water, fragrant with mint leaves, for the diners to ceremonially cleanse their hands, Jacobides allowed himself to proudly survey his table, regally laid out as usual.

Menahem's intensity was, for once, turned outward. He found himself seated across from the owner of that very pair of cinnamon eyes that had waylaid him from the synagogue gallery. He could hardly contain his irritation as they appeared and disappeared when servants blocked his view as they crisscrossed the space between their two facing segments of the U-shaped table. As the meal progressed, fascination turned quickly to entrancement.

The hymns that concluded the meal seemed interminable tonight, with far more than the usual repetitions, cheerful banging on the table and clapping. When he was sure his father was not about to start in on another Psalm, Menahem jumped up and attempted to make his way to the kitchen, where his mother had been supervising the meal's final courses. His behavior at the table was not lost on his father, who stood up to block his way. "I can tell you all you want to know about the young lady," he enticed his son. "In any case, I want to speak to you, so let us find some privacy."

Father and son retired to the room Jacobides used as his office during the week. That puzzled Menahem; ordinarily, it would be closed for the Sabbath. "No one will expect this room to be occupied on the Sabbath eve, and that is why we meet here," Jacobides answered his son's unspoken thought. "Not one jot of what I have to tell you must reach any other ear." Menahem looked at his father sharply at the sudden, unaccustomed intimacy in his tone.

In a low, rapid murmur, Jacobides confided to his son what had transpired in the home of the Roman governor. Menahem listened with bowed head, hoping against hope that the final words would not come. But he knew his father too well. In all things, the father saw the son as his right arm, doer of his bidding. For this purpose did men father sons.

The words that Menahem dreaded came next. "I want you to take upon yourself a task that I cannot ask anyone else to perform."

"There dwells among us secretly a leader of the Sicarii. It is Simon, the blacksmith. He has been among us since the earliest days of the Judean revolt, but I have known for years that he was more than just another Judean refugee. His real name is Joseph, son of Naqsan. He was one of the first to be thrown out of Jerusalem by his rivals when the Jews retook the city and the Temple. Eventually, he made his way to the mountain fortress called Masada with others of his party. But he left Masada some years later, escaped Judea, and settled here. Ever since, he has been sowing his seeds of revolt, agitating against Rome from within our community. He knows better than to show his face in the synagogue, but keeps company with others of his ilk. He despises me as a traitor to his hellish cause. He is the husband of the woman you are so taken with. Had I known who this woman was when I redeemed her in Jerusalem," here Jacobides lowered his voice even further, speaking as if to himself, through gritted teeth, "never, *never* would I have brought her here."

"The woman believes her husband to be dead. For the good of the community, I want you to see to it that he soon will be."

Menahem felt his hands and feet grow suddenly cold. Words rose to his lips, but none emerged – his father's eyes, fixed on some far-away point, invited no dialogue. Menahem understood one thing at least: From now on his life would no longer be dictated by the next arriving shipment of cloth, the prices in the Alexandria market, or the whims of his young friends sharing good wine from Rhodes or Cyprus.

"Where is Simon now, Father?" Menahem, said, recalling that he had not seen the blacksmith for a few months now. "If he is in the city, his informants must surely have told him of his wife's arrival, and he is on his way even now to reunite with her."

"He may by this time be on his way back here from one of the bronze caravans on its way from Cyrene, which he uses on the pretext of selling his wares. But I have been informed that he also carries information to his compatriots there. From what I hear of the turn of events in Cyrenaica, I can guess that this is precisely where he has been, probably at the side of that maniacal Jonathan, who has led the Jews out of the city of Cyrene into the wilderness to kindle a rebellion. The best thing for you to do is to follow his trail back from Cyrene."

Jacobides seized his son by the forearm and lowered his voice further: "I want you to leave as soon as possible, to find him and to do what needs to be done."

Menahem did not hesitate. "It will be as you say, Father," he lied softly. Surely his voice must have faltered just then; surely every nuance of the plan that he had been formulating even while his father was speaking must have been revealed in those seven compliant words. He stared at his father, certain to see a wave of suspicion ripple across the high, deeply lined brow. But his father's features remained, as always, frozen.

"I will leave immediately after the Sabbath has ended," Menahem announced, emboldened by the success of his pretense. Father and son exited the room and turned in their separate directions to retire for the night.

With those words, Menahem launched the first of several deceptions that would bring to a head all his years of secret longing. When the time was ripe, Menahem would leave his home city. He would never see his family again. For he would never carry out his father's order.

Chapter 21

Miriam had been through more in the weeks since her departure from the fortress than other women experienced in a lifetime. Yet the next day, when Menahem entered the courtyard where his mother and her sisters were passing the long, languid hours of the Sabbath afternoon, the young woman's strong, dark eyebrows rose in anticipation, and her eyes lit up in the way of all young women at such moments.

The other women threw furtive, knowing glances at each other, for Menahem had just then been the subject of a number of guarded remarks.

"Jacobides, praise God, is a fine businessman and a pillar of the community, to be commended for saving Miriam's life," Menahem's mother had just finished saying to no one in particular. What she really meant was that her husband's business acumen was completely unmatched by any understanding of affairs of the heart. He would have given no consideration at all to precisely the turn of events his wife recognized as inevitable the moment she caught Menahem staring across the Sabbath table at this strange young woman with no family and no dowry. She was worried.

Menahem stood before Miriam and cleared his throat uncomfortably. The women fell silent; the better to catch every word the young man spoke to their houseguest in case they would be asked to report on it later. "If it pleases you, I would like to show you our city. We can walk to the palace and the gardens." Grateful to be away from the scrutiny of the women of this household, Miriam agreed.

As they walked, Miriam avoided looking at Menahem. It was not difficult – she hardly knew where to look first at this glittering city. It was as if she was dreaming this wide expanse of gleaming street, the joyful plunk-plunk of water in the marble fountains, the white-robed priests and priestesses gliding silently up and down the broad marble staircases of the shrines. If Caesarea merely dulled in comparison with Alexandria's dazzle, then the Jerusalem she had left behind seemed like a dark, decaying nightmare peopled by shades from She'ol.

The Jews of Jerusalem and those of this city hardly seemed to belong to the same people, she thought. Their dress, their food, the very air they breathed was as different as moon-gleam from sunlight. But how could the beautifully coiffed young man at her side understand any of this, she wondered, allowing one quick sideways glance at him. She was half a head taller than Menahem and when she turned, she caught him looking up at her with undisguised admiration. What could he ever know, or want to know, of the things she had seen? But a conversation had to take place, if only to mask her discomfort at the way he was staring at her. She plunged in.

"You must be impatient to learn about the situation in Judea," she offered.

"I, ah, yes, I am, very impatient." Menahem had realized that he was staring. The smooth olive skin and golden-brown eyes of his companion made him think of ripe wheat sprouting from dark, fertile soil, and at that moment nothing could have been further from his mind than the situation in Judea. Dutifully, though, he began to question her about the things of which he saw she desired to speak.

She spoke, and did not stop speaking until they had left the Jewish quarter far behind them. As he listened, the plan whose seed had been planted the night before began to germinate in his mind. In it, this enticing young woman would have the most important role.

They had walked so far they were now passing the palace, rising lustrous from its vast expanse of gardens like a pearl in a bowlful of emeralds. Miriam's childhood home had a tiny garden, as did most of Jerusalem's Upper City villas, but a garden such as the one she now glimpsed ... the closest she came to even hearing about such a place was when she was a little girl, and people spoke of King Agrippa's palace – terrace upon manicured terrace of medicinal and aromatic herbs for kitchen and sickbed perfuming the air and citrons, pomegranates, and dates hanging heavy in their season. Miriam saw all of these this evening, along with several species that had never reached Jerusalem, but thrived in Alexandria's moisture-laden sea air.

The burgeoning greenery was indeed an astonishing sight, and Menahem stopped so Miriam could take it in fully. But he could see that the garden gave her no joy, although he could not know why not. He could not know that it only served as a reminder that in Jerusalem nothing – from Agrippa's sumptuous palace garden to the little herb patch in her parents' courtyard that cook had allowed her to help tend as a child – had survived the flames of Rome's rage against her people. Menahem had never met anyone over whom hung such an all-pervasive sorrow, he thought.

Night had fallen. Menahem led Miriam to the causeway separating the city from the Island of Pharos, where the glow of the lighthouse was shooting a fiery wake across the water. He watched her take in the scene, knowing the effect it would have. When it seemed that she would remain rooted to the spot forever, he finally placed his hand lightly on the folds of her cloak at the small of her back to wake her from "Pharos' Reverie," as Alexandrians called this all-too-familiar stunned response visitors had to their first sight of the brilliant gigantus.

"I never thought such light could exist that was not the sun," said Miriam, enthralled by the sight in spite of herself. The tower was far higher than anything she had ever seen, dwarfing what she remembered of the Holy of Holies in the Jerusalem Temple. She started to count the rows of windows that rose into the sky, and lost count when she reached thirty and saw no end in sight. She watched as a steady stream of porters came and went, transporting wood to the pulleys that brought it to the rooftop to feed the flames. Above the lower floors, an octagonal tower was planted firmly, and above that, the circular light chamber with its otherworldly brilliance that she half-heard Menahem tell her came from some sort of mirror. Miriam could not imagine how that could be; the only mirror she had ever used was a copper one in which she could barely make out her own reflection. She sensed Menahem's hand resting at the small of her back, but she could not move.

Then it struck her. This was the triumph that she had begun to dream of in the synagogue at Masada. It was a triumph of bricks and mortar, true, and not a human life, not her life. But still, if God could inspire human beings to create a thing of such beauty and power that could rise above it all, could God not help her do what she had willed from the moment she smoothed the last bits of soil over the scroll of Ezekiel that she had buried at the fortress? Could she not return to the land she knew and loved, prove to all who had died hopeless that hope survived wherever life did?

She felt invisible now, as if the lighthouse had enveloped her within its glow. But here was the young man, still beside her, here was that unfamiliar, uncomfortable sensation of his hand upon her. She realized that he was speaking to her. "Perhaps," he was saying in the pleasant tones of a host used to explaining his city's greatest attraction, "on certain days, the smoke did unpleasantly darken the sky" – but did she know that at night its light could be seen one hundred stadia out to sea? That the reflection of the sun's rays from its wondrous mirror could set fire to the enemy's ships right on the water?

He was speaking to her of science and of shipping, but to Miriam, the beacon and the smoke were reminders that the Holy One, blessed be He, had been a pillar of fire to His people by night, and a cloud by day. He had not abandoned them. He had instilled strength in His people so long ago, as He had in her on the mountaintop. The radiance of Pharos' flame had become a most unlikely sign. Her sign.

When Menahem finally managed to propel her forward, Miriam felt like a tree uprooted. She tried to look back at the sky, still glowing red above the warehouses behind them. Vaguely, she was aware that the young man, having discharged his duty to show off the greatest wonder of his city, had begun to speak of his own life in his father's house. Of growing up with the twin understandings of faith in one God and the nation God had forged, both of which were in constant competition with the pagan rites that surrounded them. Of his father's way – emphasizing the moral aspects of their faith, proving to the community that they were on a higher plane than their pagan neighbors, downplaying their connection to the Jews of Judea. They took care, he told her, to walk the thin line that would allow their community its continued prosperity. Miriam's thoughts were still at the lighthouse, and the young man's recitation was at first of little interest to her. She understood his Greek, but the ideas he was sharing were foreign to her. She knew no more about this kind of Judaism, she thought, than she did of sacrificial rites to the pagan god Mithros she had stopped to gawk at outside of a temple in Caesarea before Jacobides had pulled her away. It puzzled her to realize that people who believed what Menahem did, who lived their lives that way, were her brethren. Then, it dawned on her: If she were to rebuild her own foundations, to rekindle her life, then her mortar, her fire, would be the ability to listen to anything and respond to anyone who could further her plan. On the walk that night she began to both listen and respond, as they returned to the house she had resolved to begin thinking of as her home, without realizing, at first, that it was one that her Joseph would never know.

As the days went by, Menahem sought Miriam out, under the disapproving eye of his mother. She didn't have to be a priestess of Eros, Iscah startled Jacobides one day by telling him, to see what could develop here. A match between her son and this young stranger was out of the question. The sooner the refugee left their house the better it would be for their family. Jacobides agreed, although his reasons were different than Iscah's. It was his task to keep this woman and her kind away from both his family and his community, even if he had to sacrifice his son to do so.

Miriam saw that she delighted Menahem when she quoted as well as he could from the works of Philo of Alexandria, although her Greek, peppered with the gutturals of her native Aramaic, was strange to him. She also saw that this young man was the embodiment of what her father had invoked the philosophers of the nations to teach her – that those who read them forgot the true twinning of faith and nationhood for which they had been fighting.

On her seventh Sabbath in Alexandria, they were taking what had become their customary end of Sabbath walk to Pharos.

"When I…" Miriam began.

"Do you not know another way of beginning a sentence?" Menahem interrupted her. "'When I return to the land,' is beginning to sound like the refrain to the longest epic poem in the history of literature," he chided her gently. "And do not tell me again that I cannot possibly understand."

"I will tell you again. You cannot understand. You have told me yourself that your father never allowed you even to speak of the events of Judea."

"True. But I have ears, and there are no secrets in Alexandria. I know you fought like lions. I want to feel that kind of fire."

Miriam looked down at him disdainfully. "What did you hear? The burning walls of our fortress, our synagogue… our Temple? Of the priests that cast themselves into the flames?" She could not go on. She placed her hand against her belt, where the scroll lay hidden, in what had become a habitual gesture. She wanted to ask Menahem if he had heard precisely how her husband, and everyone she knew, had been killed because of one man's vision. She wanted to ask him what he knew of Roman siege tactics, about a murdered little girl, about Elisheva her mother, the village of Carmel, the arena. Menahem's ignorant burst of enthusiasm dishonored all these memories.

"You should know nothing of them," she finished firmly, collecting herself. "Your father may have taught you more wisely than mine taught me. Between the Wicked Empire and the blind fury of some of our own who loved life too little, Judea has devoured those who loved her. It is a land of sorrow and devastation. And my own husband? Did he sacrifice himself to a Roman blade, or did he die at the hands of other Jews who hated our ways? Will I ever see him again?" Miriam fell silent, for she felt her throat closing, and she would not permit tears.

Menahem was glad that Pharos reddened everything in its path, because he feared his sudden blush at her last words would give away the knowledge of her husband's whereabouts that he unwillingly possessed.

"I must return to Judea. With or without my husband. I cannot let Masada be the end," she added, giving voice for the first time to her vow. "But you, you are not like me, what your father calls 'the wild seed sown in Judea.' You have a choice. Take it."

But in the days and weeks that followed, Menahem realized that he had no choice. That impassioned, honey-timbered voice and the story it told had enthralled him. The secret he bore, that her husband was still alive and might return at any moment, made his next move urgent. He told himself that by keeping her from her husband, he was helping her to begin her life anew, exactly what she said she wanted.

Jacobides knew his son too well to expect Menahem to share his plans with him, even if secrecy were not of the utmost importance. In the first days after Jacobides had given his son his mission, he watched intently for signs that Menahem was putting some plan into action. One morning, a few weeks later, it seemed, Jacobides noted with satisfaction, that the young man had made his first move.

Jacobides said nothing as Menahem left the store with a bolt of saffron Damascene cloth tucked under each arm, even though he had obtained the cloth at great cost for a certain foreign buyer who he knew would not arrive in Alexandria again for several weeks. Neither did he comment when later that day, Menahem returned with a wagonload of inexpensive cotton of the type Jacobides had not stocked since the boy was swaddled in it and he could afford nothing else. Clearly, funds would be needed for the journey, to pay for information, and perhaps for bribes. His son was skillfully covering his tracks, conducting business as usual, the community's business, Jacobides dared hope, the nation's business. Each day that passed, Jacobides expected to learn that Menahem had left. Each day, he was disappointed.

Jacobides was never to discover that Menahem had made straight for the port with the Damascene cloth that day, and boarded a ship due to set sail for the western islands, where one of his father's clients was waiting for him on deck.

"Here is your merchandise," said Menahem with none of the usual, essential preliminary courtesies. The young man had his hand out for payment even before the other man had a chance to untie his purse strings – Jacobides would be ashamed at his son's peculiar rudeness, the merchant reflected briefly. But the cloth-dealer readily counted out the fee Menahem had named on their previous meeting – he could not believe the low price he was paying for this fine merchandise. Jacobides probably had more to be ashamed of than his son's rudeness, the man thought. But remembering his own indiscretions as a young man, he chuckled as he patted the young man on the arm. "Your secret is safe with me son, I promise your father will never know of our transaction. How fortunate you are to be able to discharge your gambling debts with nothing more than a few bolts of cloth from your father's stores."

A curt nod was Menahem's only answer. He had one more stop at the port before going back to the shop. The silver dinars Menahem had received were not going to pay for caravan passage to Cyrene to seek out Joseph the rebel, as his father might have imagined, but for passage by ship to Caesarea, for him and for Miriam.

As for Miriam, she played the role required of her in her new life. She had no trouble heeding the warning Jacobides had given her while still on shipboard that she say nothing of her past to anyone in Alexandria, except when it had come to Menahem. If there was one thing she understood from the day of her arrival, it was that anger against the Sicarii burned in everyone she encountered. Her skin would crawl when she heard the people who had raised her, who had died around her, the man she had married, grown to love, and lost, maligned as "the scourge of our existence," "our misfortune." One thing became clearer to her with each day that passed: There was no way that her Joseph could have survived the mire of virulent hatred for the rebels and all they stood for.

Obediently and efficiently, Miriam completed whatever task was set her by Menahem's mother. She made herself appear to listen as the women of the household spoke to her of suitable matches, and to appear not to hear as they spoke behind her back of the difficulty of marrying off this refugee of mysterious and dubious background. In the future in which she was rapidly becoming enmeshed, the possibility of her return to Judea seemed slimmer than that of encountering Joseph among the living. There were even days when she doubted the veracity of her vision by the lighthouse; days when it was simply easier to forget.

Chapter 22

It was the second time the men were meeting in Jacobides' study. It would be too dangerous to do it a third time; all would have to be decided and arranged tonight. The men gathered around the merchant. Their faces, especially that of Aaron, son of Joseph the priest, were dark with anger. "You promised the governor to solve his problem, and you assured us that you could solve ours as well. Now, instead of doing what you convinced us all had to be done to save our temple and our community, we hear rumors of a match between your son and that Judean refugee you harbor. She is of the same ilk that got us in to this trouble in the first place!" the priest fumed. Do you think we are fools? That out own sources had not informed us of the Sicari troublemaker Simon, and that we had not guessed he must be the target of your so-called plan? For all we know, this troublemaker Simon you promised to eliminate is already on his way back to Alexandria. Who knows where things will lead then? Who is to say that he will not be able to infect more of our young men with his Sicari poison? If the rebels are successful in convincing Jews anywhere in Egypt to withhold taxes, any chance of saving the Temple at Leontopolis will have been lost. In less than a year, they say, the emperor will dedicate the Temple of Pax in Rome. Must we see them open another new temple to their gods, while they burn our temple here, as they burned the one in Jerusalem?"

The circle of men closed in on Lucias Jacobides. He felt his throat close as if the circle was their hands tightening around his neck. He fought the urge to run his tongue over his lips, which had suddenly grown dry. Slowly, as stone-faced as always, he took out a document from beneath his robe and held it up to them like a shield.

"This is a letter from Elijah of Cyrene."

The name of one of Cyrene's leading Jews caught the men's attention and they stopped their advance.

"Every Jew of any standing in Cyrenaica has begun to suffer from the false accusations of rebel affinities. Government coffers are filled with the confiscated property of Jews who, if they refuse to join the Sicarii, are falsely denounced to the governor for sedition by the Sicarii themselves. Most have lost everything. The poorest Jews have left the cities to follow the Sicari leader Jonathan into the desert, and Elijah reports that our own Sicari agitator, Joseph of Judea, the one we know as Simon, is more bent than ever on sowing mayhem, is indeed on his way back to Alexandria. You are right, my friends," Jacobides tried to mollify them. "We have every reason to believe that he will continue his malicious work among us here. If he chooses to denounce us before the conqueror, which one of us in this room will withstand his accusations?"

He looked into the eyes of each of them in turn. They could not mistake his meaning: He, Jacobides, was the one in gravest danger. None of them had redeemed, then harbored in his household, a Judean refugee. But none of them, Jacobides thought to himself, had a son to whom he had set the task that Jacobides had set Menahem. Despite his fleeting hope something was finally afoot the day Menahem had taken the cloth, nothing further had transpired. He now saw that he could wait no longer for Menahem to act.

"I myself will meet the caravan when it stops at Berenike," was all he said, opening the door of his study. The meeting was adjourned.

Three days later, Jacobides assembled a small camel train carrying damask for delivery to the markets at Berenike in Cyrenaica. On its return, the animals were laden with bronze vessels that Jacobides had exchanged for his cloth, which no one could doubt justified the trip. With him also was information, which he conveyed to Tiberius Julius Lupus in person: Of a certain young man, known to some by more than one name and to most by no name at all, dead at the hands of an unknown assailant, bleeding into the sand on a moonlit night in the Egyptian desert.

When Jacobides returned to Alexandria, he did what he knew how to do best: keep up appearances. He forced himself to make his return to Alexandria appear like a hundred others. He even agreed to be honored on his return by reading the Torah that Sabbath in the synagogue. But his disappointment in Menahem dug into him like the sting of the biting flies of the desert from which he had so recently returned. He was too proud to reveal to his son directly what he had done. But he already knew how he would make sure Menahem did not escape that knowledge.

Menahem sensed that his father was taking pains to put an even greater distance between them than usual. Even though he had known he would never carry out what his father had asked of him, he almost relished those weeks after his father had made the demand. As long as Jacobides believed that Menahem was preparing to carry out his will, he had shown his son what for him almost passed for affection.

That Sabbath morning, all eyes were upon Jacobides as he left the row where the textile merchants sat and made for the raised wooden reader's dais in the center of the synagogue. The deep and perfect tones, which had served over the years to increase his stature, entranced the community no less this morning. Even the most boisterous of the children lapsed into a rare and respectful total silence.

"So Joseph dwelt in Egypt, he and his father's household," Jacobides concluded the morning's reading. "And Joseph lived one hundred and ten years. Joseph saw Ephraim's children to the third generation. The children of Machir, the son of Manasseh, were also brought up on Joseph's knees. And Joseph said to his brethren, 'I am dying; but God will surely visit you, and bring you out of this land to the land of which He swore to Abraham, to Isaac, and to Jacob.' Then Joseph took an oath from the children of Israel, saying, 'God will surely visit you, and you shall carry up my bones from here.' So Joseph died, being one hundred and ten years old; and they embalmed him, and he was put in a coffin in Egypt."

Jacobides rolled up the scroll of Genesis, and gave it to the *gabbai*, who returned it to its storage chest, draped with a beautifully embroidered cloth of the finest gleaming linen, which Jacobides himself had donated to the synagogue. The merchant then settled himself imperiously in the imposing, stone preacher's seat at the front of the synagogue. He began his commentary calmly, in such a low voice that even the caller standing closest to the chair had to strain his ears to be able to pass on the words to his counterpart standing at the hall's midpoint. Having read the sacred words, he would now apply their message, as every good preacher knew how to do. The congregation, including those who reported to their overlords, would hear a message meant to enrich and guide the lives of the congregation. But it would also contain private tidings to the leadership, and, most important of all, to his son.

"My brothers and sisters, Joseph, son of Jacob lived a long life, did he not? It had been a life of service to his family and his people. He had overcome the hatred that his brothers bore him, foiled every plot to kill him, be it from within the bosom of his family or from foreigners who feared that they could not dominate him."

Menahem felt a strange sensation forming in the pit of his stomach. He looked up into the gallery, as he always did of late, and met Miriam's eyes, which revealed nothing. Unlike Menahem, she had not even an inkling of what his father had in store this morning.

"Joseph overcame all his anger," Jacobides went on with his homily. "In fact, one of the last things he did in life was to forgive his brothers all the evil they had done to him, for the sake of their father Jacob."

"To proffer forgiveness to all of our brothers who have sinned." Jacobides uttered the last word with the barest questioning up-tilt of his voice. His words seemed to waft through the congregation like a cold winter wind from the sea. People began to glance at each other uncomfortably. "We too seek to bring back our brethren who have sinned against us. Is there a higher calling than this? Some among us cannot do so, I know. They even believe that, God forbid, murder is the answer to a better future for us here. Perhaps someday we can find and cast out all those who have taken the lives of others in order, they believe, to further their cause. For now, however much we want to, we will not be able to, because these murderers are too well hidden among us. But, my fellow Alexandrines, each of us can strive to be like Joseph of Scripture, Joseph, a true leader, who died here, in our land." Jacobides finished, his black eyes roamed across the congregation. They flickered briefly at Aaron the priest. They rested slightly longer on his son, then roved uncharacteristically upward, to the gallery, where Miriam stood, looking down. "Joseph, dead in our very own land; his death, and his life, are a lesson to all of us, all fathers and sons, all families," Jacobides intoned piously, his hearers, except those few who needed to know, missing the irony in his tone.

Menahem ground his teeth together, fighting for control. How like his father to transmit information meant for his ears, not taking him aside again after the Sabbath meal, nor during the long hours when they stood next to one another in the shop, but from the Seat of Moses in the synagogue, in front of the entire congregation. To gloat over the achievement of a goal he had set for his son. Menahem could never win, he knew it for certain now. It was just as well he had put his own plans into motion. He raised his eyes once more to the women's gallery. Miriam's knuckles were white as they grasped the railing in front of her. She, too, had understood Jacobides. Her Joseph had been right here in this city. And somehow, she knew: She would never see Joseph again.

Early the next morning, the first day of the week, Miriam, her face an impenetrable mask, found herself once more accompanying Jacobides' wife and their cook to the market. They had spent all morning replenishing the kitchen stores, and two house slaves trailed them, the carefully balanced baskets overflowing with fresh produce on their heads. Iscah bade Miriam inhale the coriander, then the cinnamon, to teach her, the older woman said, as she never seemed to tire of repeating every time they went to the market, the difference between the pure spice and that which had been mixed with dust from the carpenter's shop floor. She did as she was told, keeping her grief far below the surface lest the wailing of her soul burst forth right there in the crowded street. Had her feelings begun to become adulterated, like inferior spices? That, too, was a reason for grief, she thought. The fragrant grains were still tickling her nostrils as, Miriam noted with relief, they seemed to be starting for home. The charms of the Alexandria market had begun to wear thin over the last month, and today, as she mourned Joseph, they did nothing but repel her. The filth of the beggars or the smell of meat too long on the hooks now attracted her attention more than the antics of the bright-eyed, costumed monkey from Africa or the flamboyant feathers of the parrot from India.

But they were not heading for home, she saw. They had turned onto the Street of Fabrics, where footsteps and voices were muffled by swaths of colorful cloth that hung like signal flags from every stall. The crowds were thinner here – this was a street that not everyone could afford to visit. The garments of most people, even the wealthy, were woven at home by wives, daughters, or servants. But now and again, expeditions were made to seek out a fine swatch of linen from the south, or even silk from far away Se'en in the east, for a very special outer cloak or a bride's tunic.

Miriam had an eye out for the landmark she had taught herself to recognize in the vicinity of Jacobides' shop. There they were: the black and white fabrics for covering chaises and sofas, some elegantly striped and others busily plaid, which hung from the stall next door. The entourage came to a halt outside Jacobides' shop. He too, had cloths hanging high on display in front of the stall. But his finest textiles did not hang in the shop entrance, to be groped and sullied by the groping hands of passersby. Everyone who had the money to pay, knew that Jacobides was the purveyor of the finest woven linen garments available in Alexandria. He also had fabric available for the small but persistently profitable niche of pious upper class Jews who adhered to the biblical prohibition against weaving together fibers from wool and flax plants.

As usual, Jacobides was in the back negotiating with a client, surrounded by bolts of his most expensive material. Menahem was at his side. When Iscah entered the shop, the merchant raised his eyes from the negotiations for only as long as it took for him to signal her to keep silent until he was done. Spying his mother, Menahem's eyes immediately swept the space behind her in the street to see if Miriam was with her. Unnoticed by either his father or the client, Menahem slipped out the door.

Out on the street, Menahem pretended to closely inspect the produce his mother had purchased, lifting the straw cover of this basket, peering into that one. As he passed Miriam, his head lowered, he whispered: "I have a plan. You will have your wish to return to Judea. I have booked passage. Before dawn, I will come for you," Menahem managed to add, just as his mother exited the store, eying the pair of them suspiciously, as she always did.

Miriam was too shocked to reply. But her mind was racing. Over the past weeks, she had forced herself to dull the desire to go home, because each time she had begun to formulate any kind of plan, the sea that separated her from Judea seemed to beat her back with a cold wave of realization that unaccompanied, she would be too conspicuous ever to cross it. But the words Jacobides' had uttered yesterday from the Moses Seat, in juxtaposition with his diatribe against the rebels, obtuse as they might have been to others, were clear to her. The Jews of Egypt would not let her Joseph live. It was time to go home, and this strange young man was the solution to her greatest obstacle.

She did not see Menahem for the rest of the day, and by the end of the meal, her nerves were "as taut as Judah's bowstring," as her father used to say, and she could wait no longer.

Two words were all she had time to whisper as she passed him after rising from the table. "I agree."

That night, Miriam lay awake through both the first and the second changing of the household guard, their voices floating in from the central courtyard through the latticed window of her sleeping chamber. But finally, tension opened the gate to sleep. The guards' voices, amplified in the stillness of the night, began to weave their way into her dreams. She was in a noisy, crowded place, the market of this morning. When she looked into the faces of the people jostling her, instead of the strangers of Alexandria, who every moment since her arrival reminded her of her own foreignness, here she knew everyone! It was the market, but it was Masada. Here was her mother, Samuel, and the other children from Masada. Elazar was there, too. And her Joseph. Everyone was doing a dance, but with a bizarre, limping cadence. Then she saw why. Each of them had a limb missing. Some a leg, some an arm. The stumps, though, were not fly-caked and oozing like those of the beggars who haunted her childhood nightmares and to whom her father had given alms at the Gate Beautiful. In her dream, all the people she loved seemed completely unaware of their missing limbs. What is the matter with you? She tried to ask them, can't you see yourselves? But in the way of dreams, no sound emerged. Then she looked in the direction of the black eye of the cave where her father was buried. Yes, she remembered that he was buried there, he wasn't here in this market. So perhaps this was not a dream? Father, why do these people not know of their misfortune? How can they pretend all is well? They will die if they are not cared for. "Daughter, listen to me," her father's voice came to her. "They will not die. Even without an arm or a leg. After all, what other choice do they have? Can they choose to die?" and the dark eye of the cave seemed to wink open and closed with her father's bitter, rippling laughter.

The guards in the courtyard exchanged yet another joke to keep awake through these, the hardest hours of their duty. Their raucous laughter jolted Miriam from her dream. Her cotton night shift was soaked through with perspiration, right down to the belt that she never removed.

It was the right thing to do. She would join forces with Menahem, pay him, when the time came, in whatever currency he desired. She put her hand upon the *get* that lay against her belly. It would remain with her, reminding her of what had been and what need never be again. If death would come, it would have to choose her. She would not choose death.

She was ready when Menahem came for her, during the third watch, when the guards succumbed to sleep as they inevitably did. They crept out of the house and made for the port to await the opening of the gates to the quay. By the time the morning sun glinted gold on the water, they were underway.

By the next evening, Jacobides' house was in an uproar. The kitchen maid had just received a kick from the cook, which happened just after the mistress of the house had summoned the cook to deliver a scathing evaluation of the latest dishes to emerge from her oven. The cook willingly admitted that on occasion her tripe with fennel cream sauce may have turned out a bit vinegary – everyone knew the perfect effect was hard to achieve. But to claim that the ginger marinade for last night's guinea hens was "pale", that the milk of her cheese pudding had made the household ill? The cook, whose sensitive nose recognized the least hint of spoilage long before the offending ingredient might be used… "Well, it was inexcusably and patently unfair," she had whined.

But the cook's sixth sense told her more than when to throw milk out into the street. If this family was ill, she told herself, it was from the evil humors that had invaded the house since the master brought that mysterious young woman here from Judea. Back in the kitchen, they rarely even caught a glimpse of young Menahem, and so the fact that they had not seen him that day meant nothing to them. The rest of the house, however, was in chaos. It was a carefully controlled one, though; it wouldn't do to have outsiders know anything that could upset the master's business or this family's standing. But the cook could tell chaos when she saw it. The mistress' red eyes had nothing to do with a lack of ginger in the sauce or spoiled milk in the custard. Raised voices in the dining room and the bedrooms told the rest of the story. The household had awoken to find the master's son was missing, together with the strange houseguest. Good riddance to that Judean woman, said one and all. Though how this family would survive the loss of the young master, and under such circumstances, was anyone's guess.

Chapter 23

Fragrances, warm and sweet, pungent and savory, filled the air as clay jars large and small were hauled up from below deck and passed from hand to hand onto waiting carts on the quay at Ashkelon, their first port of call. Miriam moved off to a corner of the deck to dodge the scurrying crew as they offloaded their cargo of myrrh from Arabia and pepper and cinnamon from Ceylon. With an eagle eye, overseers glared at their workers, and roughly reprimanded any man not handling the valuable merchandise as carefully as if it were a newborn child.

Miriam wished she were handling her unfamiliar feelings with as much care. In the two days of their voyage she had begun to find herself intrigued by the young man whose Alexandrine ways had only a month ago been almost as strange to her as those of a gentile. As the Mediterranean breeze and the Nile current drove them northward she had begun to discover in him a kind of Jew she never knew existed: a Jew who struggled in the land of his birth to be seen as equal to the gentile. It was a way of life no Judean would ever consider. And yet, her Jerusalem and its struggles seemed to call out to this particular young Jew so powerfully that it had alienated him from his surroundings, even from his family.

She had never met anyone who writhed with the inner conflict she saw in Menahem. The lives of everyone she knew had always been set out clearly for them, the lines clearly drawn between them and others. Miriam began to understand that while she had agreed to take him on as her protector on the journey, she was also his leader on a quest.

On the morning of the fourth day, the ship departed from the port of Jaffa, where it had taken shelter for the night, for the last leg of their journey to Caesarea. The sun was overhead when the city pulled into view. The other passengers gathered on deck to gawk as the finely proportioned, gargantuan pillars of the Temple of Augustus glided into view atop the bluff that crowned the city, as the sailors began once again to scurry in preparation for landing and offloading the rest of their cargo.

Menahem stood very close to Miriam. Close enough for her to rethink her plan, close enough even to contemplate the parting of their ways. She stepped firmly away from him. Menahem had no difficulty in interpreting the move, but kept his voice steady.

"I had hoped that you would allow me to accompany you once we land. I can offer you protection. In return I will need your help in translating until we reach Jerusalem."

Quite right, Miriam thought wryly, but said nothing. This man cannot put two words together in the language of her countrymen, though even most the gentiles here spoke Aramaic. Like every newcomer, Menahem thought only of Jerusalem, Jerusalem, Jerusalem. But the Holy City of his dreams was the nightmarish devastation of her all-too-recent reality. She wanted no part of it. The twelve silver shekels from Elisheva were all she needed to start her new life. With the money, she would purchase a few *plithars* of land as far from Jerusalem as she could get, where she would set down new roots.

They alighted together. Caesarea's lighthouse, one of old King Herod's greatest accomplishments in his showcase city, was no more than a poor man's Pharon to Menahem or the other Alexandrine passengers, barely rating a second glance, and everyone made quickly for the port's gate.

Miriam slung her bag unceremoniously over her shoulder and plunged into the crowd without a backward glance at Menahem. He squeezed through after her, breathlessly catching up after they had left the row of warehouses behind and were passing the magnificent inner gate that led to Sebastos, the royal anchorage.

"I believe I see a group of travelers over there," shouted Menahem over the din, pointing to a dusty gathering of chattering men and women at the south gate of the port. "If they are on their way to Jerusalem, perhaps we can join them."

Miriam looked at him out of the corner of her eye, her lips pursed and raised slightly to one side in what he now had come to know expressed her disdain. But this time, the look also signaled that things were about to take an unexpected direction. "We," Miriam paused as if the word did not sit right with her, "are not going to Jerusalem. "I" – another pause to give voice to what she had decided only a moment before – "am going to Beit Govrin."

Menahem remembered the name. His thought of his father's gold and silversmith friends, who had spoken with impatience of their shipments, en route overland to Damascus, which were sometimes held up for weeks at this Judean lowlands crossroads town. Here was the place where caravans transporting their goods under guard to the port of Gaza did or did not materialize for shipment, subject to the whims of a dozen middle men.

"I am acquainted with Beit Govrin through family business dealings," he blustered with what he hoped passed for a dignified tone. "But what do you seek there?"

"Land is cheap there. I will indenture myself for ten years if I have to, but I will settle there. I will buy an olive grove, and that is where I will live."

Chapter 24

SPRING, 75 CE, CARMEL

Samuel had seen more and learned more in his eleven years than many of the oldest people in Carmel who were five or even six times his age. But one of the first and harshest lessons only the elders could teach him was that in his new home of Carmel, he was never to speak of his past life in the fortress of Masada. In the beginning, it had been a struggle. A few days after he arrived, he had his first test.

The father of the children whose sleeping pallet he shared took him aside and explained to him that the woman who had brought him there had decided to leave and seek a new life elsewhere. He believed she had said something about relatives in the north. Samuel, he said, was to live with them now; he was to call this man "Father."

The day after Samuel arrived at Carmel, the boy had begun to tell the man about his real father, who he had seen for the last time less than one Sabbath ago. The man had placed his finger to the boy's lips, still chafed from his four days in the desert, silencing him in mid-sentence. Then the man explained the meaning of the puzzling thing Samuel had seen that very day: a huge crowd of people, scampering children shouting with pleasure and swooping down on pieces of sweet grain that were being tossed out at them. Samuel had been wondering about it. A game? A celebration? There was one man who looked very sad, so maybe this was the theater he had heard that they had in the cities. No, said the man he would call Father, it had been neither a game, nor a celebration.

The sad man Samuel had seen did not have enough grain to pay the conqueror so the conqueror had taken his land. This was the way the man's neighbors were helping him say goodbye to his old life.

"You should have seen the place where I came from," Samuel started off proudly in response. "You should have seen how we had those Roman soldiers on the run. For weeks and weeks!"

"And what happened then, my son?" the man asked, so kindly that young Samuel could not discern the edge in his tone. "Where are those Roman soldiers now? Where is your own father, your own brothers and sisters?"

Samuel never forgot how he closed his eyes and struggled with the unfamiliar sensation of tears burning behind his lids.

The man was still speaking. Now he was talking about remembering. That the whole village turned out that morning was about working hard to remember, he had told the boy. Samuel could have a good life here if he too would remember what he had heard and seen that day. But he would have to do some forgetting as well. There would be no fighting against the Romans here, and no talk of fighting.

For a while he took comfort in their rules. The forgetting helped to douse the fire of shame that burned whenever he remembered himself standing before Silva, believing the promise of mercy from those unclean lips, tricked into revealing the identity of the woman who had saved his life.

Samuel learned other things as well in his new home: to stay out of the way of the legionaries when they came into the village, especially as time passed and he caught up on his growing. He was not tall, but he was muscular, just the type to catch the soldiers' attention, always on the lookout as they were for a strong local boy to serve in the camp. If the arrival of the soldiers caught him in the street, he was taught to keep his eyes cast down, as if that could help make him invisible.

Samuel worked daily beside his new family at whatever they taught him to do. Unlike his father who had spent all day by the shoemaker's bench, even after they had moved to the fortress, Samuel's new family worked out in the fields, turning the eastern hillsides green in the spring, then golden with ripe barley at Pentecost. But then, they gave two thirds of the harvest they had sweated over, guarded and nurtured, to the conqueror. Samuel could never bring himself to understand how they could do it, year in and year out, never complaining.

It was just after his second Pentecost in Carmel that the soldiers came again. His day's work done, he was playing with the other boys, calculating that the last light was just enough for one final, good toss to win the game and take home the last of the pile of walnut shells they had been aiming at. From the step outside the courtyard door, Samuel had a good view all the way down the main street of the village.

There were twenty of them, many times more than the usual contingent that came to take away the village grain, olives, or whatever was in season. Two by two, they split off to enter every second house. People in the streets and courtyards stopped what they were doing, confused, as frozen as shade-seeking goats under a rocky desert ledge at midday. People in the houses the soldiers had entered were pushed out into the street.

Every family kept their dry harvested grain in their own storerooms next to the *trakleen,* the main room of the house. Some stored their grain in upper story bedrooms as well. So there was no lack of fuel to consume the houses when the soldiers touched their pine-resin torches to the grain and the rough wooden furniture. Next to every cooking stove, a generous supply of *gefet,* the waste from the last pressing of the olives, waited for the merest spark to crackle into a ravenous fire. Soon the blaze lit up the night.

By morning, the gleaming plaster walls of the house of Samuel's family were black with soot, overlaid with clinging gray ash from the fires that had consumed the houses on either side. After a sleepless night during which the family did not dare venture outdoors, Samuel, his tone infused with an irony well beyond his years said, to no one in particular: "So, the families whose houses were burned must have withheld grain from the Romans." The woman who had sought to be his mother cringed with her husband's response, a resounding slap that split the boy's lip.

The next day, a dozen homeless and bewildered families, red-rimmed eyes gazing from soot-blackened faces, left the smoldering embers of their homes behind with whatever they could carry for wherever their legs would carry them. Like a magnet, the road to Jerusalem pulled them northward.

Samuel, too, set out on the road that morning, peeling off the life that had pressed upon him like an ill-fitting boot, and peeling off the shame.

Chapter 25

SPRING, 75 CE, BEIT GOVRIN

The same sun that beat down on the broken little party from Carmel melted rivulets of sweat through the dust on Miriam's brow. She closed her eye against the sting. Shifting the squirming burden in her arms to one hip, she set down the basket of food she carried under the giant sycamore tree at the edge of the grove. Never, griped the elders of Beit Govrin, had there been a spring as hot as this one. Miriam had nothing to compare it to, for this was only her second spring in the region, and the first in her life spent mainly out of doors.

The previous year had passed in protracted negotiations that ended successfully when Miriam took out the last of her coins from her cracked leather purse to pay for the rights to the land on which she now stood. The time had also flown in caring for six-month old Gabriel whom she now carried, as she did each day during plowing season, to see his father at the midday meal.

Miriam could already detect the tiny olive at the base of the almost translucent green flower. By the Feast of Tabernacles, four months hence, it would be shaken and beaten free of the tree, to become part of their first harvest.

When Menahem caught sight of Miriam, he passed the reins of the donkey to their laborer, and made his way to her. He loped unevenly across the deep furrows punctuated by thick clods of moist earth still unbroken by the plow blade.

"We have a guest," Miriam said to Menahem, volunteering no other words or gestures of greeting. Menahem was not surprised by the shortness of her tone. He was her husband and the father of their child, but he had finally stopped waiting for anything more. He was married to her, he used to think sometimes, but she never seemed married to him in the fullest sense of the word.

"A man from Galilee, with news. He awaits your arrival."

Menahem tickled the palm of Gabriel's pudgy outstretched hand with one soil-encrusted finger and was rewarded with a coo of pleasure. He lifted the baby from Miriam's arms onto his shoulders. They were broader now, with muscles no longer hardened by exercise in the gymnasium but by a farmer's plowing and hoeing.

Together the little family ascended the path leading from the grove to the town. Their tiny house was on the outskirts of Beit Govrin, only a few minutes' walk from their grove. From here they could see only the green fringe around the Jewish part of town, undulating against the heated blue of the sky. From the Market Place of the Jews, however, they could smell the incense the gentiles offered to their deities in the temples whose carved architraves rose atop magnificent colonnades in the newer part of the city. But like their neighbors, Miriam and Menahem had no reason to venture into the part of town where the Romans lived.

Ducking into the doorway, Miriam put the baby down and stood aside so that her husband could enter behind her and greet their visitor.

"Peace unto you," opened Menahem.

"And unto you, peace," rejoined the man in the time-honored fashion. Menahem motioned to the man to join him as he lowered himself to the woven mat that covered the beaten-earth floor. Miriam busied herself in the pantry. Soon olives, cucumbers in fennel, and a dip of cooked vegetables appeared before them, and, of course, bread for dipping. Menahem poured wine from the pitcher Miriam handed him into a clay drinking bowl, and passed it to the man.

As the stranger watched the liquid flow into his bowl, Menahem eyed him discretely. His clothes were presentable, and he seemed no dustier or unkempt than a week or ten days on the roads would warrant.

Menahem decided that their visitor was not one of the itinerant "prophets" to whom people threw the occasional bronze *issar* just to silence their wails and shouts as they made their way through streets and markets all over the country these days.

The man helped himself to the meal before him, which he consumed lustily and in silence. Miriam and the baby had left the room, probably, Menahem thought, to the courtyard behind their house. The man took one more long swig of wine. After commenting on the fine quality of the beverage and the tastiness of the food, the long silence returned.

Finally, the man let out a prolonged gust of a sigh. "You are indeed fortunate to live where you live, brother." It was an enigmatic statement, but Menahem knew better than to interrupt with a question. With his opening words, the practiced storyteller-traveler, as Menahem now realized his visitor was, was sure to catch and hold the attention of his audience, even if in this instance its was merely an audience of one.

The man dabbed fastidiously at the corners of his lips and the tips of his fingers with a pliant piece of leftover flat bread. Finally, he continued.

"Yes, indeed. Not that our olive groves in Galilee give less fruit or our market days less livelihood. Our wine still makes our hearts glad, as Scripture says. Of Jerusalem most of us try not to speak. We have buried our dead, and we are getting on with our lives. Yes, we have been getting on.

"But who would believe..." – the man paused just long enough to emphasize the importance of his next words – "that some among our people have had the audacity to sit with Emperor Vespasian, to teach him our sacred books? Believe you me," the storyteller sniffed smugly, "others have paid the price for such unnatural behavior. From such as these he has learned that our king-messiah is of the house of King David. And so, the emperor sent his soldiers among us, seeking to do away with the king's descendants. The first to be arrested were sons of the brothers of that teacher and healer born in Herod's time, Yeshua of Nazareth, said by some to be the Messiah and crucified by the Romans." The storyteller scrutinized Menahem. "That was many years before you were born, young man. But our conquerors had decided for some reason to actually follow their own laws for a change, and because nothing seditious could be proven against them, they were released."

Menahem finally opened his mouth to respond but the storyteller had more to impart.

"I hear tell that trouble is sweeping down your way. Don't tell me you haven't heard! Some overzealous local commander in the hill country of Judea has burned out most of the villages around Bethlehem, including Gilo and Carmel. The conqueror has heard that people are beginning to seek comfort in that story, older than our grandparents' grandparents, about a king of the Jews being born there. He must be a very busy king, wouldn't you say, to be causing all this trouble? Ha!"

Menahem cast a wary glance toward the courtyard where the sounds of his son at play mingled with those of a neighbor who had come to chat with Miriam. Had his wife overheard their guest telling of this latest oppression? Though she kept her days at the fortress locked away within her, he could tell that Miriam had forgotten nothing. Any time the oppressor was mentioned, he would see her pain rising to the surface like oil on water in the basin of the olive press after the first rain. But it was pain of which she would not speak, not even to him. Especially not to him. Menahem decided to maneuver his guest to more neutral ground.

"How fares your business?" Menahem did not have a clue what that business was. But a man from Galilee stopping at Beit Govrin could only be on his way to Ashkelon, readying for a sea journey, perhaps to Egypt, with Galilean or Judean olives. Or, as Menahem knew from another lifetime, if the traveler was heading the other way, perhaps he was coming from Alexandria with linen for the markets of Sepphoris and Tiberias.

"Not too bad for these times, not too bad," the man answered. "Alexandrine cloth can still make a man a living, even if most of his sales are to gentiles. And a man with a story is always welcome," he added, as if Menahem needed such a hint to remind him of the custom of a traveler's meal considered paid for by a good tale from afar. More often than not, a good storyteller saved himself the price of a meal as well as a pallet at an inn.

"Ah, a tale," Menahem said with what he hoped seemed like relish. His mind was on the man's business, now that he knew what it was. How close was he now to being recognized by someone who knew his father? He looked nothing like he had two years ago. The long hair that he had so fastidiously oiled and combed in Alexandria was no more. The square, aristocratic cut of his jaw was hidden now beneath a peasant's unkempt beard, and his dress was that of the simple farmers who used to make his mother grimace when they passed too close to her in the market.

Remembering his manners, he stood and opened his arms to take in the small central room and the ladder to the upper-level bedroom. "Surely you must be tired; please, take our room," he said, gesturing to the ladder, "and rest until the evening meal when we will gather our neighbors to hear your tales."

Chapter 26

Evening came and the lamps, flickering in their niches, filled the house with the pungent aroma of olive oil. The visitor, seated at one end of the long room, looked in turn into the eyes of each and every one of the twenty people who had crowded in, contracting personally with each for his or her attention for the duration of his tale. "This story, you understand, I know to be true because I saw it with my own eyes." But the man knew that veracity would be judged neither by these words nor by the look in his eye. For that matter, it would not be judged at all. This was entertainment as much as information, and the silence in the room told him that his listeners were ready, if need be, to suspend disbelief.

"In the market in Alexandria," the man began, savoring the rapt attention of the closely packed room, "a rich man named Jacobides conducts his business." Menahem kept his face as impassive as those of as his neighbors, but he caught Miriam's slight, involuntary intake of breath at the mention of his father.

"This Jacobides was well connected with the authorities and fought for our people like a lion. No, I do not mean that he took a sword in hand to kill the conqueror, God forbid..." Here the man paused. Where would his hint of opposition to the rebels lead him with these folk? One never could tell where a nest of hotheads still lay hidden, even these days. For all he knew, this very town could be sheltering those who prided themselves on their refusal to come to terms with Rome, no matter how many lives it cost. The silence, unfortunately, told him nothing more than that his listeners were hanging on his next words.

"Now this Jacobides fellow would intercede wherever he could to protect our people in that great city. He came and went from the governor's house as if it were his own. They say that when the emperor himself decreed the destruction of the Temple of Onias it was Jacobides who succeeded in getting the decree commuted to mere closure.

"And did those priests of theirs thank him for it? You can be sure they did not! For what good did it do them, hah? They were out of a job, whether their temple still stood or not!" Snickers and snorts of assent told him that he had struck a nerve. Perhaps there were no rebels in the room, but there were at least a few in this little group for whom five years was not enough to dull their rancor at the high-handedness of the Jerusalem priests when the Temple stood.

"Anyway, this Jacobides turned out to be as deep as the Great Sea and as calm as the water in my father's well. Listen, my friends, to what he did next… There was a man – lived among them for years as it turned out – everyone knew him as Simon the blacksmith. Turns out, this man was one of those Judean Sicarii hotheads. His real name was Joseph son of somebody-or-other. Well, there's always a price for us to pay to the conqueror, and Jacobides decided that this Simon-Joseph troublemaker was the price he was willing to pay to keep the community together and the temple from burning.

"People say they wouldn't have put it past the old man to ask his very own son to get rid of the rebel! Because the son up and ran off, they say, with some captive Judean woman Jacobides himself had redeemed and brought to Alexandria! Maybe he killed the Judean before he left, nobody knows. But when they found this Joseph, he had been stabbed right in the belly, they say," the storyteller finished triumphantly, all eyes fixed on his hands as they went flying up, then down to his stomach, wielding an imaginary dagger.

The storyteller had gotten it wrong, as often happened in the retelling. The audience could never know, and the more dramatic, the better. In fact, Menahem could not ever forget the sting – and the relief – of having failed his father in not killing Joseph. But now, cold had robbed the feeling from Menahem's feet and was working its way up through his body, as he saw Miriam stand abruptly. The others could imagine that she had merely just noticed empty bowls and cups that needed refilling and was using the break in the story to fulfill her duties as hostess. But Menahem knew that the news she had just heard was like a millstone around her neck, dragging her back to the abyss on whose edge she had so precariously stood from the moment he had first met her.

Later, when all the neighbors had departed, they laid out their sleeping mats in the main room, after seeing to the comfort of their visitor in their own bed in the loft. Miriam had been silent from the moment the news had been delivered. Menahem now broached the subject.

"We are safe," he whispered. "He does not recognize me. He must have started frequenting the markets of Alexandria after we left."

Miriam looked at her husband scathingly. "You know it is not about that."

Menahem knew.

"I only knew for certain who Joseph was after I had made our plans," he offered.

"But you did know."

"I did, and I thought you, too, must have surmised what had happened to him. A man like Joseph would have found the same end no matter what. You are fortunate that he gave you the *get* before he left you on the mountaintop."

"You have no idea what that scroll means to me, so do not try to pretend you could. You had no right to keep Joseph's whereabouts to yourself. I promised myself once I would leave behind the world where Jews murder other Jews. "Now," she bent to her task of unrolling the sleeping mats, her voice barely audible, "your father's actions have tied our son to it forever. I understand that my Joseph could not have returned to me once he saw his mission in Jerusalem would not succeed. He had to go to Alexandria, if that was where he thought he could fight on for our people. He never knew peace, but I will see to it that Gabriel does."

Miriam's next words were spoken with the same depth of feeling as if she were counting jars of oil in the storeroom. "I will raise him beneath our olive trees, and then, when he is grown, he will work the land in his turn. He will love the land. But I will see to it that he does not make the choice that Joseph did, in the end only to be used by the likes of your father. I vow it. He will be used neither as a tool to seek peace with the conqueror, nor for any other purpose. Only God will use our Gabriel, in God's own way, in God's own time," finished Miriam. She could not bear to look at Menahem. Her mind raced ahead. A woman alone, with a baby... she would never survive.

She lay down and pulled the blanket over herself, turning away from her husband. For the rest of their lives, she never spoke of this night again.

Chapter 27

BEIT GOVRIN, 95 CE

Twenty harvests had passed. Miriam and Menahem had prospered. So did their neighbors, always under the watchful eye of the Roman governor, his agents and his spies. And so it was that this cold mid-winter morning of the month of Tevet, Miriam, Menahem, and Gabriel had risen before the sun. They made their way up the well-worn path leading from the village to their olive-oil press. In less than one hour, doors would open, curtains would be pulled aside. Their neighbors, jars balanced on their heads or shoulders, or leading their donkeys laden with flopping goatskin bags, would ply that same path to the spring to draw the day's supply of water for their households.

But at the moment, their only companion was the silence of the hills.

Over the years, Miriam had kept her distance from the townspeople. And their neighbors did not pry. Most among them had lost family to the conqueror, in Vespasian's vengeful attacks, before or since. If asked, they presumed that Miriam, from wherever she had come, could have told a story similar to the ones they had known too well.

People preferred to keep their gossip to other aspects of each other's lives, such as the fact that Miriam and Menahem's brood never grew beyond that one son. One village matriarch even came to Miriam's house and slyly brought out from under her robe a vial of mandrake root, pulverized and ready to mix with the milk of a she-ass, in case, it was intimated, the problem lay with her husband's lack of desire. Another had selflessly braved the burning pain of the nettle, she declared, eyes rolling sanctimoniously, to harvest Miriam an entire *se'ah* of the stinging herb from the edges of her summer field. She took the younger woman forcefully aside one day in the market and pressed a roughly woven bag of the remedy into her hands, instructing her to take no more than one dried date's worth in size ten times a day. Another waylaid Miriam at the well to regale her with the salubrious effects of milk-thistle tonic, good for the blood and for color. When Miriam was not around, the women discussed her incessantly, wondering whether she had availed herself of the open secret of preventing conception by mixing old olive oil, honey, and cedar resin applied to fine wool, or two parts pulverized pomegranate skins to one part oak galls. During those years after the visit of the storyteller, no one knew to ask her if she had ever wanted to conceive again.

Gabriel would have covered the distance to the press in half the time had he been on his own. But they, especially his mother, believed for some reason that he could not accomplish this task by himself. Had he not all but carried it out alone for the last six of his nineteen years, he thought irritably. But he dutifully slowed down to match his parents' pace. As she progressed, he saw his mother's eyes staring off, as usual, into some unknown place far beyond the cave that was their destination. His father was his usual reticent self.

Some three months ago, the oil press had rolled to a halt for the final time after crushing the last olives of the season. The last of the grove owners had received their share of the golden oil the wooden screw had squeezed from the crushed fruit inside its column of flat baskets. Buying the press had been his father's idea, one of the few times Gabriel remembered Menahem eager about anything. The Greek tax agent who owned the stones was about to leave the country after becoming embroiled once too often in debts to the authorities, Menahem had reported to his wife and son. The press, and the cave that housed it, right up the path from their house on the on the edge of town, could be theirs for nearly nothing, Menahem said. They could certainly use the extra income they would earn from the fees other farmers would pay for pressing their olives.

Gabriel's mother was less enthusiastic. Ownership of the olive press would bring people closer than he knew she preferred. For that matter, they could have every farmer in the district seeking them out each year to press their olives. Still, she had to concede, the income would stand them in good stead. By the next harvest, Miriam and Menahem's crushing stone and screw-press was working day in and day out for a month, halting only on the Sabbath eve, resuming on the first day of the week.

Additional chiseling over the years eventually opened up rooms behind the front chamber of the cave, where the crushing stones stood next to the press. There, jars of oil were placed after the pressing, each in its own hollow on the floor, jar after jar, row upon row. Narrow channels led from one niche to the other, so that if a clumsy worker dropped and broke a jar, the precious fluid would drain through the channels and could be collected again.

Miriam saw to it that these additional rooms in her cave kept their secrets. Against the day when the tax agents of the wicked kingdom would come to their town, she took three out of every ten jars of olive oil from her own harvest and placed them beyond the Romans' reach.

It was not the desire to increase their wealth that led her to do this. The whole village knew that Menahem gave away at least that much when called upon in synagogue to help a bride or an indigent. He was even among those who, for the sake of good relations, insisted that some of the community's charity monies go to the poor among the gentiles. No, the hiding place was for the anger that had never ceased burning in Miriam. Keeping whatever riches she could from the conqueror and his minions was now the only revenge she knew.

This was what she had intended when she set out for the cave early that morning, long before her neighbors had begun to go about their business and to pry into hers. She unlocked the wooden door of the chamber behind the press, where the storage jars stood row upon row. She touched her torch to the wicks in the oil lamps in their niches and the room sprang into shadowy relief. Fifteen rows of ten jars each bore witness to the bounty of this fall's harvest. No grower could possibly have harvested more, or so anyone would think who surveyed the contents of this room, calculating how much might be concealed elsewhere to keep taxes from the Romans. The small size of the room had been carefully calculated to impart a sense of fullness. Now was the time to hide the evidence of that bounty from prying eyes.

The festival to the idol the gentiles called Isis would bring many idol-worshippers to the town of Ashdod, a day's journey from Beit Govrin. Travel to the festival would give the conqueror's agents the opportunity to explore the surrounding towns, conducting the legalized robbery from the Jewish villagers known as tax-farming. Miriam saw it as her responsibility to see to it that, at least from her family, they steal as little as possible.

Gabriel edged past his mother to the place calculated always to be in shadow, even if the torches of the tax collectors were to light up every corner of the room. With his right hand he took an awl from his belt and he felt with his left over the smooth white wall until he detected the crack that only he and his parents knew was there.

He inserted the awl in the crack, and pried until an entire segment of the wall came loose. Menahem came forward to help Gabriel push the heavy block aside. Gabriel eased himself through the opening. Squatting, he then turned himself around and thrust his arms back out. Miriam had begun carefully to lift jars from the rows, alternating rows and locations in the rows so as to mask the missing containers. She selected only jars in perfect condition – even the tiniest crack would have left behind a telltale oil stain. Jars passed from hand to hand until the prerequisite three out of ten in the chamber had been repositioned by Gabriel in the inner storage room.

On the way home they stopped at the spring to wash away the light dusting of chalk that had coated them during their labors, and to fill the water skins that would provide the pretext for their early morning foray.

In the coming weeks, their lives followed the usual pattern. On fine days, Miriam sat with the other women in the courtyard to weave and keep watch over the younger children. When the boys' incessant sing-song repetition of their Scripture lesson from the teacher's house became too irritating, the women would cluck with disapproval as they always did, and nod vigorously when one or the other vowed to speak to her husband about moving the school to another location further from their homes. On rainy days they moved their work indoors, for there was always wool to be spun, wheat to be ground into the day's bread, lentils and salt to be picked free of pebbles and dirt and a hundred other tasks they had to complete that kept their families fed and clothed.

The men had rhythms of their own to pass the winter days: Menahem and the others would meet at the synagogue at the end of a day spent repairing the stone walls that supported their terraces and delimited their fields, to discuss current events and conduct communal prayers, although like everything else about their lives, such prayers were a matter of debate. Some of the men, who had been to the coastal plain town of Yavne, a two day walk away, reported that the sages who had reconvened there were now teaching prescribed prayers to be offered daily at the same hour.

Others were loath to give up their private prayers, continuing to pray, as one of them put it, in the spirit of King Manasseh who had called upon the Lord with his own words. Menahem much preferred heated discussions of the new customs issuing from Yavne to debates over current events. He never lost the fear that during a heated moment he might unwittingly reveal something of his or Miriam's past. It was impossible to tell who might be passing on information to the authorities.

Except for Abraham the shoemaker, of course. That was a different story. Everyone knew that anything told to him would find its way over the rough fieldstone walls surrounding the nearby Iron Legion encampment. If the conqueror hoped to gain useful information this way, however, he was usually disappointed. For Abraham was a stupid man, hence, his value to the community. He would pass on anything he heard without ascertaining its truth or logic, keeping the conqueror busy chasing rumors.

And then there were the others. The ones who the community feared precisely because their identity as informers was a secret, sometimes even to their own families. Had they flaunted the riches they surely must have amassed in exchange for their perfidy, they would have been easy to spot, but they were far too cunning for that. Was it only greed that made them betray their people? Were they protecting the lives of their families, or concealing some terrible secret? All wondered, but an unspoken law barred them from sharing such thoughts.

The conqueror had instilled such mutual suspicion among the Jews that even if it became known that tax assessors were on the way, each person feared to be the one to deliver the warning. And so people relied on the calendar to protect them from danger. Not their own calendar, which linked the change of seasons to the scriptural holy days of convocation, but rather the one that was attuned to the festivals of the conqueror.

Few Jews ventured into the markets of the gentiles on those days. Most of the sages at Yavne frowned on such outings, as they brought their shrine-bereft people into contact with every sort of abomination and thus thwarted the sages' attempts to create a cohesive community worshipping the one true God. But the days after the feasts, when the gentiles took to the roads, were dangerous days for many reasons. Not the least of these was the occasional tax farmer who had spent too much money on his women and his idols, who would have the Jews of Beit Govrin scraping for forgotten coins wedged between paving stones and beneath benches. Just let him have the money and be on his way, they would tell each other. No one was particularly surprised, therefore, when on the second day of the week two gentiles were seen making their way from the Roman part of town, where they had stayed the night, to the Jewish quarter. They made straight for the house of Elihu. They were admitted, and did not reemerge until several hours later, at a time almost too late to start a journey. But their hurried pace revealed less the lateness of the hour and more their discomfiture at the dozens of pairs of eyes they sensed were following their every move.

Darkness had fallen. Unexpected guests were almost unheard of after sunset, but Miriam rose immediately when she heard the scraping of footsteps outside her door. She opened it to face Elihu.

Elihu, one of three Jewish elders the conqueror had appointed to represent the Jews of Beit Govrin, had no illusions about his reception in this household, or for that matter any other in the community. Elihu had self-righteously convinced himself that at least his neighbors had a Jew to present their causes to the gentiles. And yet, he often thought crossly, they had the gall to resent his wealth, the very wealth – he often thought crossly – that allowed him to give all his attention to their problems for days on end. He was disparaged as far afield, he had heard, as

Yavne. So when Miriam opened the door, he saw no reason to waste time on pleasantries.

"The tax assessors have been to see me."

"And so? Did they require you to reassess how much your properties and groves are worth to your masters? Why should this visit be of any interest to me?" Miriam rejoined.

Menahem placed a hand warningly on Miriam's forearm. He, at least, understood that this man could hold their lives in his hands.

But Elihu ignored the jibe. "You believe all your enemies are those you can see, and that you can defeat them by ridicule, but you are wrong. Your additional sources of income are well known at the encampment of the Ninth Legion. Even the first light of dawn has eyes in surprising places." He paused, allowing the meaning of his words to sink in.

"What more could I possibly have that they could want?" Miriam responded as lightly as she could. "I suppose I could recheck our records. Perhaps at the height of the season, with all the coming and going, we sold a greater quantity of oil than I recorded." She turned to Menahem. "What do you think, husband?"

Menahem was silent.

"Your husband thinks more clearly than you do, Miriam daughter of Jonathan," Elihu said her whole name deliberately. "This is more than a matter of a few jars of oil. The orders mentioning your name came from the highest authority. In the north, they dance the emperor's dance with this foolish rushing about arresting all scions of the house of David. Here in the lowlands of Judea they are much more practical. Where a man's family can be traced to the accursed rebels of Masada, they regard it as no more and no less than the perfect chance to steal his wealth. And I don't mean only his lands, I mean his true wealth."

"It's Gabriel! They want Gabriel." There was no question in Menahem's words, only a statement delivered in a hoarse whisper.

Miriam's eyes went lifeless as comprehension sank in. These years in Beit Govrin with Menahem and with Gabriel, had not been a new start; they had been no more than an interlude. The conqueror, who had once before penetrated her life to the core, stealing everything and everyone she held dear, was about to overtake her once again.

"Gabriel…" she began, but her voice trailed off. Her son appeared from their inner room in time to hear his name spoken, and see his mother's eyes bulge and dart like those of a cornered rat. He took it all in: his father's stooped shoulders, the councilman in his finery standing ill-at-ease in the center of their small living space, avoiding Gabriel's questioning glance. Whatever had transpired in the room, it was his fate that now hung in the balance. His questioning eye finally caught his father's. "Keep silent!" his father's burning glance warned him, more powerfully than if he had actually spoken.

"Gabriel son of Menahem," came a gravelly voice from beyond the door, "you are required to surrender yourself to the emperor's representative for interrogation."

By custom, the Romans did not enter the homes of the villagers. And there was usually no need to do so. The fear the conqueror had instilled, a fear that most were born with and died with for longer than any storyteller could remember, was so powerful that men found themselves unquestionably obeying disembodied voices that reached for them through bolted doors and stone walls. Miriam's mouth dropped open and her eyes narrowed as she turned toward the councilman. "You have led them to us," she hissed.

She allowed herself only that single moment's luxury of venting her hatred of the man and everything he stood for. Miriam knew what she must do. As spryly as a young girl, she mounted up the ladder to the bedroom she and Menahem shared. As at Masada so long ago, a loose stone in the wall of her home concealed money and her *get*. But this time, she set aside the scroll; it was the coins she was after now. Ripping Menahem's pouch off the hook near the door, she plunged into it the coins earned from the last harvest and pressing, and clamored back down the ladder. It happened so quickly that the three Jews still stood in the room below just as she had left them.

The sight of the pouch roused Menahem to action. He pushed past Elihu, headed for their small storeroom and emerged with a dagger. He pressed the handle into his son's hand. Miriam averted her eyes. The sight of the weapon conjured up long-repressed images of her doomed cousin Elazar, of her mother, of all of those left behind. It was a waking nightmare, dragging her back to the horror of those days.

"Quickly, my son," Miriam grabbed hold of Gabriel from behind. She slammed the pouch into his one hand as Menahem placed the dagger in the other. Both parents propelled him toward the door. "Run, take the stairs to the roof," she whispered urging him to make good escape by disappearing over the flat housetops adjacent to theirs.

But when Gabriel pushed open the door, he found the tax assessors, together with two legionaries, blocking his path. They were talking in bored tones, annoyed by the proceedings, which had interrupted their plans for a fine end to a fine festival. The surprise on the soldiers' faces was reflected in the light of their pine-resin torches, as the young man burst through the door like a startled gazelle.

"Take him," commanded one of the taxmen diffidently over his shoulder to the legionaries.

The soldiers moved in on their quarry, but too slowly. In his panic Gabriel forgot that a simple turn would bring him to the roof and safety, and ran straight into his pursuers. "Gabriel, no! Just run! To the roof ! Save yourself !" Miriam screamed, but it was too late. Before Gabriel even remembered that he held a weapon, the dagger had found its way deep into the fleshy folds of the belly of the governor's tax collector, who fell to the ground with a grunt. Gabriel looked at the bloody dagger in his hand, and down at the fallen man. The two legionaries were no longer laughing. They stood rooted to the spot, squinting into the shadows as they tried to make out what had happened.

"Gabriel!" Miriam screamed again, and this time the sound spurred the young man. He made for the stairs to the roof, and in an instant the darkness swallowed him.

"You dimwit!" shrieked the other taxman hysterically, "Find him!" Both soldiers started up the stairs "Not the pair of you!" he bellowed at them. "You! Stay behind to guard the prisoners!" gesturing to Menahem and Miriam. He gazed down at his dead colleague, collecting himself. When next he lifted his head his cold eyes bored into Elihu's own. "Including you," he sneered.

By this time, cracks of amber light had appeared all around the courtyard and Miriam felt dozens of eyes upon her and Menahem. For a moment she allowed herself to imagine doors opening not a crack, but wide. She pictured the conqueror's men running for their lives as her neighbors rushed to the aid of her little family. Of course, it was not to be. The remaining legionary pushed the three of them roughly to the ground and planted himself firmly above them.

"If I might... just a word," stumbled Elihu.

"Silence," barked the soldier, a well-placed kick of a knobbed boot opened a gash in the man's head. Seeping blood slowly stained Elihu's fine white linen robe. The cracks of light disappeared one by one.

Labored breathing and the shuffle of footsteps announced the return of the first legionary. "He's gone," the man reported unnecessarily.

"You fool," the taxman spat out sourly. "Give me one of those torches. I will return to the camp. Remain here with the corpse and the prisoners." He turned on his heel and crossed the courtyard. "Reinforcements will be sent in the morning," came his voice from beyond the courtyard wall.

Morning found the three Jews lying in the same position as the taxman had left them. Their two guards, however, were seated with their backs against the wall of Miriam and Menahem's home, putting as much distance between them and the Jews as they dared and still keep a wary eye fixed on them. With sunrise, the flies had discovered the body, and they swarmed around the prisoners as well. An eerie silence reigned over the adjacent courtyards. Not a family had stirred, nor would they until the soldiers had left.

They did not have long to wait. Before the sun had risen above the houses, ten legionaries appeared in the Jewish quarter. They pounded on door after courtyard door until they found their prisoners. The body of the dead tax collector was flung across the back of a donkey confiscated from the neighboring family. Wordlessly, they hauled the prisoners to their feet and bound their hands behind them with lengths of hemp. The detachment avoided speaking to the two guards – they would pay the price for their part in the previous night's fiasco when they returned to camp, so the less said the better.

And so, for the second time in her life, Miriam found herself in a Roman military stockade. This time Menahem, father of the son she knew she would never see again, sat with her. They had not spoken for hours.

A shroud of suffocating sadness settled on Menahem. How had it come to this? It had been his hunger for a meaningful life with Miriam that had bound him to her in Alexandria so long ago. Miriam had been sated with the struggle and he had encouraged her – convinced her – to once again choose to fight the Roman beast. And now it had risen up to devour their son.

A soldier appeared and motioned Menahem to stand. Menahem sought Miriam's eyes one more time, and what he found there cried out louder than the ululation of the mourning women at the houses of the deceased. He had never known Miriam to shy away from the truth. Now, the pity he saw in those honey-flecked eyes told him that he would pay with his life for the death of the tax collector and for Gabriel's escape.

It was only fitting, he decided, and he looked away. A wave of relief washed over him when he realized that it would probably not be long now before his last ordeal began. His last thought was of Miriam, who he knew would survive, as she had always said she would.

The next day, a single soldier escorted the prisoner from the camp back to the Jews' quarter. But first, he had orders to take the woman to the execution grounds just beyond the camp gate, and make sure she saw her husband hanging, bound and lifeless, to a stunted tree-trunk.

Miriam knew too well what she would see if she looked up. She refused to allow her last sight of Menahem to be his surrender of life in a crushing agony of pain and defeat. The soldier saw that his prisoner was keeping her eyes fixed straight ahead. What did he care? This woman was obviously of no value to his superiors, and certainly of none to him. All that ruling this accursed posting amounted to, he thought glumly, was punishing the locals one way or another and seeing that taxes were collected that seemed to line everyone's pockets but his. He had never gotten anything out of these Jews. No local delegations arrived at the camp bearing gifts in exchange for Roman adjudication of their quarrels, gifts even the foot soldiers could wangle a share in, the way he heard it was elsewhere. No, only their own were good enough for these Jews. So why should he do more than the minimum his orders required. He would take the woman to the road back to Beit Govrin. Let her look, let her not look, it was all the same to him. The debt had been paid. Another fresh widow's presence back in the Jews' quarter would douse any future plans of revolt, until the next time this accursed lot found a new way, or one of a dozen old ones, to make his life a misery.

Chapter 28

The freshly shed blood of two days ago had sunk into the dark beaten earth in front of Miriam's door without a trace. Everything was as they had left it. Everything and nothing. The noxious fumes of defeat and despair now pervaded the room. If she stayed, she would be poisoned.

She would not stay.

Then she heard a voice calling hesitantly from beyond the door. "Miriam? Menahem?" it questioned. And then, more firmly, "Who is in there?"

It was Heraklea, their neighbor. Miriam opened the door.

"Where is ..." Heraklea began when she saw Miriam. But she fell silent when she saw the answer in the other woman's pale, pinched face.

"Neighbor! I thought I heard noises. I came to see if you had returned, or if an intruder had broken in here, as well," Heraklea said.

Miriam stifled the desire to ask Heraklea where she had been when her neighbors had faced the conqueror's men alone. There was no point. What would she have had the woman do? Fly out of her house brandishing a pitchfork?

"What do you mean, 'as well'?" Miriam demanded. "Where else have they been?"

"They have been to the olive press," Heraklea replied. "They have emptied it out. You have nothing left."

Miriam's mind quickly calculated the likelihood that Heraklea could be hinting that she knew of the secret hiding place – other families probably used the same methods – but decided that there was no way the other woman could know.

"You should come to stay with us," offered Heraklea in a thin voice. Her offer was one the sages required be made to a new widow by those who could afford to. No one should remain uncared-for in the community, the sages taught.

"I thank you, neighbor, but I believe I will manage with certain resources."

Her neighbor's raised eyebrows and the puff of breath that escaped the woman's pursed lips told Miriam that Heraklea was relieved that her offer had been refused.

"I will leave you then," said Heraklea bowing slightly as she backed toward the door. "May He who comforts mourners comfort you from Zion."

"Amen. May it be His will," Miriam responded instinctively.

Heraklea's visit to Miriam and Menahem's home was enough to spread the word throughout the quarter. A steady stream of neighbors began to arrive with food and comfort for the widow. The men spoke in hushed tones about the need to beg the body of Menahem from the Romans. Even as they said the words, they looked sideways at the widow, hoping she would relieve them of a task both gruesome and risky.

Why put myself in harm's way, each thought. Out loud, they spoke of the unimaginable risks of life these days. Anyone could be taken – a rumor could seal one's fate with the slightest careless word.

"Even the emperor's own cousin," whispered one comforter to another, "the Consul Flavius Clemens had been executed because of such rumors." The gentiles' market, the comforter went on, had been seething with the rumor that the consul's crime had been atheism, as punishment for which their gods had supposedly deprived him of heirs.

"What?" cried another, too loudly for the occasion. "Everyone knew that the consul and his wife had become Jews."

One of the men in little group laughed uncomfortably, before being silenced by his wife with a prod and a jerk of her eyes toward the mourning woman.

"Who would want to join us who had not been born into such a burden?" another asked rhetorically.

Miriam gave no sign that she understood anything they were saying. The comforters took this to mean her distress had rendered her incapable of speech. Hints were dropped as to the whereabouts of young Gabriel, but Miriam remained unresponsive. Clearly there was no one to relieve them of the burden of begging the body of Menahem from the Romans so it could be laid to rest, and so they set about discussing the practicalities of this mission.

Night fell, and the last of her comforters finally departed. How like Miriam to retreat into silence among her neighbors not because of her loss, but the better to put together a plan for her future. A plan that she set into motion that very night.

She waited until every sign of movement in the other courtyards had ceased. Then she went to the pantry and selected a bowl from a low shelf. Within it she placed an oil-filled lamp, lighting the wick with a reed ignited from the embers of the cooking fire. Throwing on her cloak, she slipped out of her door and the courtyard, making for the path leading for the cave of the olive press.

One look at the door verified Heraklea's report. It lay ripped from its hinges, its iron stays loose, it wooden slats splintered where it had been tossed aside. The tiny light that glowed from within the bowl was enough to see that not one jar of oil remained in the open room beyond the olive press. Casting a furtive glance behind her out of habit, her heart in her throat, Miriam groped to the back of the room toward the secret doorway which so short a time ago Gabriel had sealed behind him.

Satisfaction drew the corners of her mouth upward into a thin crescent that could not quite be called a smile, as she ran her hand over the undisturbed entrance. Behind that wall lay the means that would help reunite her with Gabriel.

For the first six days after her return Miriam made certain that she complied with custom. No one saw her leave her house. When the delegation of Jewish villagers returned from the Roman camp with

Menahem's body, it was laid to rest without her. The wailing of the mourners and the doleful tones of their flutes wafted from the town's old cave-tombs on cool gusts of winter air and in through her small, high windows. It was as loud, she thought wryly, as if she had paid a fine sum for it. Finally, it ceased, telling her that the sealing stone had been placed across the cave. The interminable visits of her neighbors resumed, all unable to disguise their desire to be elsewhere as quickly as possible.

When the seven days of mourning were over, Miriam walked to Ashkelon to meet her purchasing agent. Her request that he meet her the next night at the press was unusual, but his curt nod told her that he knew her situation and would ask no questions.

At the appointed hour, after counting the number of jars in the secret room, he promptly bid half of what she knew the lot to be worth. Just as promptly, Miriam accepted his offer, hoping that her lost profits had truly purchased his silence.

Over the next month she led a double life. Days saw her gradually return to her routine. She even took to sitting with the women in the courtyard in the afternoon hours. She had begun to weave complex patterns in her linen cloth, having announced that she would take the finished items to market to supplement her income and fill her time until the spring plowing of her orchards. She let it be known that soon enough, when work in the olive grove began, she would be seeking hired labor. But each night, except for mid-month full moon, she stole out to the oil press to meet the purchasing agent from Ashkelon and watch as he emptied yet another small portion of jars from the storeroom, loaded its contents on donkey back and headed back to the coast. On the tenth night he placed a leather pouch into her outstretched hand and wordlessly turned away for the last time.

Early one spring morning toward the end of Adar, when the village stirred and neighbors met in the alleyways upon returning from emptying their chamber pots or setting out for the spring, Miriam was not among them. At noon her door still had not opened.

Heraklea was delegated to investigate. She nudged open Miriam's unlocked door. Gingerly, she stepped inside. Climbing the ladder to bedroom, her eyes swept the chamber, empty of its sleeping roll. In the house's inner courtyard, she laid a hand on the stove. It was stone cold. That was all she needed to know. Miriam was gone.

Chapter 29

JERUSALEM, 99 CE

"She was the wife of Elazar of Masada, I'm sure of it," whispered one woman to the other as they picked their way along the street near the garrison.

"I heard she was his sister," said her companion, bending over to pick up the rotting rind of a pomegranate. She turned it over carefully this way and that, peering at it as if she was inspecting a fine piece of produce.

"Keep your voice down, they'll hear us."

"What are you talking about? In five years we've never been caught, and it's not because they haven't heard us, you twit, it's because they don't even see us! I can pick through their garbage from now until the moon grows a beard, and they'll never notice."

"Anyway, as I was saying," the first woman continued testily, "this old crone told me something about being of the family of Elazar son of Ya'ir."

"She must be mad, if she came around *here* boasting of *that*," opined the other.

"Noooo, there was more! She told us she was looking for her son, who ran away after he *supposedly* accidentally did in a legionnaire down in Beit Govrin. Been all over the south, and she's on her way up north looking for him, she said. Stupid enough to admit that she has money to give him, if anyone sees him. She asked to stay with us, but who can take in strangers, when we've only got Roman garbage to eat."

Her friend looked at her in horror. "You didn't turn her away?"

"Of course not!" The woman's skeletal wrist flicked the very idea off into the air between them. "Days, we brought her here with us, to the dump. She stayed with us for a while. And then one day she stopped coming back with us at sunset. I guess she stays here now," the woman said. "Ehh, look at this, the woman said, picking up a whole clay drinking cup. "Ten years old if it's a day. Probably belonged to one of those high-class people who could afford to throw it away if they found a little mildew in it, God forbid," she snorted, placing the cup in the sack tied to her waist. Who knows, she thought, it could still bring in a *pruta*. Aloud, she returned to her subject. "She's not the only one. Anyway, by the looks of her she won't last long."

Miriam lasted five more years.

On her better days, she joined the garbage pickers beyond the tents of the small military detachments encamped strategically around Jerusalem. Her "territory" did not include the best pickings; far from it. Those were to be had outside garrison headquarters where sometimes, even in this godforsaken place, the occasional dignitary would arrive who had to be wined and dined.

By then she was certain: No one had seen Gabriel. There were only three or four Jewish families left in Jerusalem and she had spoken to all of them within days of her arrival. She had interrogated even the youngest of the city's waifs, in the hope that a pair of hollow young eyes in one of those aged faces had caught a glimpse of her son. Nothing. Now, that could be a good thing, she sometimes thought. Her Gabriel was young and strong. Why should he even pass through this dying city, where the gentile soldiers outnumbered the pitiful dregs of Jewish inhabitants by the hundreds?

Toward the end she neither spoke nor was spoken to, and took to spending more and more of her time among the rock-cut tombs beyond the city limits. There were others here, their gray hair a matted bandage over the running sores on their scalp and face, rags barely covering their nakedness.

Despite her forty-nine years she could fight like a lioness for her scraps and the regulars took to giving her a wide berth. One day, as she laid a hand on a gamy shank bone, another hand grasped it at the same moment. She raised her eyes to meet the tired gaze of a man about half her age.

The man gasped as if he had seen what the gentiles called a shade. It could not have been her appearance, she knew, for the man was afflicted with the same sores and covered with the same rags as all Jerusalemites.

"Miriam of Masada?" the younger man rasped. "Do you not remember me? I am Samuel, the boy you saved. You left me in Carmel."

Miriam jolted as buried memories clawed their way to the surface. Her heart sank. Samuel, the brave young boy who had been her companion on the journey from the Roman camp below Masada to Carmel. A tear, glinting in the corner of her eye, was enough to tell Samuel that she had not forgotten.

"Good folk took me in, even before you left," he told her. "They stayed clear of the conqueror and got on with their lives." If he remembered anything of how such good folk had treated Miriam on the day they forced her out of Carmel, he did not show it. That there really was no keeping clear of the conqueror, who returned to Carmel with a vengeance, there was no need to say. Everyone who had lived through that time knew it too well. And so he went on.

"But what were they to do when Carmel burned? They took the road to the city, hoping to find a way to just stay alive. I was twelve years old or so by then, old enough to fend for myself, and so I lost contact with them many years ago. I do not know what happened to them." These words emerged without passion, which, like speech itself, was a commodity too precious to waste when every ounce of strength was spent keeping alive from one sunset to the next.

Miriam grasped Samuel's forearm with such talon-like strength that his eyes opened with surprise and not a little pain. "I stole you away from death, from the captivity of the wicked kingdom. I brought you through the wilderness to give you life, a new life. Would I have done so if I knew it would be for this?" She motioned vaguely to the surrounding stinking heaps of refuse. Some of the other hunched-over denizens of the cave had inched closer to glean something of value in the heaps of refuse that these two, foolishly wrapped up with each other, might now very well miss.

"And what, then, would you have done?" Samuel asked. "Left me for dead or enslaved by the conqueror?"

Seeing her again, the torments of his life overtook him once again. In spite of the elation he sometimes allowed himself to feel in surviving fear, hunger, cold and fights to the death with others like him, nothing could assuage the humiliation. It overcame everything else whenever he remembered that he had betrayed his protectress to the Romans, long ago in the camp.

But looking at the old woman, he knew there would be no confession from him, no absolution from her. He could see that even the few words she had spoken had exhausted her. And yet, releasing his arm, she went on.

"At the age I was when I found you, if I had known…" Her voice faded, though her thoughts swirled and echoed within. Her hand moved toward the belt around her threadbare robe, resting on the small bundle beneath, on the scroll with which she had never parted.

She spoke of her marriage to Joseph and about Alexandria. She forgot he was there as she conjured up the images of those who had peopled her life: her parents, Joseph, Elazar, the father-in-law and mother-in-law who lived a life in Alexandria completely unimaginable in Jerusalem, of hapless Menahem who had linked his fate with hers. Even the man who had given his life in the arena for the one he believed was the Messiah. And of her beloved son Gabriel. She spoke of and to each of them.

Samuel leaned closer so he could hear her hoarse whispering of names. Her mother, her father, a Joseph and a Menahem. And then, with a shock, he heard the name of Elazar, the leader of their community. His hero. Yet this woman spat out his name with a vehemence that belied her frailty. "Joseph…ah, my Joseph, how he worshipped you, Elazar! And you sent him to fight in Jerusalem!" she cried out.

She clawed at her belt and pulled out the scroll of her divorce. In her final beclouded moment on earth, she opened her eyes wide and looked straight at Samuel. "Gabriel! Thank God! You are here! Here, take this," and pressed the scroll into Samuel's hand. "Please, my son! Take it.

Treasure it! It speaks of a great love, of a sacrifice that should never have had to be made. This was my life. Do not let it be yours."

Samuel saw the old woman was beyond reason. He was still not sure who Joseph was, or Menahem, but she had had a son, Gabriel. That much was clear. He took the scroll gently from her trembling hands and she became calm.

She closed her eyes, as if resting for a moment. Then she leaned over bit by bit until she lay prostrate on the heap of refuse, her last breath scraping and rattling like pieces of coal raked out of a cold brazier.

Samuel inserted the scroll carefully into his own belt. But the most important thing now was to lay Miriam to her eternal rest. He stooped into chamber after chamber in the tomb in which she had spent her last days, bearing her nearly weightless form easily in his sinewy arms, seeking an empty niche. Most held the bones of Jews who had been interred here in the days when the Temple had crowned the city hundreds of years before. Finally, he found a place. It was as far back inside the rocky heart of the mountain as the ancient diggers had ever reached when they cut these resting places for those they believed one day would rise again.

He had no spices with which to anoint the body. So he picked a few sprigs of myrtle and lavender that grew wild in the valley among the refuse. He placed them in the bottom of a broken clay vessel of the type that littered the valley in the hundreds. Then he brought the vessel down the valley to the Siloam Spring and dipped it into the rushing water. Carefully balancing its contents, he bore it back up the hill to the tomb where he had placed Miriam.

He laid her torn and filthy robe aside and, unwrapping the rag that protected his head from the sun, he immersed it in the bowl of liquid. With gentle motions he washed the grime from the frail figure. His thoughts of her were of a kind unfamiliar to him. He would not have called them prayers. But he imagined her claiming her peaceful dwelling place in that city which, even in its degradation, a voice from deep inside him whispered, was holy.

The two garbage pickers were waiting for Samuel when he came out of the burial cavern. Though neither was willing to admit it, they wondered what the man's connection to the old woman could have been, and whether the old woman had given him – or whether he had stolen – anything of value from the corpse that they could find a pretext to force him to share. "There! There's the scroll. I told you!" The woman jabbed her finger excitedly at the item protruding from Samuel's belt, deriving some ludicrous pleasure from the confirmation of a tale of the past retold only to forestall the pain of the present.

And then, to Samuel: "Don't think you've stumbled upon directions to the house of a rich relative in Alexandria there," the woman scoffed. "It's nothing but a *get*. A fat lot of good it ever did her to drag that thing around, she finished." Samuel looked down at his scroll as if seeing it for the first time. But the look in his eyes when he raised his head again drove her a step backward toward her friend. "I... think there is an heir to that document, though," the woman fawned, suddenly fearful. "The old hag talked about a son... Gamliel... no... It was Gabriel!" she dredged up the name in a kind of desperate triumph. "But where could you possibly find him? Before the last words were out of her mouth, Samuel handed Miriam's frayed robes to the woman, and turned away, the scroll resting securely within his belt.

As the sun rose, he climbed to a bluff overlooking the Gehenna Valley and carefully unrolled the scroll. His reading was poor, but he had learned what he needed to, enough to know that the scroll in his hands bore the name "Masada." Then he made out more names. Miriam's own, and Joseph, no doubt the man she had mentioned in her rantings. A *get*, the old women had said it was. Miriam's divorce document from this Joseph? Sealed and delivered at Masada.

He could not make out much of the rest, but he had seen enough. A scroll issued at his beloved Masada! Something like this, in the right hands, could become the key to making his people live free again in their own land. Surely that was what Miriam also would have wanted, he told himself, as he stood to finish his climb out of the Valley of Gehenna.

Chapter 30

Seeking was a skill that Samuel had honed carefully over the twenty-four years since he had left Carmel. Seeking, and finding, were a matter of survival. He therefore now put his scavenger's mind to a problem far more complicated than where his next meal was coming from or how to avoid, or sometimes hopefully sabotage, the occasional Roman patrol.

Here was the chance to change his world. In ordinary times he would be considered almost an elder – thirty-six years old, as nearly as he could calculate. Never in all that time did he feel the exultation that filled him at this moment.

He made his way up from the tombs of the Valley of Gehenna to the caves that dotted the rock face above the Potters Field. He whistled softly into the empty air. An answering whistle came as if from nowhere, his permission to climb the rock ledge and enter the cave.

He had been privy to this secret signal ever since he had begun to run errands, too long ago to remember, for the men in the cave. No matter how often he scurried back to the cave to deliver what he thought could be valuable information, no matter how often they praised him for it, he thought he could always discern a slight look of contempt on their faces. It was almost as if they somehow knew his secret shame, his betrayal of Miriam so long ago. Never mind, he would tell himself, the next report he gave them of a heavily laden caravan they could raid, the next piece of information about a Roman-loving Jew who had met a mysterious death – would surely be the turning point that made him one of them.

Samuel bent through the low cave opening. He was greeted by the smell of mildew mixed with sweat, which had long ago become the sweet fragrance of the only home he knew.

He found the men huddled, as usual, in a circle around the glowing coals of the day fire. Their intense murmuring told him they were planning yet another of the sorties he longed to join.

"Samuel!" one of them hailed him, motioning energetically for him to join the circle. "Let's ask Little Man what he thinks of our plan." The man laughed good-naturedly, but Samuel still winced inwardly to hear the nickname they had given him when he first came to them.

When they had discovered him sneaking into the cave behind them on his first night in Jerusalem, they had grabbed him by the scruff of the neck and some were ready to take a knife to his throat. Others had diffused the moment with a warm guffaw when they saw that he was just a boy. When they heard his story, "the little man from Masada" seemed the only nickname that would do. All they chose to hear was that the boy had survived Masada. They did not hold it against him, they told him. Quite the opposite, they saw his arrival among them as a sign that God was speaking directly to them, telling them that the struggle was far from over. From that day on, they had raised him in their image. Now, finally, he had a plan that would win them all over and put his past to rest.

The men watched warily, out of long habit, as Samuel reached into his robe. But it was Miriam's worn and soiled *get* he drew out, waving the scroll dramatically before them.

"With this document," he said slowly, "I will move our cause ahead as it has not moved for the last twenty years."

The cave-dwellers waited for the younger man to continue, some with more patience than others.

"I believe we can use this scroll to rally our people," he opened.

"What good can a roll of parchment do us, Little Man," the headman finally ventured.

"It belonged to the woman who saved my life at Masada," Samuel answered eagerly. I found her at the walls, and before she died, she made very clear to me her last wishes as she entrusted me with the scroll. Once I make known to people that I have actually met her, I can lead them to realize that only God could have brought us together, and for a holy purpose. I will tell them what Miriam of Masada, widow of Joseph, closest comrade of Elazar Ben Yair himself, as much as told me on her deathbed: 'Do not give up the fight. This document, the last evidence of our struggle at Masada, will light the way to a future as free men.' That is what I will tell people she said to me."

The coal fire picked up the odd glow in the eyes of the sandal maker's son. "Miriam told me she has a son who fought gloriously for our cause and has been in hiding for years. I will find him and convince him to join us."

"We have all seen that you can find anything you want, Little Man," said the headman. But the others sensed the doubt in his voice.

"You would better serve our cause by helping us scout out the territory for our next raid, instead of dreaming up lost sons of dead women," one of them said, to a murmur of ascent.

Though Samuel had never been able to see it that way, what he saw as their contempt had been no more than the easy way older brothers tease a younger one. And he never knew that once they realized he was their last living link to the last stand at Masada, they had sworn to each other to protect him and never to allow him to join them on a raid. Today, those among them who remembered Elazar saw that this one burned with the same passion as the leader of Masada. He would do exactly what he said he would.

"No, our Little Man is right," declared the headman. "If he is successful in his mission, and uses this scroll wisely, we will be able to rise up in like a shooting star on a moonless night. And we are in need of such stars."

The men took Samuel into their circle, and began deliberations that lasted all night. When the sun rose, Samuel bound Miriam's document tightly in his belt, and took to the road. The search had begun.

Chapter 31

SEPPHORIS, 117 CE

The only sound in the chamber was the steady scratching of ten reed styluses on ten papyrus sheets. As Gabriel strode into the room the scribes raised their heads in unison.

"Jacob," he called to one of them. The man rose and approached his employer, awaiting instructions. "A messenger has arrived to inform me that our latest shipment of olive oil and wine was never delivered to our clients in Egypt. It must have been captured by another raid of bandits," Gabriel said.

With the instinct born of a decade of service to the merchant, Gabriel's chief secretary immediately grasped the urgency of the situation, and continued Gabriel's train of thought effortlessly. "I'll have to get a new shipment on the road immediately, or the next messenger our client sends out will be one bearing a request for a new order – to your competitors in Sachnin. It will be done today, sir."

Jacob returned to his desk to write out the necessary documents, leaving Gabriel with brow furrowed as he mentally calculated the cost of this latest fiasco. With a sigh, he turned to the papers on his own desk to see what other messages had been marked for his attention. These attacks were as much a part of their lives as the visits of the tax collectors, and usually not even as expensive.

All told, the last few years had been good ones. Roman domination of the land had had no effect on the love affair Jews everywhere had with its fruit. The fact that no self-respecting Jewish home would consume wine, oil, or fruit from anywhere else if they could afford it had allowed Gabriel to build a faithful stable of clients. And there was no better place than Sepphoris for his business.

Sepphoris had earned its peace and bounty, its very future, by allowing the tidal wave of the Great Revolt to flow around it forty years ago, instead of over it, thus sparing it the ravaging the rest of the land had endured.

But no one was safe from bandits. Mostly zealots who had turned to a life of highway robbery to support themselves and their cause, they hid in plain sight among their own people. And few were the people who would risk turning them over to the gentile authorities for fear of being caught up in the bandits' own net of reprisal against their families.

And so the banditry went on. Gabriel's clients happily paid the higher prices necessitated by his occasional losses on the road. They were convinced that he provided them with the pick of every grove and vineyard, outshining his many competitors. He entertained them with lavish meals, sending them home laden with gifts. His charming manner diverted their attention from the fact that he calculated the cost of the gifts right into the price of their next order.

When Gabriel's wife Hannah and his daughter Rebecca took their places at his sumptuous table, or appeared in the market place to supervise the shopping for their busy household, their beauty and business acumen only added to the aura of his success. No one could ever have imagined that, less than two decades ago, this same Gabriel had fled across the rooftops from another life.

Gabriel usually had no difficulty keeping his vow to blot out those days from his thoughts – except when the Zealots invaded his new life, as they had today. Then he had no choice.

And so this afternoon, in his mind's eye he found himself once more scrambling across the rooftops of Beit Govrin.

Nothing but the force of life itself had propelled him that night. Until then, he had been like any other young man in his prime, whose modest family business would ensure his future. If not for the events of that night, his parents would soon have begun seeking a suitable bride for him among the better families in Beit Govrin. Until that night, when Gabriel lost that life forever.

He exchanged day for night in avoiding the patrols during the first days of his flight. The easiest thing for him to do, or so he thought, would be to make for the coast – for Yavne, where the sages held court. Even if he could not make his plea publicly because of the loyalty of some of the sages to the conqueror, surely a covert appeal to the right men in power would result in someone in the community extending a helping hand to a young man in such trouble with the authorities. But if the actions of his neighbors on that last night at home had not been enough to disabuse Gabriel of this notion, a day in Yavne convinced him that this city would not save him. Like everywhere else, the coins that the Jews of Yavne exchanged in the market place were minted by Emperor Domitian, and embossed with the words "Judea Capta." A Sanhedrin that led a captive Judea had too much at stake to shelter a fugitive from the Romans.

And so Gabriel changed his mind. He moved northward and left Judea behind. The rolling hills of his childhood home soon gave way to the mountains of Samaria, its expansive valleys carpeted with fields of greening barley and wheat. Olive trees, almonds, and still-bare grape arbors covered its terraced slopes. The early spring sun, which coaxed the glorious white blossoms from the almond trees, darkened his already dusky skin. Many a burning midday he took shelter in a rocky cleft, where the sweet barley kernels, which he stripped from their stalks in the fields he passed, were his only sustenance. Sometimes, as he rested in a thicket of oaks, he came across shepherds with their flocks of sheep and goats. These were days of uncertainty, and the shepherds seemed as content to avoid him as he was them.

Eventually, the threat of pursuit abated and Gabriel began to travel more freely during the day. Still, he avoided the larger towns where he could be accidentally caught up in a Roman net, ever trolling for rebels.

He remembered the other dangers too. In Be'erot, only a half-day's journey north of Jerusalem, he had come across a man who told him that further to the north, in Galilee, Emperor Domitian's men had arrested two grandsons of Judah of Nazareth, brother of Yeshua, whose followers some said were divisive troublemakers and others miraculous healers. The two had even been sent to Rome for trial. Not that they did not deserve their fate, the man had pontificated, reciting a Proverb for good measure: "Remove thy way from her, and come not near the door of thy house," his finger piously pointing heavenward.

Gabriel realized that he had too many predators. He had to find a way to blend into his surroundings the way a wild goat blends in among the mountain boulders. And so he made plans.

Even now, standing at the window, surrounded by his own beautiful and fertile land, Gabriel could still remember the first work he found in Jewish-owned fields, orchards and vineyards that he came across. At first, as soon as the mealtime break was called, he was so hungry that he raced through the required ablutions before the meal, especially if the foreman was not watching. At sundown, he willingly settled for a meal of lentil soup and barley bread as his only reward for a day of toil that had begun at sunrise. The meager fare was grudgingly doled out by dour-faced men who had once owned the land they now managed for another – someone who had been quicker than they to please their Roman overlords. Other workdays ended more successfully when a denarius, or even two, would be placed into his callused outstretched hand. Eventually Gabriel became an expert in negotiating with the landowner or his agent. As the days turned into weeks, a cache of coins grew within the folds of his belt.

No matter how many years went by, Gabriel could not forget his first view of the shining city of Sepphoris. He had arrived after the last of the summer grapes had already been harvested, and he settled down beneath the burgeoning olive trees that surrounded the town. In a short time, he judged, there would be work at the harvest. As the days passed, other day-laborers joined him and a little encampment took shape.

One day, an event in the grove north of the city where he was staying changed his life. He had gone out as usual, to put in a day's work at the tanner's workshop on the outskirts of town. He had come back later than usual to the encampment because the tanner had promised an extra half-denarius if Gabriel finished scraping the last of the goat hides on order and plunge them into the tannin before he left.

On his return he found the grove alive with the news. Emperor Domitian had been murdered. "The seed of the destroyer has in turn been destroyed," the runner had whispered before speeding on to the city with his report. "God Almighty has seen our suffering and has snuffed out the life of the son of the destroyer of our Holy Temple," cried out a man whom Gabriel and the rest of them had taken to avoiding because of the strange fire in his eyes, and because every word he uttered told of the bleeding and battered Jerusalem those eyes had beheld. This time the exhausted laborers, throwing caution to the winds, nodded in assent. The destruction of the Holy City was a crime none of them had witnessed but of which all knew they were the victims, and they all shared in the satisfying taste of revenge.

The second bit of news circulating in the grove turned out to be the most valuable Gabriel would ever receive: The owner of the grove had been forced to sell his land. Who, the worried laborers asked each other, will now send this harvest to market? Who will pay our daily wage if we work here?

Most left before the sun rose for the groves of Sachnin to the north. "You should leave as well," several people had advised him.

But Gabriel's mind was already off in a different direction entirely.

He did a quick calculation. In the four months he had been on the road, he had accumulated 200 denarii. Enough to put down half of the money they would probably be asking for the small, four-*plithar* olive grove.

Gabriel would never forget that year's harvest, which began two weeks later. He worked alongside the harvesters, this time not as a day laborer, but as owner of the grove toward whose purchase he had indentured a portion of the harvest from his new holding.

At the next year's harvest, people looked askance at this stranger to their region who, when his own harvest was in, hired himself out to surrounding farms. But within two years, Gabriel had increased his tiny property tenfold. Then he bought the adjacent vineyard and wheat field.

Times were very bad. Upheavals plagued the Jewish world in Egypt, Cyrenaica, Libya, and Cyprus. And exhausted, desolate Judea was set upon yet again, with the arrival of the ruthless Lucius Quietus, charged by Emperor Trajan to quell the Jewish rebels. Yet, true to the conqueror's pledge, Sepphoris remained untouched.

And through it all, Gabriel prospered. His olive trees and vineyards now covered the terraces as far as the eye could see. In the most important of the town's synagogues he sat with the other prosperous landowners on the stone benches, nearest the Seat of Moses, right next to the Torah shrine. When it came to giving charity, Gabriel, like his father, was more generous than any of them. If Gabriel took a liking to a man who had fallen on hard times, he would give him as much as twelve denarii, some of his employees grumbled, the same amount he paid one of his scribes for a week. Gabriel was fast approaching the age to be considered for a position of leadership in the community. All was well.

His adopted town was perfect for the life he was building. Sepphoris was famous for its single-minded concentration on one cause: itself. Of course, before the destruction of the Temple, Sepphoris, too, had sent its tithes. Sepphoris pilgrims, like all travelers to the Holy City, returned with open-mouthed tales of the Temple's magnificence. But when the time came, and Jewish generals appeared to exhort the people of Sepphoris to do battle for far-off Jerusalem, they did not listen.

They had opened their gates to the Romans. Prosperity had been their reward. In the eyes of many, this made the Sepphorites no better than traitors. When Gabriel strode forward to lay claim to his new life, he left behind plenty of people with fire in their eyes in the grove, people who had nothing left to lose. Every time he lost a shipment to the *listim*, the highway robbers; every time the rebels burned a field or an orchard – as much in revenge against those who were trying put the past behind them as to deprive the Romans of taxes they would then be unable to pay – it was a reminder of the path he had not taken. But, over the years, when, like today as he stood at the window, thoughts of the old days flew at him out of the blue like restless hunting falcons, he shielded himself in the assurance that this was the life his parents would have wanted for him.

Gabriel forced himself out of the past and concentrated on the magnificent vista framed by his counting room window. In the distance lay the valley of Beit Kerem. Through its green expanses ran the east-west highway connecting the port of Ptolemais to the town of Julia and points further east. A byroad led away from it toward Sepphoris, appearing and disappearing as it wound its way from the valley floor through the hills north of the town.

At this hour, the road was likely to be silent and deserted, baking in the midday sun. Travelers, even those bound for Sepphoris, would await the cool of the afternoon to continue their journey. Gabriel gazed into the distance. A small plume of dust signaled that one traveler was still on the move. The midday heat had not slowed him down, quite the opposite, Gabriel noticed. He was hurrying down the road as if evening was imminent and the gates were about to close. Gabriel wondered briefly about it. But a clerk drew his attention away and the traveler was forgotten.

Chapter 32

It was evening before Gabriel had cause to remember the traveler again. He and his small family were reclining on their couches behind the low tables of their dining chamber. Servants had appeared from the adjacent rooms bearing trays laden with cool, smooth yogurt mixed with fresh cucumbers. Hannah, Gabriel's wife, had seen to it, as she did every day, that lotus jujube juice, her husband's favorite beverage, was on hand, in addition to dried fruit, apples, figs, pears, nuts and spiced black olive paste in which to dip their bread. Wine was poured from delicate glass decanters that had just arrived from the finest workshop of Dor.

Hannah looked closely at her husband. It seemed to her that the furrow between his brows had deepened since she saw him that morning. She had not had heard about the lost shipment, but she had lived with Gabriel long enough to know the worries he faced building a business in a world where a man's lifework and his family could be wiped out by a few whispered words from a slighted business rival into the ear of the conqueror. But Hannah did not speak, and she watched the lines in Gabriel's face relax as father and daughter conversed.

Gabriel's daughter Rebecca was regaling her father with the story of that day's visit to the market together with the cook to purchase vegetables. A dancing bear from Syria had been shown in the town square and the entertainment had been wonderful. Hannah let out a sigh of relief when she realized that the subject tonight was not going to be the one her daughter always seemed to harp on after her visits to town – the "scourge of the Romans," as Rebecca had taken to calling it, from the smoking incense outside their shrines to their tax collectors with their yawning maws of purses ever hungry for profits from the Jews.

Hannah saw that the spectacle of the dancing bear had turned her daughter, if only for one evening, back into the carefree young woman Gabriel was so proud of. Night had fallen, and the laughing eyes of father and daughter sparkled in the torchlight.

Rebecca was Gabriel and Hannah's chief joy. Her thirst for knowledge, even as a child, had often led Gabriel to remark that had his daughter been a boy, he would have brought the finest tutors in the region into their household to educate her.

Hannah and her three sisters had in their own youth been provided with the knowledge they needed to run a household: There were servants to manage, purchases to be made, and wool and flax to be spun and dyed for the household. She had always performed adequately at the reading, writing, and ciphering tasks she had been set that would allow her to run her future home. She could not understand her daughter's insatiable intellect, or even recognize it as such. But then, Hannah had never known the grandmother from whom her daughter had inherited her brilliance.

Like Jonathan of Hanablata more than a half-century ago, Gabriel would proudly watch the tilt of his daughter's head as she labored over her letters with perfect concentration. Over the years Gabriel would find himself anticipating the moment he would see Rebecca's eyes light up when, every so often, he succeeded in answering one of her innumerable, breathless questions to her satisfaction. Rebecca never missed the opportunity to be present in the synagogue when a teacher passed through town. Gabriel would smile indulgently when he observed her changing her seat several times to sit as closely as possible to the sage, so that when a full house required his words be relayed from repeater to repeater back through the crowd, she could boast that she had heard them first-hand. Recalling the many nights when as a child his mother had regaled him with endless stories, from the Torah as well as the ancient Greek fables, Gabriel had no doubt as to the well from which such intellectual curiosity sprang.

A servant approached the couch on which Gabriel reclined, and whispered into his master's ear. Gabriel raised his hand for silence. His daughter stopped speaking, her slender hennaed fingertips drumming the smooth stone tabletop as she waited to find out what had interrupted their evening. As the servant finished speaking and withdrew, Gabriel wiped his hands on a piece of flat bread and got to his feet just as a stranger entered the room.

The two men had never laid eyes on each other before. Each, however, knew what was expected, of the other and of himself. Gabriel immediately invited the stranger to join them at the table. "Please – help us do justice to the meal," he offered, hands sweeping the air before him magnanimously. Though hospitality was a virtue practiced by the patriarch Abraham himself, the enhanced reputation of the host could certainly do no harm; a guest traveling onward with pleasant memories of a host's wherewithal and magnanimity could spread that information far and wide.

It was not lost on Hannah that in between dips of his bread into the numerous dishes set before him, the guest hardly took his eyes off her daughter, except when he thought others were looking. In turn, Hannah watched him. She had an eye for strong men. It was that same eye that had caught and held the glance of an unknown young man in the Sepphoris market long ago. That, and an iron will had brought her under the marriage canopy with Gabriel despite all her parents' pleadings.

Their guest's advanced years had robbed his muscles of some of their bulk, but his arms and legs were taut as well-ropes under the bronze skin not covered by the short laborer's tunic hanging loosely from his angular frame. He had washed his hands and feet before entering the room and drops of water glistened in his close-cropped, stone-gray hair as well, though it had done little to clean away the white dust of the road. Hannah noticed that he was missing the little finger of his right hand, probably lost in some brawl somewhere, she told herself.

If he were a younger man, the man's glances at her daughter would immediately set Hannah to plotting and planning. After all, had she not married a newcomer from who knows where? But what could this man want with Rebecca?

She could not have imagined in her wildest nightmares that Samuel knew more about her family than she did. His inquiries of the townsfolk regarding Gabriel's household were a ruse designed to present himself as an ordinary traveler seeking shelter and food from a wealthy man, as was the custom. Samuel had already discovered everything he needed to know about this family to add the final chapter to his mission.

It was a mission that had taken years to accomplish. He had watched for the *listim* along the road who, like him, had easily passed the test of a finger's amputation to join the ranks of their leader Ben Cosiba. Such men did more than waylay and rob strangers to feed their families. As much as Gabriel had tried to keep his past a secret, these men had made it their business to know and to pass on the knowledge. That knowledge had finally led him to this family and this table.

Talk remained impersonal. It turned to the sages, men whose pronouncements had become increasingly important in all of their lives. The stories about them made entertaining and stimulating dinner conversation, too.

These days, it was Eleazar Ben Azariyah's name that was heard most often.

"Eighteen years old! Really! It is scandalous to think that such a man could succeed the great Rabbi Gamaliel as head of the Sanhedrin," Gabriel remarked this evening.

"And they say you are still too young to take up a post in the city," Hannah teased her husband, while pretending to count the gray hairs in his hair and beard.

"Don't forget that it is said that a miracle occurred and Eleazar's hair turned gray overnight," Rebecca rejoined. "Thus, the Holy One, blessed be He, showed everyone that this rabbi was His choice and had all the wisdom of an elder full of years," she finished reverently. Samuel let his glance linger thoughtfully on the young woman for a moment more than he should have.

"More likely, the day he realized he had a room full of sages to mediate among, his hair turned gray with terror," Gabriel retorted wryly.

Rebecca's almond eyes moved back and forth between her parents. Like practically everyone in Sepphoris, she, too had been at the synagogue the day that Rabbi Eleazar had last come to Sepphoris to preach. Everyone had been there. "I have heard it said," Samuel offered casually, "that Rabbi Eleazar has opened the study house to all who wish to learn." Rebecca started to add that she too wanted to study, but her father interrupted her.

"Not even his great wealth will keep him in his position." Gabriel silenced his daughter with an uncharacteristically dismissive swat at the air. "Rabbi Gamaliel will be back, you'll see. Such a man knows how to keep us out of the path of the storm." Everyone around the table knew what Gabriel meant. Even though nearly fifty years had passed, the story continued to circulate: Rabbi Gamaliel had risked his life to carry Rabbi Yohanan ben Zakkai out of Jerusalem in a coffin so that Rabbi Yohanan could ask Vespasian to allow him to reconvene the Sanhedrin in Yavne. "Such a man! I'd wager him capable of going to Rome and getting anything he wants, even from the emperor himself !" Gabriel said.

"Thanks to him, we know how to conduct ourselves these days, when even a circumcision knife must be hidden," Hannah said.

"That foolishness again?" Gabriel's voice rose. How many times have I told you that the emperor has *not* forbidden circumcision, but rather, he has outlawed castration. That has nothing to do with the sign of Abraham's covenant. All rational people, including our Roman overlords, know it."

"And let us suppose for the moment that the fear-mongers are right," Gabriel continued, "and it is circumcision that is forbidden. Where exactly does conducting our rites in secret bring us, my dear? If we circumcise our sons in spite of Rome, does that make us free of Rome? Must I remind you what happened to the Jews of Alexandria? How, precisely, did their currying favor with the wicked kingdom, or the rebels among them, help them? It is said that farmers in Egypt have no need to fertilize their soil, it is how rich it is thanks to the blood of the Jews who have been slaughtered there."

Hannah saw the old anger, her husband's constant shadow for as long as she had known him, rise again; she had seen it boil over before, but she had no way of knowing it was about anything but a threat to his business. "Is a few years too long for you to remember how we all suffered when Emperor Trajan's army last marched across Galilee?"

Gabriel continued to fume in silence. Nothing must interfere with Rome's trade route. No one knew this better than Gabriel. Trajan had smashed his way across Galilee on his way to Armenia to topple the puppet of Rome's old enemies the Parthians to prove just that. Then, when the emperor had suspected the Jews of Mesopotamia of conspiring against him, he ordered Lucius Quietus, a commander who had vaulted up through the ranks, to suppress the revolt. As a reward for bloody services rendered, that same Quietus had been given the governorship of Judea, where he proceeded to unleash his particular brand of terror upon the already ruined province.

Gabriel forced himself to return to their guest, whose face, Gabriel noticed, had remained as impassive during their conversation as if they had been discussing the latest heat wave.

"You are fresh from the roads. What news of the Moor?" Gabriel asked Samuel, referring to this same Lucius Quietus.

"Praise God, he has been ousted from office."

A murmur of pleasure rippled through the room.

Samuel ignored the effect his announcement had on the other diners. He had waited for this evening and this moment, planned for every day of his long years of searching for this household, and the assignments that had come in between. The time had come to tell the tale. "Jerusalem has suffered," said Samuel, letting out a heavy sigh.

"The mountain of the Temple lies deserted of course, as all know." Turning respectfully to Rebecca he addressed her directly for the first time. "Rabbi Elazar himself has been to Jerusalem and reports as much when he preaches in synagogues elsewhere.

"The most shameful moment of all should have been the most glorious – when the sound of the chisel was heard once again on the Temple Mount. But it had not been put to work in order to rebuild God's house – it was to place a statue of their moon-goddess where our Holy of Holies once stood. I saw the roads lined with crosses bearing the dead and dying – those who dared protest, writhing until they drew their last tortured breath. Sometimes their own family members broke their legs in the hope of hastening their death." Now that Samuel sensed he had Rebecca's full attention, he turned away from her, and his tone turned more casual again.

"But those times, praise God, seem to be over. Hadrian's diplomats are working at rebuilding bridges to the Parthians, and even to the Jews. As you say, rumor has it that Hadrian has met with Rabbi Eleazar in Rome as well as with Rabbi Joshua ben Hananya. Some say he expressed an interest in our faith. We are watching him carefully."

We. Gabriel stiffened when he heard the word. He hoped his guest had not noticed, and he looked at the older man with new eyes. He would be the last person to shelter a rebel in the household he had struggled so hard to build. When he tried to catch his daughter's eye, he could not. She was riveted by the stranger. Gabriel heaved himself up to a sitting position and then he stood. Rearranging his robes, he invited his guest to join him in the atrium. The women, of course, stayed behind at the table.

After he was sure they were out of earshot, Gabriel said, his back to his guest, "My daughter, praise God, lives a life of luxury, even though – or perhaps because – I inherited my share of trouble with the Romans." Then, Gabriel turned to face Samuel.

We. It had only taken that one word spoken over dinner, for Gabriel to sense that this stranger was going to change his house forever. The words poured out, as Gabriel began to reveal things to this man that he had told no one since arriving at Sepphoris. He was doing so to save his family, he told himself.

"I want to make sure you know whose house you have entered this night. My mother," he began, then faltered, searching for words in unfamiliar territory, "... I never really knew her. There were hints, words exchanged between my parents that stopped when I entered the room. Then, when I was older, there were other things ..." Gabriel's voice faded as he recalled his mother once lovingly cradling a scroll she had taken from its hiding place behind a stone in the wall of the upper sleeping chamber. When she had turned to meet his wide-eyed stare, she had called him to her. She held him in a rare, warm embrace, explaining to him that the scroll told of the great love she had known, and of the life she had sworn to leave behind. This, Gabriel decided, he would not share with the stranger.

"As a young woman, my mother made a stand with the freedom fighters of the ilk I have no doubt you admire," Gabriel said, staring pointedly at Samuel's missing finger. "My mother loved the land God promised us no less than you do. But she loved life more, and she resolved to put that other life behind her. It followed her, though, and eventually it tore me from her and my father. The last time I saw her was twenty-two years ago. It was then that I made a vow. I promised myself that if I lived, I would make my peace with the conqueror, even if I never see an end to their oppression.

"I have been faithful to my vow. I have made myself useful to the conqueror. In return they have left my family and my city alone. You are the first to bring news of Jerusalem into our home. My daughter knows nothing of these things."

Samuel easily kept up the pretense of knowing nothing of Gabriel's antecedents, that his superiors, after hatching their plan, had not been having Rebecca watched from the moment Gabriel's identity and location had been ascertained. "Forgive me," Samuel responded softy, "but I doubt that your daughter, as you say, knows nothing. If she troubled herself to go to the synagogue to listen to Rabbi Eleazar, then she almost certainly knows more than you think.

"She is probably making plans you know nothing about, plans that have nothing to do with the kind of useless compliance that Rabbi Eleazar teaches our nation. Although certainly" – here Samuel paused, taking in the atrium to which Gabriel had led him, from its perfectly proportioned columns to the intricate and colorful designs of its mosaic floor – "... individuals do prosper this way."

Gabriel's uninvited guest hurried on, ignoring his host's darkening face. "You were right about one thing you said back there, though," motioning with an upward tilt of his strong, square chin toward the dining room. "The small deceits some Jews practice mean nothing. But some of the things they do mark them as clearly as the mark of the trader on a slave's hand and forehead."

Over the years, Samuel had amassed practice at unbalancing men, even powerful ones, with his words. He knew he had succeeded once again with Gabriel. It was time for the next step. "I noticed that Rebecca touched neither wine nor meat during our meal, even though

Rabbi Eleazar and his disciples have said it is wrong to abstain from these simple pleasures as some do to mourn the lost Temple."

For Samuel to speak of Rebecca by name to her father was to take an unacceptable liberty that belonged to family members only. A taste more bitter than over-boiled sage crept into Gabriel's mouth. This man, who had come out of nowhere, was going to steal his daughter away.

Samuel seated himself casually on the edge of the fountain that adorned the center of the atrium. He swept his fingers absently through the water that sparkled in the torchlight. His next words belied his easy stance. "I, like you, have sworn an oath. Yours was to leave the path your mother's people set for us. Mine was never to leave it. We must never give in to the conqueror. You are right to say that our secret circumcisions do not liberate us. But they give us hope, because they are a sign that we will never belong to them."

"Rebecca will never live the life you have chosen for yourself," Gabriel retorted, one desperate step ahead of Samuel. But to his surprise the words came out more as a question than a statement.

Samuel knew differently. He almost wished he did not. Good food, good company, and pleasant Cypriot wine had nearly warmed the lonely core within him. He felt a kinship he could not explain with the younger man who stood with him in the colonnaded atrium. He wished, if only for a moment, that he could surrender as Gabriel had, that he could live out his life in just such surroundings as these. But long ago, a little boy had put away that option forever, when the man he had become pledged himself to liberate a people, and himself.

"Could she not remain in Galilee?" Gabriel asked, inwardly cursing the plaintive tone, so foreign to him, which he heard emerging from his throat.

"Galilee? Hardly the place to start a rebellion," Samuel scoffed, looking again around the beautiful courtyard. Here before him stood the owner of these beautiful premises, the son of the woman who had saved his life, in a way, almost like a brother to him. Yet Samuel had convinced himself, despite Miriam's deathbed words, that he was more of a son to Miriam than this man who had made his peace with the Romans.

Tiny drops of water splashed from the gurgling fountain onto the floor. Samuel watched them darken on the tiny tiles, bringing to life the elegant geometric pattern of black, white, and ochre. As the evening breeze blew in from the hills, the words of the shriveled old woman who had been Miriam's last earthly companion came back to him in a flash of realization. "She has a son, Gabriel, who escaped the troubles here. But who knows where he's gotten to, or even if he's still alive."

There was no question about it. This was the right place. Indeed, as he had been warned by the *listim,* Miriam's son was not what he had hoped. But his superiors were also correct that the daughter would more than do, as they had told him when they revealed their plans for her.

Samuel had seen the sorrow in Miriam's face as she left him behind in Carmel so long ago, and then once again as he heard her deathbed confession. But for his purpose, he would paint a different picture. It was now his task to introduce Rebecca to a different picture of that grandmother. In that picture, Miriam had kept her scroll of divorce as a living sign of devotion to her long-lost rebel husband, and had never given up hope of throwing off the conqueror's yoke. Through that portrait, Samuel would introduce Rebecca to Elazar ben Yair of Masada and all that Samuel's ilk believed the rebel leader had stood for. Samuel would rekindle in Rebecca the fire of rebellion, and she would do his bidding.

Samuel reached into his belt to touch the document hidden there, unwittingly imitating the gesture Miriam had repeated so often in her last years. It was time to show Gabriel the last evidence of his mother's existence. Then, he hesitated. Would this collaborator not surrender him to the conqueror for the crime of possessing such a document? After all, it attested to an ancient ritual of the conquered people, precisely at a time when every mother trembled for the life of her newborn son and every groom sanctifying his bride knew he might be sacrificing both their lives in so doing.

Samuel saw Gabriel tense when he reached into his belt, and tried now to undo the move for the scroll and insert his thumbs casually beneath the folds of his belt. But Gabriel had caught the shift of the visitor's hand to his belt with the eyes of a man who knew what it was to be hunted. He backed away. He would not have been the first landowner murdered in his own home by a brigand. He was not about to take the chance.

A sharp nod in the direction of the servant who stood at the door connecting the dining room and the courtyard set the well-practiced defenses of his household in motion. The servant disappeared, and in what seemed like the blink of an eye, eight men soundlessly surrounded Gabriel and the stranger. They did not appear armed, but Samuel knew that beneath each robe a dagger lay ready. Slowly Samuel lowered his hands from his belt and held them out to his sides, turning his palms up in surrender.

"What I have hidden in this belt is no weapon," Samuel said softly. "It is a document. One that I have reason to believe belongs to you."

Gabriel raised one dark brow. "Never having seen you before this day, I cannot imagine how you could have come into possession of a document belonging to me." Suspicion brought a note of formality into his voice. These last words hung in the air, inviting a response, and closure to this mystery. Gabriel was a man who never truly dropped his guard, a man who hesitated in doorways, who watched empty roads. He was a man who had somehow woven together enough threads of his life to cover his nakedness, but never ceased longing for the opportunity to complete its tattered edges.

"If I may be permitted…" answered Samuel, turning his wrists cautiously with palms still open. Gabriel nodded his assent and signaled with a wave to his men to stand down.

Samuel brought out the cracked leather bag containing the *get*. Still moving slowly, his finger slid beneath the ties and out came the scroll. What was this, Gabriel wondered. His mind raced. A contract? Was this stranger lowering himself to demanding a finder's fee for returning the deed to his parents' lowland holdings? No, that could not be – he had never known exactly what had happened to Menahem or Miriam, but of one thing he was certain, after his crime, their land would surely have gone to some Roman official.

Something gnawed at the far reaches of his memory and he felt the hair stand up on the back of his neck. He closed his eyes for a moment and the image of his mother's face came unbidden behind his lids. He had seen this scroll before.

Chapter 33

"Follow me," Gabriel bid Samuel curtly. They crossed the courtyard and into Gabriel's study. Gabriel pulled the vermilion tapestry curtain closed, and on his writing table he set the oil lamp one of the bodyguards had handed over to him. Starlight winked at them from the high windows. The rich aroma permeated the air of olive oil from the lamps that burned there during the day to illuminate the work of Gabriel secretaries. This most ordinary of scents, unnoticed during work hours, now seemed overbearing to the man who held daylight court in this room.

Gabriel motioned to Samuel to unroll the scroll on his desk. Gabriel began reading aloud: "*On the first of Marheshwan, the year six, at Masada. I divorce and repudiate of my own free will today, I, Joseph, son of Naqsan, you, my wife, Miriam, daughter of Jonathan from Hanablata, living at Masada, who having been my wife up to this time, so that you are free on your part to become the wife of any Jewish man that you please.*"

Gabriel stopped reading as realization gripped him. The man who stood before him had had known his mother in the life that had made her who she was. That life now rose like wisps of smoke from the curling page before him. Gabriel continued reading in a whisper.

"Now you have from me a bill of repudiation and a writ of divorce. Now I give back the whole dowry and for all ruined and damaged goods, and so let it be determined and paid fourfold. And at any time that you say to me I shall replace for you the document, as long as I am alive."

He had forgotten the name on the scroll his mother had shown him that day, but the moment he heard it again he knew that it came from that place on the other side of her life where neither he nor his father was permitted to go.

When Gabriel raised his eyes to look again at Samuel, they were different. Somewhere during the reading he had been transformed from powerful landowner, the respectable belly hanging over an embroidered belt bearing witness to his high station, back into a frightened, homeless young man.

Now, Samuel was in charge. He motioned Gabriel to sit in the chair that served the landowner during business hours, its curved back elaborately carved with intertwining grape vines. Samuel took the backless chair opposite him.

Leaning forward, his elbows resting on the fluted wooden armrests, Samuel's hands opened wide as he searched for words. The words to bring alive a whole community, a place hemmed in by despotic terror, then by death, and a young boy and a woman who had left their lives in a doomed palace on a barren plateau.

As he told his tale, clammy night air began to seep in to the room. "And so it is," Samuel finally concluded, "that I and the road are so intimately acquainted. I make my way from one outpost to another, giving encouragement, transferring funds, whatever is needed. But above all, it is you I have been seeking, or rather, your daughter, Miriam's granddaughter, cousin, as are you, to Elazar of Masada." Gabriel unclenched his hands from around the edge of his seat. When he stood every muscle ached, and he realized that he had not moved since Samuel had begun his tale. Hands behind his back, he faced the wall examining as if he had never seen it before the landscape painted on it that danced in the shadows.

The silence was finally broken by a sound at the doorway. Roughly, Gabriel pulled aside the curtain to look straight into a pair of wide, quizzical eyes. "How long have you been standing here?" he asked in a cracked voice.

The answer was in those eyes.

They were no longer the eyes of the daughter-ornament he had pampered and shielded from the life that lay beyond the veil that he, like his mother before him, had created. Gabriel reached for Rebecca's arm and pulled her into the room.

"No more than I needed to hear to know, finally, where my life will go now," Rebecca replied firmly.

Listening at the door. More than four decades ago, the grandmother she had never known had also listened at a doorway on a desert mountaintop, and turned her back on everything she had known before. "Where your *life* will *go*... What could you possibly mean by that?" Gabriel's tone now rose to a desperate pitch. "Your life will go as we always planned it. You will marry well with the dowry I will provide, that is all you need to know and all you need to do." His voice spiraled out of control and he gritted his teeth to bring it back down to a whisper. Every ear in the house, and not a few eyes, were probably fixed on the room that had swallowed Gabriel and Samuel.

Something seemed horribly off balance, a sensation he last remembered feeling as he was teetering on the rooftop of his childhood home in Beit Govrin, when he stood on the brink between his past and his future. He was falling, falling.

He sank back down. The carvings in his fine chair dug into his back and sweat pooled beneath his thighs.

"I'm sorry, Father," Rebecca said in a tone too mature, he thought, to belong to his daughter. "Ever since I heard Rabbi Eleazar in the synagogue I have known that this can no longer be my life. Rabbi Eleazar spoke with the voice of a slave who has lost the yearning to be free. This town, which opened its gates to the conqueror needs to give its children back to the struggle. I know of many others who feel as I do. You see, the markets of Sepphoris have provided more than entertainment for me."

"This is why Samuel has come to us. To me." Rebecca's next words showed Samuel how right his people had been to select her.

Gabriel shook his head vigorously in response as if overtaken by a chill that had nothing to do with the night air. Her next words told him that her passion was going to be their weapon. It had blinded her to all the logic he knew she possessed. Like an audience happily oblivious to a market-day magician's sleight of hand as they cheer at his tricks, his daughter was now ignoring the fact that Samuel's arrival in their home had been anything but coincidence. "Samuel's arrival is the proof I need that this is what God wants me to do," she declared.

Helpless, Gabriel turned to Samuel. In vain he looked for some sense of regret in the man's face. Samuel felt this bereft father's torment. But he did not turn away. One man's torment was meaningless in the face of what this young recruit could do for them when the time came. Yet, as well trained as Samuel was, he was not prepared for what happened next.

Gabriel lunged at Samuel with the shriek of a deer trapped in a hunter's blind. The older man sidestepped him easily and Gabriel tumbled clumsily onto the first row of scribes' tables, sending them flying in every direction. The crash brought the household servants running in from the courtyard, where they had been waiting uneasily since the earlier confrontation.

They found their master sprawled on the floor, blood oozing from a small wound on his forehead. Gabriel forced himself to think quickly. He could not let it be known what had transpired in the room. Sheltering a stranger who then proceeded to leave in the company of his daughter? The information would make the rounds of all the homes in Sepphoris, and reach the Romans before noon the next day. Everything he had worked for would be wiped out by this time tomorrow night. He scrambled, purposefully inelegant, to his feet.

Clasping his hands together around Samuel's shoulder he made as if to hang from him dizzily. "One bowl of wine too many, and look what it brings us to, my new good friend," he said, slurring his voice. "Why did you even come in here to offer us more, Daughter, when you see the condition I am in already? Woe is me if my Hannah finds out," he finished, comically rolling his eyes. The servants looked at each other in confusion. The voices coming from this room earlier, muffled though they were, seemed anything but those of celebrants. Now the master was dismissing them with a crooked wave of his arm. They complied with a shrug.

When they were alone again, Gabriel went as still as if he were in a restful asleep. Rebecca heard the familiar sound of labored breathing that signaled that he was deep in thought and unaware of his surroundings.

Then he refocused on her. His voice was flat. "When I left my home and everything I knew and loved, my enemies were snapping at my heels. To stop running would have meant my death. I left in order to choose life over death.

"Until that moment, my parents had raised me to believe that by denying my mother's past, I would be spared its curse. How could they know, how could *I* know that the past would stalk me down through the years to my own home, this very evening, and rob me of my own daughter?"

He strode over to the desk where the scroll lay. Deliberately, he rolled it up and placed it in its leather pouch. Looking away from his daughter, he extended it in Rebecca's direction, his tone as bitter as an uncured olive. "You are so in love with those days, with those people who brought us nothing but destruction and despair. This scroll, then, is rightfully yours. Take it with you when you leave."

No more words were spoken. Her father's fingers brushed Rebecca's as he passed her the scroll. It was the last time she would know the touch of his hand. Whispering to Samuel that she would meet him shortly, she left the room and made her way silently to her own. She lifted her woolen outer robe from the hook on the wall where she had hung it upon her return from the market, a thousand years ago that morning, and wrapped it around herself, securing it with the bow-shaped silver pin that had been a gift from her mother.

Pulling aside the curtain that hung over the wall recess filled with her clothes, she carelessly pulled a plain flaxen dress from within, ignoring the colorful disarray in which it left her other frocks and cloaks. She crammed the dress into the straw basket she had woven under Hannah's tutelage many years before. Tossing a few more essential items into the basket, she tied it shut with its leather thong and placed it on her bed. She lay down next to it to await the first glimmer of dawn, when the town gates would open.

Sleep fled before the cavalry of thoughts that thundered through her mind with every heartbeat. There would be no goodbye to her mother, who would not understand where she was going or why. It had been easier in these past years to hide her proclivities from her mother than from her father. Her father, she guessed, had seen, and denied what he saw; her mother had not even seen. Together her parents had made it simpler than they would ever know for her faith in rebellion to grow. As the night wore on, she understood that when she walked out the door, she would lose both father and mother.

But she had also gained something. As if it were a living, breathing thing, the scroll that she had spent several minutes securing in her belt under her cloak seemed to warm against her body. It was as if her grandmother herself was at her side imbuing her with the thirst for freedom for which surely she must have lived until her dying day.

Her father was wrong, she thought; surely, her grandmother would have approved of her choice.

Chapter 34

The eastern sky was pinking softly as the young girl and the older man made their way through the silent streets toward the gate. The stirrings of the day could be heard behind high courtyard walls, but shops were still shuttered and the streets, as Samuel had hoped, were empty. The night watchmen were fixing the iron rods to their hooks to pull open the massive wooden doors of the city gates, and the two travelers waited in the shadows until the sentries swung open the doors. No one saw them slip out of the city.

As the morning wore on, they met others along the road. Travelers walked or rode with their eyes down in order not to meet the gaze of others, especially those that seemed to bore into them from beneath military visors. Delays – or worse – would ensue when soldiers on patrol were ordered on the spur of the moment to search for "contraband." The contents of many a carriage or saddlebag was transferred all too efficiently to military wagons, as merchants or families looked on helpless. It was a popular method of supplementing a military salary.

Rebecca wondered if Samuel would lead her west to Ptolemais and the Great Sea, or east to the Sea of Galilee and the Bashan beyond. In any of these places they would find a shelter in a dozen homes and synagogues where, she imagined, discontent simmered, hidden from the eyes of the conqueror and his agents, and she could begin whatever mission Samuel had in mind for her.

But Samuel surprised Rebecca when he left the main east-west highway and continued along a narrow but well-traveled path that led northward between rocky hills studded with oak, terebinth, and carob. "Samuel, where are we going?" Had the older man heard her question? If so, he made no sign he was going to answer. Just as she was about to ask again, he spoke.

"Before I tell you where, I must tell you why I came to you at this time of all times. A month ago, the emperor announced that he would allow the Jews to rebuild the Temple. Everyone believed the move was perfectly in keeping with his other diplomatic initiatives. After all, he's done everything right – from finally deposing Lucius Quietus to making formal inquiries of our sages about our beliefs," Samuel explained.

"Now he has rescinded the promise to build the Temple. Worse than that, the servants of Emperor Hadrian *deny* that the promise has been rescinded. Instead, they say that we *can* now rebuild our Temple anywhere we wish – anywhere but on the Temple Mount!"

Rebecca stopped in her tracks as the significance of this last statement sank in. "But it is impossible to build the House of God anywhere but where God has chosen," she protested. She knew that the Romans were far from ignorant of her faith and she instinctively understood that this insult Samuel described was no more than one more way of forcing her people into total submission. It was an extension of the scenes she saw each time she went to the market place, or on the road: the conqueror did as he pleased, and the people submitted in order to preserve their lives and their community. Rebecca swallowed the anger that had risen in her throat. "I pray you are taking me straight to Jerusalem!"

"To Jerusalem?" Samuel snorted. "What good do you think that would do us? No, we are on our way to the village of Beit Rimon, where Joshua ben Hananya will be addressing the people. Depending on what Rabbi Joshua and the other sages say to the people we will know how to proceed and where we are needed most."

Now Rebecca was puzzled. This grizzled old revolutionary has sought her out as a companion to attend a gathering of sages, no different than those that took place a dozen times a month in some town or village in Galilee? "But we must act now," she said, making a fist with one hand and slamming it into the other. "After this latest insult, how could our sages not allow us to rise up against the conqueror?"

Her words hung in the air as they continued walking. Samuel had not even so much as looked her way in response. The scrub oaks on the hillsides now gave way to manicured orchards. The perfectly shaped crowns on each still-green pomegranate that hung from the trees promised a plentiful harvest.

"Our sages teach that the seeds in each pomegranate are the exact same number as commandments in the Bible," Samuel mused, gesturing at the new fruit. Rebecca looked at him out of the corner of her eye in disbelief. Counting pomegranate seeds or commandments seemed a useless preoccupation to the newly homeless girl. But she did not know Samuel. He was about to make his point.

"Each act that God commands us we must perform to glorify the name of the Holy One, blessed be He. Any way that we acknowledge the right of the evil kingdom over our lives, even the smallest, diminishes us in that task. The words we hear from the sages will surely show us God's will in this matter."

Rebecca had no time to respond, as they had joined a crowd of strangers funneling into Beit Rimon's narrow main street. There was no need to ask directions, the river of people was flowing upward to the choicest location in town. To the place where every self-respecting town and village in Galilee built its synagogue.

The building's long main chamber was filled to the rafters and still people were pouring in. All three tiers of seats around the walls were occupied with people cramped shoulder to shoulder. Others sat on mats spread on the floor, reaching nearly up to the wooden podium in the center of the room. Rebecca and Samuel moved toward a staircase leading to the second-floor gallery that spanned the three sides of the hall. It, too, was overflowing, and Rebecca eyed the wooden banister warily as people leaned over it for a better look at the speaker.

The room was in chaos. Neighbors called to one another to fill an imaginary space next to them, while business associates from across the district took the opportunity to advance transactions that otherwise might have to wait until the next market day.

Suddenly, Joshua ben Hananya entered the hall from a side room. Every eye followed him as he strode to the podium. His deep-set eyes seemed to look directly at each person in the room. His arms were invisible, crossed beneath a finely woven linen mantle from which ritual fringes trailed. A mane of silvery hair cascaded down his back, and a carefully coifed, snow-white beard covered his chest. Shouts turned to whispers that continued to fly through the hall, overcoming the voice of the sexton calling frantically for silence.

"This is a man worth walking six hours to hear."

"Ben Hananya will give us the word!"

"He will tell us that now is the time to throw off the yoke of the evil kingdom."

"An end to our suffering is near!"

Rabbi Joshua's voice was unexpectedly soft. Silence finally prevailed as, together with everyone else, Rebecca and Samuel leaned forward, straining to hear the rabbi's first words. "An evil man seeketh rebellion. Therefore a cruel messenger will be sent against him."

Sharp intakes of breath from the people seated closest to the raised dais. As these words from the book of Proverbs were relayed to the furthest corners of the hall by the professional repeaters, whispers rose once again to murmurs, and soon something approaching a muted roar was rolling from one end of the room to the other. Rebecca felt Samuel stiffen in his seat.

"He has betrayed us," Samuel forced the words from between locked jaws. Rebecca looked over at him. In the old rebel's tone was a kind of acceptance, of finality. Confusion settled on her like a cloud. The rabbi's eyes moved serenely over the faces in the crowd while he waited for the repeaters to complete their task. Rebecca saw them come to rest on Samuel, locking on him as if there was no one else in the room. They narrowed slightly, as if trying to place him. But the eyes moved on.

The repeaters attempted in vain to silence the audience. But it was a simple gesture – Rabbi Joshua's suddenly upraised hands – that finally quieted the room.

"I will tell you of the lion and the crane."

Ahhh, the audience sighed, familiar territory. Surely the tale to which they were about to be treated would make everything clear. True, the sage had started out his homily by excoriating the rebellion. But he had probably done that so as to better explain that rebellion would be the crucial next step, their looks said as they nodded to each other, satisfied with this convoluted logic. They settled down to listen.

"One day, as a lion walked through the woods, he chanced upon a caper bush whose succulent buds were ripe for the picking. 'What a meal this will make,' said the happy lion as he chomped off a branch heavy with the tightly closed blossoms. However, as we all know," said the rabbi, leading his audience skillfully, "the caper not only buds and blossoms, but vicious thorns as well. Together with his tasty morsels, the lion swallowed an entire branch of thorns!

"Miserable, the lion lay down in the dust as it became harder and harder for him to breathe. All at once a crane swooped out of the sky and landed nearby, a mere hand's span from the wretched beast. The crane walked all around the lion, eyeing it warily. When the lion caught sight of the bird, he called out to him. 'Dear friend crane, help me, please, help me!' The timbre of the rabbi's voice barely changed. But to the audience, it was the lion itself that now spoke from his throat.

"But the crane kept his distance. 'Why should I help you,' he shot back, 'when for such a deed I may lose my life?'

"'No, no,' begged the lion. 'You have my solemn promise, if you use your long beak to remove this thorn from my throat, you will earn my undying gratitude. And the undying gratitude of the king of the beasts is worth much!'

"Well now, this crane weighed the possibilities of his future reward for a few moments longer. Then he approached the lion to fulfill his request," the rabbi continued.

"Opening its jaws, the lion leaned toward the crane. At the sight of those jagged teeth protruding from the lion's stinking maw, the crane hesitated, but only for a moment. He dove inward to extract the thorny branch, which came free in a shower of blood and saliva."

Breathless "oohs" and "aahs" showed that the audience was reveling in the colorful details – almost as much as the moral they knew was to come.

"What reward would the lion bestow upon the brave crane, my friends?"

The tension at this point of the telling was now made all the more delicious by their initial disappointed shock at the anti-rebel stance with which Rabbi Joshua had opened his homily.

"The lion stood up to his full height and shook his heavy mane to and fro. But the courageous crane was not fearful now. Had the lion not promised to deal with him handsomely? 'I will accept my reward now, Master Lion,' said the crane.

"'Your reward…' the lion made as if to ponder. Suddenly he turned on his regal heels, his tail snapping jauntily right and left like a whip. 'Your reward shall be…that I let you live! I could have swallowed you whole with your silly beak in my mouth and yet, I let you live!' The lion roared with laughter at his own joke. 'Let that be your reward Master Crane, and leave me in peace!'"

The room fell silent. Row by row, section by section, as the repeaters did their duty, the whole audience now went rigid as Samuel had done upon hearing the rabbi's opening words. They all understood his meaning now. They were being instructed to continue to bear the blows of the evil kingdom. Not to circumcise their male babes, not to build their Holy House. To emerge alive from the lion's throat and be thankful that they had survived. Though wrapped in layers of allegory, the great rabbi had ruled. Even a child could understand it.

Rabbi Joshua rose, stepped down from the dais and exited the synagogue alone through the door of the central nave. The audience sat stunned. Samuel was the first in the chamber to rise. He pushed his way through the crowd, oblivious to Rebecca at his heels.

He strode out the door, down the wide steps, and back down the street by which they had come.

"Samuel, wait! Speak to me," Rebecca called breathlessly after him. The older man stopped as if remembering for the first time that Rebecca was with him. He seized her hand and made for the nearby drink seller, whose wares were advertised by the wide-mouthed clay jars half-buried in the ground outside the stall. He pointed to one of the jars. The drink seller ladled out two bowls of sweet, dark date juice, one eye on the task and the other contemplating the horde of potential customers pouring out of the synagogue behind Rebecca and Samuel.

Bowls in hand, they moved away from the gathering crowd onto a shaded side street where a row of shuttered shops told of merchants unable to pay their taxes to the Romans. Samuel gestured toward the locked doors. "Everyone in that room who listens to Rabbi Eleazar will continue to believe that it is better to live under Roman domination than to challenge it," he said bitterly.

Then he did the unexpected. He laid a meaty hand on each of Rebecca's shoulders and looked into her eyes. "You are the crane," he said, "who will enter the jaws of the lion. But you will not be foolish like the rabbi's crane, feeling you deserve no more than to have escaped with your life. You will enter the mouth of the lion and dig out his teeth, one by one, until he writhes in pain and finally starves to death."

There was only one question Rebecca could think of at that moment, and it revealed her willingness to accept a fate that she could not yet even begin to imagine.

"Will you be there?"

"I will accompany you to your new home, Samuel answered her. "I will instruct you. From then on, it will be up to you."

Where? How? A numbness had begun at the pit of her stomach and radiated through every limb. Bringing the questions to her lips was as hard as a servant girl trying to haul a full skin of water up from the well alone, and by the time she voiced them, Samuel had turned away.

It was time to secure a place for the night. The rooms in the town inn were all filled by now, but they found space in its courtyard. A dozen other people had done the same, most falling into exhausted sleep after time spent in the market where, in the wake of Rabbi Joshua's speech, heated opinions were exchanged more often than goods or coins. Samuel had not been the only dissenter in the synagogue.

Long into the night, Samuel whispered to Rebecca, revealing her mission in her new home. The urgency of his tone slashed away her numbness and her doubt, persuading her that not only was she perfectly equipped to perform the task his superiors had set for her, but that in fact, it was one she had been born to.

Samuel knew exactly what to say to the young girl, and if he had any qualms about his words to Rebecca that night, it never showed.

He had not forgotten the last words of his protectress at Masada, Rebecca's grandmother Miriam, before her exile from the village that refused her further shelter. She had begged him to seek life, even under the yoke of the conqueror. But the humiliation of his life, the indignity of Miriam's death, meeting her son, who had turned his back on everything for which Samuel had come to believe both their lives had been saved – these he twisted together like strands of hemp until they no longer resembled what they had been individually. Instead, they now perfectly served his cause. Giving a final twist of the rope that turned truth into lies, Samuel lightly touched the place within the folds of Rebecca's belt where Miriam's scroll now lay. "You heard your father and me in his study, so you know what this document means. Your grandmother carried it close to her every moment she could. She died waiting for someone like you to carry the torch of liberation. Possess it now, and you will feel the strength of her spirit with you always," he said. And Rebecca believed.

Chapter 35

There was little time for talk the next day, as they busied themselves purchasing provisions for their journey. The endless stream of bronze coins and not a few silver ones that came out of Samuel's purse belied his outer appearance of a wanderer no different than anyone else plying the road seeking shelter and a daily wage. Soon enough, they had the donkey to carry enough kernels of barley, together with a small grinding stone, to provide them with bread for the weeklong journey to her new home. Dates, figs and raisins would provide additional sustenance. Neatly rolled and tied down across the donkey's back was the fine woolen blanket under which Rebecca had slept at home. By the end of their trip, it would be worn threadbare by the stony ground.

Down from the foothills, plodding along the Galilee's main highway, they headed south. The Sea of Galilee glistened at their backs as they made their way to Scythopolis. Rebecca had to admit that this region's thriving capital, with its gleaming colonnaded streets, and views of fields, orchards and pastures almost all the way to the Jordan, rivaled the beauty of her own Sepphoris. A passerby directed them to the nearest inn and after Samuel placed the requisite four denarii into the proprietor's outstretched palm, they laid claim to a corner of the room. This night at least, they had a roof over their heads.

It was still night when, as they had requested, the innkeeper's wife arrived to rouse them, leaving the oil lamp she carried in a small triangular niche in the wall. By its flickering light, Rebecca and Samuel quickly tied their bedrolls and were on their way.

The sun had not yet burned away the coolness of the morning when they reached the Jordan River crossing. The rain that had swelled the river during the previous winter had long since been swept down the narrow channel on its way to the salt-heavy Asphalt Sea and the river was a calm, muddy brown. The donkey did not balk as they pulled it toward the stream, and they emerged on the east bank wet only to the waist.

The sun dried their clothes quickly. When it had passed the overhead point and was behind them in the western sky, Samuel insisted that their pace stay as brisk as the ascent from the river bank toward Pella would allow. The green thickets of the Jordan soon gave way to salt-infused plaster hillsides. They did not stop to eat, but chewed on nutritious saltbush leaves as they walked. But there was too much road between them and the city. They arrived at Pella's gates as they were closing, just in time to hear the guards shouting, "Hear now, night is upon us, find your own way until dawn. Night it upon us, closing the gates. Find your own way." Rebecca and Samuel, together with other unfortunates, would spend this night out in the open.

Rebecca took a measure of barley from the saddlebags that Samuel had lifted off the donkey before he bedded down the animal for the night. She set about the task of grinding flour for an evening meal of sorts. The rigors of the day sank into Rebecca's bones and she fought the fatigue that threatened to slow her regular back and forth movements of the grinding stone. It took an hour before enough ground flour had emerged from between the roller and its base, twice the time it would have taken the sinewy servant girl who had performed this task at home. After seeing to the donkey, Samuel joined her, bringing a basket of dried fruit to be placed on what Rebecca had now formed into a pliant, doughy disk that soon would serve as both plate and sustenance. Moments after Rebecca draped the dough over the curved clay dome that covered the fire, the bread was ready.

Families and fellow travelers had by now gathered in small groups. This was just the moment for an itinerant storyteller to ply his craft, to take the edge off the uncertainty of the night beyond the comfort of the city walls. But no one volunteered. Each group kept to itself. Next to where Rebecca and Samuel shared their meal, a rhythmic murmur rose. Normally, prayer would attract little attention – in most circles it was becoming as much a part of the evening's activities as the evening meal. But Samuel could not help inclining his ear toward the group. Something sounded different, although he could not place what it was.

One of the men in the group noticed Samuel glancing toward their circle. He disengaged from it and approached the older man and the young woman. "Peace be unto you," said the stranger with outstretched arms and palms turned upward. "And to you, peace," Rebecca and Samuel replied formally, in unison.

Samuel looked at the man while looking beyond him, feigning the mildest of polite interest while taking in everything about the stranger. It was a survival skill he had learned, like Rebecca's father, in his fugitive days. Dress, demeanor, accent and the nature of traveling companions were all unobtrusively trolled for clues to the man's identity. The man was sizing up Samuel in exactly the same way. This was never idle inquisitiveness – it was crucial to determine in the first moments – friend or enemy?

To further his efforts at identification, Samuel decided on the technique of plunging into conversation, but on a neutral subject that any two travelers would discuss.

"Your prayers have verses unknown to us in the Galilee," Samuel opened, adding, "I can imagine that a long and rigorous journey has brought you to this place."

He waited. It was the stranger's turn to reveal a general detail of his own origin. But Samuel was unprepared for the stranger's candor.

"A way that is long and a road that is arduous," the stranger replied, for emphasis using the doublet that had made its way from their sacred books into ordinary speech. "We are Ebionites." We were among the last to live in the Holy City. Tomorrow we will join our brethren in Pella. Perhaps you have heard of our community, in Galilee, the home of our teacher, in whose name many miracles of healing have occurred."

The stranger sat down next to Rebecca, oblivious to the breach he had committed by doing so uninvited. He gazed up expectantly at Samuel. But it was Rebecca who answered him in a youthful rush. "Yes, yes, indeed, we have heard of your people. They say no more than the touch of a follower of your teacher can heal all manner of sicknesses." Rebecca, once again the pampered young girl, was pleased to find such a diversion – quite a dramatic one at that – discussing that which had been forbidden to bring up at home. Most of the rabbis had prohibited any contact with the Ebionites or their brethren, the Nazarenes, but she had heard more than one whispered tale about them from their household servants as well as from the daughters of other fine families, who had gone to them in secret and returned relieved of their ailments.

"I was just an infant in Jerusalem when the Temple was destroyed. So too was our community in its infancy. My own father sat at the feet of Jacob the brother of our lord, who kept us together while the world disintegrated around us. My family knew, as I do now, that the lord has only left us temporarily, that he will return for those who await him faithfully. Too many miracles have occurred for it to be otherwise."

"And is that your family that you travel with?" asked Samuel, drawing the man out. It would have been impolite to do otherwise, although having ascertained that the man posed no threat to them, Samuel was not the least bit interested in such people, who waited for a miraculous future while doing nothing to relieve the torments of the present.

The man smiled. "In a way. We are required to treat each other as family, to share all our worldly goods with one another. Otherwise, we would not be able to make such a journey in the first place. But my blood relations…no. My father died as a witness to our path, in the manner that Isaiah the prophet spoke of David, 'I have made him a witness to the people…'"

Rebecca and Samuel reacted very differently to this last statement. Rebecca waited patiently for clarification, once the man had invoked the high-flown language of Scripture usually reserved for synagogue homilies. Samuel, however, turned his mouth down scornfully.

"He witnessed," the man continued, ignoring both reactions, "by showing perfect faith. He died in the arena rather than recant what we know to be true. I still suckled at that time," the man continued matter-of-factly. "Jacob, our leader, raised me as his own son. He taught me that my father had given his life to show that this" – at this the man gestured gently around him with open arms – "is not the only life. Who can say, perhaps someone in the cell with him that day witnessed his death, heard him tell his tale, our tale, before he went into the ring. Perhaps that person also came to know the glorious future that awaits our people."

"And perhaps," Samuel interjected edgily, "someone in that cell with your father, peace be upon him, learned something quite different from their shared moments together."

Seemingly oblivious to the insult, the man tilted his head, acknowledging a willingness to hear more, but Samuel had nothing further to say. People like this stranger were in another realm, one where the triumph or the defeat of Rome had no standing. It was a realm in which Samuel could never imagine living.

Samuel stood suddenly, and stalked off to a corner. "I will sleep now," he turned his head long enough to say. Rebecca took her cue from the older man, offering the briefest of polite goodbyes to the Ebionite before lying down. She wrapped herself in her outer cloak and her thoughts, which spun her dizzily around the events of past few days. Finally, she fell asleep to the prayerful, calming singsong of the Ebionites, which continued long into the night.

Chapter 36

The journey was proceeding too slowly for either of them. Samuel began to be uncomfortable in the company of the pampered, opinionated young woman who knew nothing of the kind of life he had led. His superiors had given a great deal of thought to the extraordinary value of selecting Rebecca, the unknown aristocratic scion of the revolt, to be placed among the people of an ordinary village in their attempt to reignite the rebellion. She would wait for the right time, and share their plans with no one.

Next came the process of selection, with word of the right family, in the prosperous town of Ein Gedi, coming to Samuel only weeks before he arrived at Sepphoris, through messengers who risked their lives to transmit the information.

As his superiors had surmised, the father would be useless to the cause. But when Samuel first saw Rebecca, her intelligence and passion told him that they had made the right choice. He followed their orders to concentrate during the journey from Sepphoris to Ein Gedi on preparing her to play the role they had assigned her. But as the road wore on, with Rebecca incessantly chattering at him like a sunbird, he could not help but wonder if the choice had not been too hasty after all.

He saw to it that silence reigned between them more often than not as they left Pella and the heat of the valley floor and climbed toward the shining city of Jerasa. Then they turned south, navigating the undulating mountain roads, stopping here and there to rest and refresh themselves and their animals at springs and wells. By the time they were five days south of Jerasa, the landscape had changed again.

"Well, it's into the furnace for us," said Samuel, in a jovial tone belied by the narrowing of his eyes as he spoke. He pointed out their new direction, westward through the tawny mountains and back down into the valley where the Jordan River had wound itself so deeply around the plaster plateaus that it could hardly be seen. The Salt Sea glinted in the distance to the south. Skirting the gray-green oasis of Jericho, they headed into the wilderness.

Raised among the green and fertile hills of Galilee, Rebecca concluded that this must be the bleakest place on earth. The air felt as heavy on her skin as a woolen winter cloak. At the same time the sun burned so intensely that it seemed like she could not possibly have any skin left on her bones. The only water near them was the briny lake, the slightest taste of whose water caused her to gag. Rebecca kept her eyes on the ground, forcing herself to concentrate simply on putting one foot in front of the other. The combination of the oppressive air and the silence was broken only by the rhythmic crunch-crunch of their sandals, which she watched crack a new spider web of lines with every step she took on the dead-white ground. The bone-dry air instantly drank her sweat, except where it hid beneath the thick curls plastered to her forehead by her scarf.

On the last day of their journey, they stepped from the salt-encrusted shoreline into the small boat that would ferry them down to Ein Gedi. Rebecca wondered how the air here could be as beneficial as it was said to be, when it reeked of an egg laying uncollected for too long in the corner of their courtyard. She told Samuel that her mother had taught her that miniscule amounts of poisons sometimes made the best medicine. The air here must have a similar effect, she mused, after she realized the older man was going to respond with nothing more than a shrug and a grunt.

By this time Samuel had ceased showing even the pretense of being a traveling companion. His mission, to deliver Rebecca, was about to end. Never comfortable around people who lived their lives outside of the cause, he was relieved that the need to speak was now nearly over. In the late afternoon, the sun suspended its onslaught. As the glowing orb sank closer to the tops of the Judean hills, Rebecca turned to look back toward the eastern shoreline from which they had embarked, and saw every crevice and valley in the gigantic Arnon gorge illuminated with a golden light.

But then, before her, a sight that truly took her breath away: Ein Gedi. It was a jewel – she had extracted at least that from Samuel the day before … no, a collection of jewels, he had continued, momentarily garrulous, spilling from an alabaster box: the emerald of the date and balsam plantations against the sapphire and turquoise of the Salt Sea, set against the pale earth that surrounded it.

With the goal of her journey now close at hand, Rebecca allowed herself to dwell upon the little Samuel had shared with her about her mission. She thought of how different her life was going to be from that of the childhood friends she had left behind in Sepphoris. If family or business ties demanded it, these young women would find themselves betrothed to men much younger or much older than themselves. A subtle hint, passed from the mother of the bride to the mother of the groom regarding the girl's readiness for marriage or lack thereof, might put off the union for a year or two at most. After her marriage, the future of every girl she knew stretched before her clearly: managing her husband's home and bearing his children.

But for Rebecca, Samuel had made clear, neither family alliances nor business opportunities had determined whom she would marry.

Chapter 37

The pair of dusty travelers entering the city rated no more than a passing glance from the locals. Almost everyone who came to Ein Gedi was somehow or other involved in the trade of a plant more valuable than any on earth: balsam. Here was a merchant purchasing the salve for resale at a hundred-fold profit. There, a doting father adding a two-day detour to his journey to Philadelphia to please his road-weary daughter with a gift of the locally manufactured unguent. After all, it would cost so much more if purchased at home.

Even the soldiers ignored Rebecca and Samuel. They did their jobs with a minimum expenditure of energy, just enough to keep their enviable post – serving in a town where bribes consisted of a few drops of the fragrant and therapeutic sap worth far more than its weight in silver.

Samuel followed the directions his superiors had sent him. He ascended the main street and turned off into the first alley. High plastered walls were punctuated at regular intervals by wooden doors, opened to admit a visitor or catch the breeze. Behind these doors lay courtyards alive with the simple tasks of home and family, from which Rebecca averted her eyes, as etiquette required. Matching the stride of the older man, as she had for the past eight days, she followed Samuel's lead as he stepped through the open door of the second courtyard they came across.

Except for its size – smaller than the house she had grown up in – everything Rebecca saw reminded her of home. Children played dice in one corner, while a servant drew water from the cistern in the center of the yard, shooing the chickens from her path back to the corner where cup-sized depressions in the beaten-earth floor served as their feed dishes.

Samuel strode to an inner door that fronted onto the courtyard. He stopped short at the entrance and called into the dim interior. "Peace be unto you." The airy linen curtain was pulled back by a man with sallow skin stretched taut over high cheek bones. His black-eyed gaze moved from the older man to the young girl without expression. The man's response came back as required: "And to you, peace."

It was starting to get dark now, but the man's ink-stained fingertips had not escaped Samuel's surveillance, and he correctly deduced that the man was the household steward. "Please tell the master of the house that the travelers from Sepphoris are here." The steward knew who they were. In fact, every member of the household, from Rebecca's intended to the cook's son who herded their goats, knew more about impending family events than Rebecca had only a few days before.

"Follow me," was all the man responded, and turned his back to mount a flight of stairs that led to a second-story room overlooking the courtyard. Inside, a large, glistening mound of a man sat hunched over a pile of documents. "Ah, Nathan," said the man jovially, addressing the steward. "I was just about to tell you the light is gone and we'll continue our work in the morning..." His voice died away when he saw that his steward was not alone.

Before Nathan could announce them, the man recognized the travelers. "Peace be unto you," he boomed. Samuel and Rebecca's requisite rejoinder was cut short by the man's excited instruction to the steward: "Go and get lady Zippora!"

"You are welcome, you are welcome," he now bubbled at the travelers, his bobbing head causing his three chins to appear and disappear over his mountainous girth. He gestured to a low couch along the back wall. A servant entered carrying a bowl of water and a linen cloth. Samuel and Rebecca removed their sandals and allowed their feet to be washed as their host continued to beam at them. Rebecca could not help thinking that the man seemed hardly able to keep from rubbing his hands together, looking at her as if she was a particularly delicious meal of which he was about to partake.

A woman now stepped through the doorway. She took in the scene with one piercing glance. "Ezra," she barked at her husband, and the hair piled impossibly atop her head tilted precariously with each syllable.

Rebecca bit back a smile, exhausted as she was.

"Why are you staring at these poor people as if they were actors in the theater? Not even offering some water to quench their thirst? Unless you think they can drink through their feet. Go!" The command was addressed to the servant who had been gathering up the washing cloths. "Bring a jug of cooled carob juice and water."

"You are fatigued from your journey," Zippora said, her habitually critical eyes roving from Rebecca's dusty hair to the travel-frayed hem of her robe. The clothes seemed pitiful next to the woman's carefully fitted saffron gown held at the shoulder with a lapis-studded bronze pin. "You will want to rest and refresh yourself. Then you will meet Itamar. Nathan will show you both to your rooms."

Nathan proceeded ahead of them down the tower stairs. Rebecca and Samuel paused to take in the scene below. The open space was much busier now, and the sun seemed have flared again. Shielding his eyes, Samuel stiffened when he saw that the brightness was not sunlight, but the flash of its dying rays gleaming from the polished armor of six Roman foot soldiers standing protectively in a half circle around their commander, a centurion of the Fretensis legion.

Not many soldiers were stationed near Rebecca's home in Sepphoris. In return for the city's loyalty, the Romans had kept the most onerous signs of their presence outside the town. The closest garrison, units of the VI Ferrata and their support personnel, were stationed more than a day's march away at Legio. Nevertheless, Rebecca had seen her share of legionnaires, and was not perturbed at the sight below. She had not developed Samuel's instincts, born of a lifetime of conflict, and she did not even sense the change in his demeanor when he spied the Romans.

It was the young man speaking to the centurion who had her undivided attention. He was slender and not very tall, especially compared to the centurion, who towered over him. One finely sculpted bare arm was outstretched, the hand proffering a sheaf of documents. Hanging gracefully over the other arm were the folds of the richly dyed, lupin-blue stole, partially covering a sand-colored linen shift. The man's black hair cascaded in perfect curls to his neck, the oil that anointed it glinting in the sunlight. His eyes, framed with thick, long lashes, were as dark as olives left behind for the gleaners after the harvest. Those eyes moved momentarily in the direction of the newcomers, then back to holding the officer's own eyes in a tight grip. A strong nose centered comfortably in a benevolent face. It took Rebecca only a moment to know that the man she so carefully perused was the one about whom Samuel had told her on their journey. Her future husband. She was not displeased.

It was unseemly for the newly arrived guests to be observing the goings-on in the courtyard so openly. But the moment Samuel realized the identity of the young man standing below, he knew that he had about as much chance of shifting Rebecca from that spot as of moving the rock palisade that rose high above the town on the west. So he waited. Without warning, the conversation between the two men ended, as the soldiers turned on their heel and exited the yard.

"If he came to squeeze another aureus or two out of this family, he was disappointed today," Samuel said to Rebecca with a satisfied huff. But Rebecca was not listening. The young man had now turned his full attention to her and Samuel.

With a bow of his head first in the direction of the older man and then in the direction of the young woman, a smile lit up his dusky features and he said, "I am Itamar. Welcome to our home." Those eyes took in everything without appearing to. He knew who Rebecca was and, like her, approved of what he saw.

"I am Samuel," came the gruff response, then adding, unnecessarily, "and this is Rebecca."

"Itamaaaar," came a shrill cry from above. "There will be plenty of time for introductions later. Let them get to their rooms." A slight pursing of his lips was the only sign of Itamar's annoyance at his mother's intrusion. Turning aside to allow them to pass, he gestured toward their rooms. "I look forward to speaking with you again later this evening," he said formally with a little bow. He watched Rebecca until she entered her quarters.

Rebecca knew his eyes were upon her, although she never looked back.

Chapter 38

In the reception room, low tables and couches had been set out for the evening meal. "Now, my dear," Zippora said to Rebecca, arranging her robes carefully around her as she took the couch opposite the one on which her husband sat. "We are delighted to welcome you and your guardian to our house and, of course, to our family. It is not often that our community wins a bride from one of the finest families of Sepphoris." Rebecca was weighing her first words to her future mother-in-law carefully. She would reveal nothing, as Samuel had instructed her during their journey. She was simply a dutiful future daughter-in-law, ready to contribute to the welfare of her new family.

She opened her mouth to answer, but before she could do so, the lady of the house continued what turned out to be a lengthy monologue about their life in this Salt Sea oasis. Rebecca's first words would not to come for what seemed like hours. When finally they did, Zippora completely ignored them. Rebecca was to learn very quickly that monologues could be interrupted only for the briefest moment while a breath was taken, a beverage sipped, or an order given to a servant. That time had to be quickly taken advantage of in order to get even a few words in edgewise.

Zippora was so used to the speech she was giving that she had no idea how ridiculous her false humility sounded to an outsider. The wealth of what she called their "humble community" – thanks to the balsam groves that they worked, long ago for the Herodian family and now for the Romans – had reached every corner of the land. There was more than one young woman, Samuel thought, who would have changed places with Rebecca. But not every young woman's family could afford the dowry Rebecca had unknowingly brought with her.

Neither, in fact, could Rebecca's father, despite his lands and business. As their hostess prattled pompously on, Samuel mused over the fact that she would not be so welcoming if she knew that the dowry, 300 denarii, one third more than the usual bride-price, came not from Rebecca's father but from Samuel's purse, the purse of the rebels. It was meant to ensure that this marriage would go forward, not for the sake of one fine lady's pride, but to play its role in a nation's liberation.

The flow of words was finally staunched when Zippora turned to give orders regarding the meal. A succession of servants brought out beautiful dishes, placing them on small tables in front of the diners. Exotic fruits, tiny succulent quail, vegetables marinated in sauces delicately spiced with coriander, black cumin, and redolent with cinnamon – virtually everything grown right on the hillsides behind their homes, Zippora told her guests proudly.

Chapter 39

EIN GEDI, 117 CE

The marriage celebration of Rebecca and Itamar was the talk of Ein Gedi for years to come. The bride had been living in the groom's parents' house these past few months so there no real need for the usual procession through the city, but Zippora wanted to be seen. So a procession there was – wending its way through the streets and back to Zippora and Ezra's home, oil lamps borne by the young women and torches by the young men lighting up the night. Rebecca wore a finely woven white linen tunic that gleamed where a magnificent sky-blue robe fell aside to reveal it. Aromatic oil burnished her olive skin and her wrists were heavy with gold and silver bracelets. On her head she wore the bride's golden crown – the first Ein Gedi bride to wear one since Hadrian's new laws permitted it once again. Behind her, four donkeys followed, laden with household goods, gifts for the young couple. The gifts were wrapped in palm fronds for protection, save one side, left strategically open so that each fine bronze, silver, and glass item winked in the torchlight and could be admired by all.

After the seven days of celebration, it was time for Rebecca to begin her duties in the household. She would never quite get used to her mother-in-law's shrill-voiced commands, criticisms, and corrections but she did finally discover the one means of getting through her days without incident: The only right way to do things was the older woman's way.

In the early months, Rebecca stayed close to home, learning the family accounts under Nathan's patient tutelage. The steward approved of the young woman. She had obviously been brought up in a home where she had been well prepared for the task of managing a large household.

Those were busy days and wondrous nights. Rebecca's husband turned out to be so charming that there had been no need for the monologue Zippora had forced upon her describing her duties as a wife. And she hardly noticed Samuel's departure, except for his parting words. They had been a riddle that left her wondering when, if ever, she would be called upon to continue her mission. Above all, he had admonished her to put her old life aside, as she did her grandmother's scroll, which she secreted behind a loose stone in the wall of the wedding house – the new couple's small room off the main courtyard.

But to Rebecca's frustration, her new life turned out to be even more restricted than her life had been in Sepphoris. At first she thought she would never leave the family compound. Her movements were restricted to the route from their room to the dining room where the family took their meals, the kitchen where Zippora supervised preparations, and the storerooms. It became the younger woman's task to catalogue the household supplies and arrange for the purchase of replacements when they ran low. The family and the forty servants who lived in the compound were dependent on those supplies, as were the grove workers who occupied the rooms that hugged the hillsides at the height of the date and balsam season.

The ink had hardly dried on their marriage contract when Itamar told her that her duties were to be extended. She would be in charge of putting together supplies for the family's pilgrimage to Yavne, where Rabbi Tarfon sometimes taught. The coming celebration of the Feast of Weeks would be their first opportunity to see and be seen in a new setting. It was an opportunity that Zippora was not about to miss.

When Rebecca was growing up in Sepphoris, the pilgrimage was a trip that her father would never have contemplated, except at the urging of his headstrong daughter. Only a few months before Samuel had appeared at their door was the last time Rebecca had pleaded with her father to make the journey. Before the rumor reached them that Hadrian had rescinded his permission for the Jews to rebuild the Temple on the Temple Mount, many Sepphoris families were anxious to join the crowds of Jews streaming toward Jerusalem to see their beloved shrine begin to rise from the ashes. Most continued to Yavne; and some to other centers, like Lydda, where prominent sages also held deliberations and made rulings.

But Gabriel had put her off with his own set of rumors. Human bones had been discovered on the site of the Temple, he told her. The ritual impurity of death had made an indelible mark on their sacred mountain. That would be enough, he had said, for the sages to put an end to the project. But as always, Rebecca was ready with her response: "Our sages must eventually decree the site ritually clean. After all, what do you suppose happened to all the bones of those who died when the Babylonians besieged Jerusalem and destroyed the Temple of Solomon? Did not the new Temple arise anyway, in the days of Ezra and Nehemiah?" She could not know how much, in her debates, the daughter echoed the grandmother. And neither did Gabriel, for his mother had banked the embers of her fire by the time he grew to the age of understanding.

But the father-daughter debate was to become moot. The Samaritans, went the newest rumor, had intervened and gotten the emperor to renege. "Certainly now it is a waste of our time and money to carry out a pilgrimage to ruined Jerusalem, a Jerusalem where Romans and Samaritans have more to say than I do," Gabriel had declared. "And what do I need the sages of Yavne for anyhow?" she remembered him saying. "We have our own elders to decide what needs deciding." And that had been the end of that.

But at Ein Gedi, the sentiment was very different. Of course, no one went three times a year any more, as Ezra's and Zippora's parents had done when the Temple stood, and hardly anyone went to Jerusalem. But every family tried to go at least once a year to see the sages, wherever they were meeting. For two months before departure, in every household and every chance encounter in the market, discussion revolved around the best time to leave Ein Gedi in order not to miss the public reading of the Torah, held at the time when the greatest number of sages would be present.

As the years went by at Ein Gedi, from Rebecca's first memorable journey as a young bride with her new family, she began to look forward to the annual pilgrimage. It was a chance to break the chain of monotony that bound her to her life.

From time to time, if the harvest of dates or balsam had been a disappointing one, Ezra would complain about the expense of making the journey, one that he found exhausting at the best of times. But never had his complaints prevented the trip, and they would not do so this year either, Zippora had promised herself.

She had found a new reason to undertake the pilgrimage. No fruit had resulted from Rebecca's union with Itamar and as time went on, she feared that none would. And so Zippora embarked on a well-planned campaign of broad hints. Perhaps, she pleaded ingratiatingly to Itamar out of Rebecca's earshot, on the next pilgrimage the elders could be consulted as to the reason for Rebecca's barrenness. Not in front of the entire council or in public audience of course, but privately, before the most intimate forum of five sages. Might there not be some point of law the family could observe more rigorously that would result in a grandson?

Ezra made the mistake of attempting to reason with his wife. "The last time I was there," he told her, "I myself heard the sages say it is better for a man to stay home with his family than to make this exhausting journey. Perhaps if Itamar and Rebecca stayed at home, if we all stayed at home, it would be the ideal solution for their problem." But Zippora prevailed, and the journey was planned.

It was almost Pentecost, the fourth day of the week, four days before their scheduled departure. Rebecca was at her usual task in the storeroom, calculating how much wheat they would need to bake bread for fourteen souls, the four of them and the ten servants that had been awarded the privilege of accompanying the family this time.

A scream pierced the cool interior of the storeroom. Rebecca threw her measuring scoop carelessly atop the overflowing jars of grain and dashed out into the sun-washed courtyard. Her in-laws were nowhere to be seen, resting in their room as usual at this hour, and Itamar had left before sunrise for the date plantation. People were running to and fro. Rebecca grabbed the hysterical wife of the plantation overseer and whirled her around.

"What is it? What has happened?"

"Nathan! It's Nathan," came the woman's breathless response. "A viper."

Rebecca ran to their steward's quarters. Nathan's lanky figure lay quivering on the bare floor. Rebecca remained calm, but her heart sank. Snakebites had been part and parcel of her life ever since she could remember. A carelessly lifted rock in her father's vineyard, a hasty shift of the courtyard water-jar – a whipping blur from a dark corner, and within hours the victim would be beyond help. Here at Ein Gedi the threat of death in writhing pain came in a slithering package half the size of that which she had known at home, one that was nearly invisible against the pale rocks. But the result was the same. She recognized it immediately in the blood that oozed from Nathan's ears and eyes, and the foot, swollen and blackened, that had stepped on the viper only moments before.

Out of long habit, the servants tending the man rose deferentially when Rebecca entered the room and moved aside.

"What can be done, what can be done for him?" Rebecca murmured helplessly.

Silence. Then, "There is something. Someone."

The servant who had spoken did not raise her eyes from the task of bathing Nathan's brow, even when she felt Rebecca's questioning eyes upon her.

"The healer."

"What do you mean?" Rebecca answered, her voice tight with desperation. "Our doctor cannot help us here. This is not a boil to be covered in asphalt or an eye affliction to be washed with collyrium!"

"Not the doctor. The healer," repeated the servant with infuriating serenity.

"There is one among us, a disciple of the Nazarene, who we have seen work miracles when all seemed lost."

What was this? Could something – anything – that went on in their family compound not have filtered through to her through gossiping servants or her in-laws' incessant chatter at mealtimes or during languid rooftop evenings? She could recall no mention of this healer. On second thought, she should not be surprised. These disciples of the Nazarene were disdained wherever they were found, except of course by those who had joined their ranks. What would the family say if she allowed this mysterious person near Nathan? On the other hand, the crimson-tinged water in the bowl by Nathan's head told her she had little to lose.

"Send for him," she commanded.

As soon as the man stepped through the door, she recognized him as one of their own household workers. For all she knew, he might have been waiting outside, unnoticed, when she swept into the room. Looking him up and down, she saw that there was not much that warranted notice. He was a small man, his skin as dark and desiccated as all the other servants, young and old, from life under an unrelenting sun. The usual yellow coating of spring dust covered him from his short hair to his bare feet. He knelt down beside Rebecca at the stricken man's side, and then glanced back at his mistress. Though as far as the family was concerned he existed to serve their needs, the look he gave her made clear that her station did not impress him. His hazel eyes glowed with a strange power. Rebecca backed away instinctively.

The healer breathed deeply and closed his eyes. He placed both hands on Nathan's quivering chest. His lips were moving, but the only sound in the room was the death rattle that had just begun to emerge from Nathan's tortured throat. Then it stopped.

"It is done," murmured the man without lifting his head.

Rebecca felt the tears welling up in her throat. "Go to the master and mistress and tell them of the steward's death," Rebecca ordered the servant standing by the door.

"No," said the healer firmly. "Nathan's ordeal is over. He has been spared."

"What?" Rebecca almost shouted. She motioned the man aside so she could get a better view of Nathan.

Her mouth dropped open. The steward was breathing softly and steadily, deep in a serene sleep.

"This is truly amazing. What potion did you administer to bring Nathan back to us? I know the master and mistress will want you to manufacture enough to have ready the next time one of the household is stricken."

The man smiled. "No potion, young mistress, but the power passed down to me by those who came before me. Those who came before them received it from the Nazarene himself. His spirit was present in the room with us, and it is thanks to him that Nathan lives."

Now that the danger to Nathan's life had passed, it dawned on Rebecca that she had stepped on a viper of another sort entirely. In Sepphoris, the *minim*, like the Ebionite she had met on her way to Ein Gedi with Samuel, were becoming more numerous. The sages had forbidden Jewish families to consult their healers. She had no reason to believe it would be permitted in Ein Gedi. But it had already been done, and she had been the instrument. Rebecca glanced at the door and saw that the servant she had instructed to report Nathan's death had disappeared. Soon, the entire household would hear.

Sure enough, only a few moments passed before Zippora and Ezra came flying into the small room like pigeons startled out of their roost. The room emptied out instantly, except for Rebecca and the healer. Nathan's eyelids fluttered open at the commotion.

"What is…" started Zippora in a shrill shout that ended in hoarse whisper that struggled to escape from between her clenched teeth when she caught sight of her prone steward, "…the matter here?"

The healer inclined his head much too slightly for Zippora's taste in acknowledgement of her presence.

"Husband, ask this man what has happened here."

"Well?" blustered Ezra, turning to the *min*.

"By the grace of the Almighty, Nathan has been healed of a snakebite," said the healer, his voice level.

"Husband, I told you this man was trouble," Zippora bristled. "We should have gotten rid of him the moment we heard that he was of the *minim*. Now look what it has come to. What will people say?" Addressing the healer now: "I suppose you expect some sort of thanks for sowing such discord in our house?" intoned Zippora, at her haughtiest.

"Wife," Ezra pleaded, "our steward has been restored to us from the brink of She'ol. Indeed we must thank this man. Then we will send him on his way," he cooed. "Furthermore" – Ezra's need to placate his sputtering wife set him to thinking more quickly than usual – "to set your mind at ease, I will go to the elders and ask their opinion about what has transpired here."

Zippora sniffed. "As long as this man is out of my sight. Then I will deal with whoever allowed him to enter this room."

Rebecca finally spoke up, issuing a rare challenge to the older woman. "Would you rather Nathan had died, mother-in-law? For that is what would have happened."

"Sorcery, sorcery, sorcery, sorcery," Zippora intoned weakly, as she felt the now-conscious Nathan eying her. "What will people say?"

Chapter 40

True to his word, on the fifth day of the week, the very next market day, Ezra asked for permission to appear before Ein Gedi's elders at the synagogue. Unwilling to endure the public shaming that she was sure awaited the family, Zippora had feigned exhaustion in order to avoid accompanying her husband. But Ezra had insisted, a rarity for him, and she knew she had no choice.

Rebecca, however, had specifically arranged to attend to market duties herself that day so that she could be present at the synagogue. She had even asked Itamar to be with her. And so, on the appointed day she found herself seated next to her husband on the long stone bench that lined three of the synagogue's four walls, as once she had sat with her father in Sepphoris, and that one time at Beit Rimon, years ago, with Samuel. She watched people's lips moving as they stood for the silent recitation of the benedictions. Her father, she recalled, had his own copy of the eighteen benedictions among the scrolls in his library. But long years of observation had taught her that something in his mysterious past did not allow him to gain comfort from the supplications, if and when he needed it. Itamar's lips, she noticed, moved with fervent devotion, as her father's never had.

Caught in her reverie, the beginning of the oral recitation of the benedictions startled her. The leader of prayer proclaimed in stentorious tones: "We praise you, Lord our God and God of all generations, God of Abraham, God of Isaac, and God of Jacob. Great, mighty, and awesome God, God supreme."

"Amen!" the congregation responded enthusiastically.

"Great is Your might O Lord, eternally…You heal the sick… and bring freedom to the captives… Blessed are you O Lord, Who revives the dead."

"Amen," shouted the congregation again, and Rebecca resisted the attempt to look sideways at her mother-in-law, who never failed to make sure that her voice was heard above all others. Finally, the last of the eighteen, "Blessed are you O Lord our God, whose Name is good and to Whom it is fitting to give thanks," and the last enthusiastic "Amen" of the worshippers.

All now looked forward to the beginning of the sages' weekly public debate. These forums were called to present to the people with the guidelines for godly living. But they also laid to rest the many questions people had about the veracity of this or that story making the rounds from rooftop to cistern to workshop. They sometimes revealed a spicy slice of their neighbor's life, without, of course, resorting to gossip, which was sorely frowned upon by their rabbis.

When called upon by the sexton, Ezra stepped forward.

He presented an account of the events that had occurred in his household, from the moment it became known that their steward had been afflicted, until the healer had restored Nathan just before he breathed his last. The congregation listened closely to every word. Not that the story was new; it had found its way into virtually every Ein Gedi household by sunset on the day it happened.

Debate raged for what seemed like hours. Rabbi Yosei was astounded that the issue was seen as having two sides to argue about. "We have only just now recited the words of the blessing intended to exclude forever from our midst such sinners as this so-called healer! 'Blessed are You who breaks the enemy and humbles the arrogant. May the apostates have no hope unless they return to Torah,'" he intoned. "Have we not called upon our *hazan* to repeat those words as many times as necessary to ensure they were heard even by those at the back of the synagogue or in the balcony?"

"Rabbi Yosei," admonished Rabbi Hiyyeh gently turning to his colleague, "those words were never intended to refer to those who have followed that man from Galilee."

"You dare to oppose the ruling of Rabban Gamaliel?" snapped Rabbi Yosei.

The two of them then began to contend the fine points of whether healing, when it occurred through faith in one whom the healer believed was the Messiah, had anything to do with idolatry. Most of the sages present believed that it did not, and interrupted the colleagues frequently to tell them so. But when Rabbi Jacob, the leader of the town council, shook his fist in the direction of Ezra's little family and shouted, "Heresy! Apostasy! Remove thy way from her and come not near the door of her house!" Rebecca noticed that the people sitting on either side of them actually moved away. Their whole family was about to be accused of *minut*, apostasy, Rebecca thought.

Finally, the council rendered the decision of the majority: Because the act of healing had been done in private and not in public, it was not to be regarded as an act of apostasy. The family breathed a sigh of relief. But few neighbors stopped to congratulate them as they filed out of the synagogue.

That evening, in private, Ezra broached the subject again with his irritable mate. He was immediately sorry he had done so.

"I hope you will now be satisfied that our elders have not ostracized us. All is well."

"Husband," came the all-too-familiar, brittle reed of a voice in response. "Our own Rabbi Jacob's ruling will do nothing but fuel the fire of contention." Her next words told Ezra his wife must have been busily ruminating all day over what had happened.

"And why should I accept his ruling, when two or three days' walk at pilgrimage time can bring me to the great Rabbi Tarfon himself at Yavne?"

Making sure his back was to his wife, Ezra rolled his eyes in frustration.

"I know you think I go too far, husband. You go to the market more than I. But when I go, I hear the talk against our family to which you choose to be deaf. And don't forget, wherever Rabbi Tarfon teaches, in Lydda, Yavne, and everywhere in between, he is known both for his great learning and his great compassion. He will rule fairly. If he rules in our favor, I can be certain that no one can speak further against us. If he rules against us, he will also determine how we can wipe out this stain on our family's reputation, and there will be a chance that all will be forgotten."

Ezra knew, once again, that he had been defeated. Discussion was at an end.

Chapter 41

Nathan's health had returned, and he wished that the small puncture scar on his foot were the only reminder of his ordeal. But his mistress let him know, in every look and nuance of her voice, that she had not forgotten the intruder that had threatened the status of her family.

Still, life went on, and the day of departure for Yavne finally dawned. Rebecca saw to it that the loads of supplies lashed to the backs of the three donkeys were secure. Then she inspected the courtyard to see that all doors were locked, and the heavy iron elbow keys well hidden. In their own quarters, out of habit, she cast a parting glance at the place behind the wall where her grandmother's scroll lay concealed.

Ezra and Zippora's little band were not alone at the entrance to the town when the day of their departure dawned. As Nathan slapped the rump of the last donkey, he had to jostle for position with knots of men, women, children, and beasts of burden. His position at the rear made it easy to avoid contact with the young mistress. Over the years his respect for her had only grown, and he did not want to upset Rebecca's position in the family and the community any further than her life-saving act of courage already had. Staying away from her was his way of protecting her.

The day passed in an uninterrupted march upward along the narrow goat paths leading upward from the Salt Sea valley to the Judean highlands; the group stopped in the shade of the thorny acacia trees only as long as the sun was directly overhead. They finished making camp for the night just as the sun's last rays disappeared behind the high mountains of Judea. The cool breezes of Jerusalem reached out to them enticingly. Fathers and mothers excitedly pointed out to exhausted and dust-caked children the mountain in the distance from which, they said, the Mountain of the Holy Temple could be seen. Tomorrow they would see where the Holy Temple itself had once stood.

But when the next day did find them standing atop the Mount of Olives and looking out to the mountain of the Holy Temple, the view filled Rebecca only with bitterness. From beyond the jagged remains of the eastern rampart, every shattered and blackened wall of their once glorious Temple spoke of the devastation that was Jerusalem. And mocking it all, new, half-built marble walls gleamed in the morning sun – Emperor Hadrian's shrine. Itamar and Ezra joined some of the older men busying themselves unrolling the scroll of Lamentations to read. But Rebecca knew she would find no solace in the ancient words. Instead, for the first time in a long time, she allowed herself to dwell on Samuel's almost-forgotten promise that someday she was destined to take part in reversing this travesty.

The reading of the ancient dirge in full view of the devastation was too much for many of the travelers. Tears were staunched with the swipe of a sleeve or the corner of a robe, and the party soon departed west toward the lowlands and the coast of the Great Sea beyond them.

The sun was setting once again by the time they reached the gates of Yavne. Zippora's worried nagging hastened their pace down a crowded street to the inn they had stayed at on their previous journeys. Ezra tried to calm her. "Each time we come here you say the same thing. You even said it when we went only as far as Lydda to hear the rabbis. 'We will have to sleep outside the gate... there will be no place for us,' and each time we find room before long. This time will be no exception, you will see."

Ezra was right. The family was given a room off the main courtyard of one of the larger inns, their servants joining those of other families in one of the front rooms whose high tiny windows faced the street.

Exhausted from their journey and tense with concern over what the next day's appearance before the sages would bring, Rebecca and Itamar retired long before the last of the travelers' tales had been told.

The sun had still not risen high enough to warm the stones of Yavne's dwellings, and only a few people had arrived at the forecourt of the council house when Rebecca's family made their way into the building. Later, the crowds might be so thick that there would be nowhere to place their mat and still hear the voices of the sages, but at this early hour they still found room right behind the first ring of the elders' disciples, as close as they could possibly get to where the sages already sat, deep in conversation. A black-bearded man, the linen folds of a spotless white robe falling gracefully across his portly form, was standing and addressing the group. The silver buckle at his shoulder gleamed as he turned this way and that. "Look, Rebecca!" whispered Itamar. "It's Rabbi Tarfon himself!"

"Of course," the rabbi was saying, "once Ruth the Moabite abandoned the ways of her people, who worshipped the idol Chamosh, she was completely purified from those ways."

"An appropriate subject of discussion for Shavuot, to recall Ruth, who met her future husband Boaz while harvesting the wheat of his fields," Ezra offered to no one in particular, hoping to appear capable of contributing to the scholarly discussion.

"Husband," Zippora whispered, "this is the perfect time to ask our question, with talk of idol worship in the air. Ask about the healing… Ask, Husband." Zippora propelled her hapless mate forward until he stood awkwardly among the disciples seated right in front of the sages.

"Rabbi, hear… ahh, if you please the humble question of a householder from Ein Gedi." Rabbi Tarfon and the other sages turned their attention to the petitioner, and Ezra was encouraged to continue.

"There was in my house a servant who was bitten by a snake. He was breathing his last, the death rattle was heard. Then, his life was saved."

"And you would like to know the appropriate thanksgiving gift for the community coffers?" inquired the sage in a tone that said he knew he would hear this question a dozen more times before the day was out.

"In fact, I wish to relate that… the servant was healed by a *min* who was brought to him…" Ezra finished hastily, "by persons unknown to me."

The rabbis stared at Ezra for what seemed to be an interminably long time. Then Rabbi Tarfon broke the silence. Slowly at first, at a pace that his disciples, scratching his words on parchment, could easily follow. "Well done, man of Ein Gedi, to bring up this matter while we speak of Ruth the Moabite. We must learn how to conduct our lives with such people of this persuasion as live among us. My esteemed colleague Rabbi Eliezer of Lydda admitted once to being charmed by the words of a *min*," the sage continued, stroking his beard. "He never forgave himself for his lapse. Nor can I. But it is not Rabbi Eliezer we are discussing here. I have said that I would be willing to lose my sons if I did not see to it that books of the *minim* be burned, even if those books contained the ineffable name of the Holy One. And furthermore I say to you" – by this time Rabbi Tarfon's voice had lost its musing tone and reached a fevered pitch that even those outside the door of the council house had no trouble hearing – "that a household that allows healing by the *minim*, even in private, is a household no better than those who worshipped Chamosh and did not, like Ruth, turn away." The Rabbi spit out his last words with a vindictiveness that caught everyone in the room off-guard. Ezra stepped back suddenly and stumbled, comically, over the first row of Rabbi Tarfon's open-mouthed disciples.

Itamar's parents felt only their own shock and humiliation, but Rebecca sensed an intense animosity against the family, stifling and stinking as a sodden goat hair tent after a desert cloudburst. The family turned to flee the hostile room.

But their way was blocked. A knot of men burst into the chamber, screaming unintelligibly. Between them they half-dragged a third man. Rivulets of blood trickled their way through the dirt that covered all but the man's exhausted, fear-filled eyes, and his robes were so torn and filthy that it was impossible at first to identify him as Jew or gentile, redeemed captive, or prisoner.

The crowed parted. Even the rabbis' disciples and scribes stood to allow passage, and soon the men stood directly before the sages. "What is the meaning of this," demanded one of the rabbis. "A man in this condition should not be brought before us. He should be taken immediately to the doctor, unless you men want to be accused of standing idly by the blood of your neighbor."

"The blood of our neighbors that this worthless *listos* has spilled is like the Great Sea compared to few drops that leak from his wounds, your honor," shouted one of the men. "He has wrought terror on those who travel the road to our town, and does not desist even on the festivals."

"What do you mean '*even* on festivals,'" interrupted another. "The festivals are when this stinking thief makes his best living." The prisoner's knees buckled under him and his head fell forward. His captors jerked him back to a standing position. Another of the men whispered to the pair, who roughly and reluctantly set the nearly unconscious man down on a stone bench hastily vacated by some of the disciples. The same man now stepped forward and addressed the sages.

"Having been appointed by you to look after the safety and security of the pilgrims plying the roads to and from the city during the festivals, I could do no less than bring this highway robber to justice. He resisted our attempts to capture him; hence his condition. Still, he should be grateful to us for not turning him over immediately to the centurion."

To turn a wanted criminal over to the Roman courts had always engendered deliberations as prolonged as they were fiery. If the Torah demanded the sheltering of even a fugitive slave from his master, how much more should a fugitive freedman be protected from punishment by the conqueror, some said. It was not the same, argued others. Did not the good of the community outweigh the good of the individual? A single suspect hiding among them had more than once brought about the deportation of a whole village.

But highway robbers were considered special cases. So many of them had been led to their criminal actions after being victimized by Roman overlords, turned out of their homes and thrown off their lands. Many districts had still not recovered from the unbearable burden of financing Emperor Hadrian's recent journey through the land, which fell heaviest on the most prosperous farms. Many farmers had even endured the humiliation of seeing their fields and orchards turned over to other Jews who had found favor with this or that local official. Fathers sometimes found it impossible to pay their daughters' dowries, or ensure their sons the inheritance due them. Even the sons of some still-wealthy landlords had turned to highway robbery to vent their frustration and anger.

"What is your proof that this man has been involved in the acts you describe?" one of the sages inquired shrilly, looking down his nose at the men.

"He has left his family and has been living in the foothills east of Yavne," one of the captors confidently volunteered.

"The fact that a man has left his family without support in these days could be cause for action of the court. But the fact that he has gone to live in the grazing lands does not necessarily make him a highway robber," Rabbi Tarfon said.

"Indeed," joined in another rabbi, "his wife may have consented to this time spent away from home, well spent immersed in Scripture. Such was once the custom of many in the days of the Holy Temple. This man may not be a reprehensible criminal, but an admirable fellow." Zippora and Ezra continued to push their way out of the synagogue, where the crowd had forgotten their existence. All the couple could hear was a confused babble as the petitioners, angered by the sages' unwillingness to validate their accusations, continued to rail against their prisoner.

But they had other worries. They now had to decide the status of the man who was their most trusted servant, and at the same time the cause of the wrong turn their lives had taken. Their status in the community was never more at stake. But Rebecca and Itamar lagged behind, captivated by the drama playing itself out in the synagogue. They held their breath while the sages continued questioning the prisoner, as people shushed each other so they would not miss anything. "They will never turn him over to the Romans unless someone can identify him directly," Rebecca whispered to Itamar, who acknowledged her observation with a nod while never taking his eyes off the sages.

"We cannot condemn this man to the Roman courts unless someone can come forward and identify him as the bandit who has been plaguing our roads of late," concluded Rabbi Tarfon, and his colleagues murmured their assent. The council secretary now stood and announced in a formal tone: "He who has suffered from the hand of the man who now stands before us in judgment, or who has personal knowledge of one who has suffered – let him come forward." The silence that now gripped the room was broken only by the heavy breathing of the injured suspect.

Finally, Rabbi Tarfon spoke. "No convincing evidence has been placed before us in this matter. However, if this man appears before the conqueror to be judged, no such evidence will be required. They care not how many Jews are condemned to their justice by other Jews."

Now his words became deliberately vague. "Men who are suspected by the community of wrongdoing should not be condemned by rumors. But such men would do well to seek a future for themselves and their family elsewhere, and none should interfere with their departure."

The man's captors bowed before the council. But they were fuming. Not only had their attempts to rid the community of a renegade troublemaker been stymied; sentiment in the crowded room was with the suspect. No one knew if the unlucky man was guilty of the charges brought against him, people were whispering to each other. The sages had all but ordered him to leave the region, but at least he had been saved from crucifixion. Even bandits deserved better than that. Rebecca did not know what to think. These sages had rendered the saving of Nathan's life invalid because it had been accomplished by what they had determined to be idolatrous means. Then, she realized angrily, they had proceeded to save the life of one who may have been the cause of continuing misery and loss, of property and even lives.

Once they had returned home, she knew which decision she would heed and which she would not. She only hoped that she could convince Itamar and that he in turn could persuade his parents not to turn Nathan away.

The homeward journey following every other pilgrimage had always been one of good cheer. People regaled each other with the favorite moments of their stay, vying to add the most drama or comedy to one or the other of their many experiences, and the telling made the hard hours on the road fly by. Not this time. It was a journey of silence. Nathan served them as attentively as always, but was more retiring and distant than usual. Ezra, who normally dodged his wife's barbs with long-suffering good humor, was morose.

Upon their return, it did not take long for the household to return to its normal daily tasks. But nothing was really the same. Itamar kept his distance from Rebecca, as if she was the cause of the malaise that seemed to have invaded their home. Rebecca was saddened that his affection for her was so compromised. But much more important, she sensed that her future here was at risk, and thus, her mission endangered. Something had to be done.

At yet another tense evening meal, Rebecca finally broke the silence. She addressed Ezra. "You are the head of our household – a household and manor that is in Ein Gedi, and not in Yavne. You know within yourself…you all know" – here she looked into the eyes of each member of the family in turn – "that the decision of the sages in Yavne was a hasty one, and that it was not suitable for our lives here in Ein Gedi. Nathan was healed by one who believes that the Nazarene is the Messiah. Is this a reason to upset every aspect of our lives forever after? People are starved for understanding the reason that the pagan powers have control over our lives. Perhaps the Messiah *will* come before this age of evil is ended. The fact is, Nathan was healed. It was a miracle. I saw it. We all saw it. We, not the rabbis from Yavne, not Lydda and not even Ein Gedi."

Itamar kept his eyes down. It was the longest speech he had ever heard Rebecca make. Ezra and Zippora simply stared at her, open-mouthed. Then they looked at each other. She was right.

From the pantry behind the dining room where the servants received empty dishes to refill and pass back to the dining tables, word of Rebecca's speech spread to the kitchen. Nathan had escaped expulsion from the only home he had ever known.

Chapter 42

Respect for the young mistress rose to new heights among the servants after she took her stand for Nathan.

So did speculation regarding the young couple's childlessness. Some thought they knew the reason why Rebecca remained barren. During the accursed regime of Quietus there were many who had grown up as the only child of their parents, with aunts or uncles who had made promising marriages, like Itamar and Rebecca's, which had not produced issue. It was the only way in those days, said some, to get around the unthinkable choice between failing to bring a newborn male into the covenant of Abraham, or of suffering martyrdom if the act was discovered.

In the early days of Hadrian, these onerous bans were lifted for a time. But Rome was Rome. The emperor could not hide for long his contempt for foreign cults. Jupiter-Zeus *would* replace the One God in Jerusalem, and mutilation of the genitals – for Hadrian it was nothing more or less – *would* cease. If the only way to do this was to ban circumcision, to revoke Judaism's status as *religio licta,* then so be it.

And so began the practice of abstaining from marital relations in order not to bring a child into the world. But more than one woman, unable to reconcile her enforced barrenness with the yearning to bring children into the world, especially boys, at least one of whom would grow up to support her in old age, made her way to wherever the sages were meeting, to obtain their counsel.

The decree of Rabbi Ishmael ben Elisha was well known by this time: "Should we not eat meat or drink wine because we are in mourning for the Temple? Because the pagan conqueror's evil decree does not permit us to gather for the Week of the Son, should we not beget children? No! Let the Jews continue to bear children! Let not the seed of Abraham die out!"

Could it be, people asked themselves, that in spite of the ruling, Rebecca and Itamar still abstained? No, this woman – whose father was known to have ingratiated himself in every way possible with the Romans in her home town of Sepphoris – would not hold to such principles. None of them did up there, they told each other. And who knew anyone these days who would take such a stand against God, against nature, her family, the rabbis. Against the rabbis, wagged the tongues? Hah! She already had done that – remember what she said at that evening meal. Oft-repeated, amplified, and distorted, that speech, spoken in the supposed privacy of her family circle, had marked her as an independent, if not outright rebellious woman.

And Rebecca? She could not help but know that her life was a subject of discussion. Although her reasons for coming to Ein Gedi were not, as all assumed, to enter into a good marriage and enrich a local family, it had never occurred to her that children would not come, and her continued childlessness was a shock to her at first. The gossipers were right about one thing at least: In a household such as her father's one did not learn to oppose Rome by such means. But with the ever increasing presence of Roman troops in the town, she found that, though she did not know why it was so, she could not be sorry that her belly did not swell each year or two like that of the other women her age. Every time a young man of Ein Gedi was arrested on the pretext of acting against Rome, every time word came to them of another family who had lost its holdings to the conqueror, Rebecca sensed that the time was coming near when she would be called upon to act. And so she turned a deaf ear to the rumors, threw herself into managing the household, and awaited the day of reckoning.

That day came, and with it, the largest contingent of Roman soldiers since the Great Revolt marched into their town and other towns and villages all over Judea. The issue of healing through faith in the Nazarene and the number of children in this or that family became the most trivial of their concerns.

Chapter 43

Ein Gedi, for all its wealth and exotic salt sea scenery, was really no different than any other city when it came to human nature. Side by side with most of its inhabitants, who opposed the conqueror every way they could, it bred its nests of informers. And so, on that fateful morning, the soldiers therefore knew exactly which houses to go to. Piercing screams followed the soldiers who emerged from two of the courtyards, one holding an infant upside down by the heels, the other carelessly clutching two of the community's sacred scrolls, one in each meaty fist.

Rebecca found herself driven, together with Itamar and his parents to the plaza at the entrance to the city. Some people called out encouragement to each other, some wept, and confusion reigned. "Silence!" bellowed the officer in charge. "Rome has been patient. But Rome will not tolerate acts of rebellion, such as those with which this community has been charged. Rome's balsam shipments have been attacked by bandits whom this town has chosen not to give over to the justice they deserve. Thus Rome punishes its enemies."

A nod from the officer in the direction of the man holding the scrolls was the signal for the man to throw them to the ground. He took a smoking torch from the hand of the soldier nearest to him and touched it to the parchment, which blazed fiercely. Faint cries were heard from the crowd. Another nod in the direction of the soldier holding the infant. The *sica* he held in his other hand rose, and flashed through the air. With a sickening gurgle, the infant's howling was silenced.

But the officer was not finished. His eyes swept the cowering crowd. Then he said something in a low voice to three of his men. A cry went up as the men fanned out among the townspeople. When they emerged, each held a struggling young girl roughly by the arm.

Only then did the contingent turn and file down the road, the nails in the soles of their boots striking the horrific tattoo against the paving stones the Jews had all come to know and fear.

Wailing filled the air. The family of the slaughtered baby gathered around its mother and walked her away so that she would not see her child lifted lifeless from the blood-clotted dust. Families whose girls the soldiers had taken turned their faces away from neighbors, writhing in each others' arms in agony at the thought of the fate that awaited the daughters they would never see again.

Rebecca returned alone to their room, where she allowed the darkness to envelope her. As if overtaken by a spirit not her own, she rose, moved the bench aside, and pried loose the stone in the wall behind which her grandmother's scroll lay. It had been years since she had last looked at the document. In the good times, she had allowed it to become little more than a vague memory.

Why did it call to her now? She tried to divine its message as she held it in her hand. The horrors of days gone by were revisiting them. Rebecca's jaw tightened. These days would end. When the time came for her to fulfill her role, they would end, she swore to herself, and they would be free.

Chapter 44

EIN GEDI, 132 CE

After the Roman raid, life returned to what passed for normal. Summer came and the family spent their evenings on their rooftop as they always had. But on this particular evening, the sultry air seemed particularly oppressive. Rebecca sensed the familiar restlessness creeping up upon her, especially now, with her belly swollen with the child she had never wanted.

Itamar's mother now treated her with a sickly sweet deference, making frequent references to "your son," but more often to "our grandson" and "our heir." Rebecca was relieved when after two hours of the usual seeming pleasantries, Itamar's mother finally stood and began to bombard the servants with the last directives of the day, the signal that the evening was finally drawing to a close.

Rebecca and Itamar were the last to climb down the ladder from the rooftop Itamar came down close behind his wife, carefully watching her descent lest she miss a rung. "The balsam plants will soon be ready for harvest," Rebecca said nonchalantly as they made their way to their room abutting the courtyard. But Itamar had come to know over the past sixteen years that, unlike the rest of the household, nothing Rebecca said was for the sake of idle conversation. He waited patiently for her to continue.

"Nathan is dividing his time between the date groves and the balsam plantation. With the arrival of the buyers, you will have your hands full working with your father – their code word for preventing Itamar's father from doing more damage than necessary with his loose tongue – to obtain the best prices. I would like to supervise the balsam plantations myself," she finished firmly.

Itamar did not answer immediately. He was thinking about Nathan. He knew she was right about their steward, and that if consulted, Nathan would deem Rebecca up to the task. His mother's opinion on the matter merited only a passing thought. She would have no objection to the plan as such – he had often enough these days seen her eye rest in cool approval on her daughter-in-law as she went about her duties. But she would doubtless protest at her shrillest that a lady of means, certainly one who was with child after so many years of barrenness, should be laboring like a common field hand.

Then he tried to imagine Rebecca super vising the balsam workers. Those gaunt, earnest men who avoided not only the company of women, but seemed to prefer the company of each other to any other person. Each day, by the time the sun's rays burst over the mountains of Moab, they would already be at work, and they continued long beyond the time when the heat drove all the other workers to seek shelter. In the afternoon they would immerse in their ritual pools, eat a meager meal, and retire to the caves above the oasis to study the sacred scriptures. Their ascetic ways were strange, but there were none better at working the balsam groves. Would they accept Rebecca's presence among them, much less her authority over them?

"I have had enough dealings with them to know that they will accept me," Rebecca said, as if he had spoken to her aloud. "Last year, when the harvest was poor because the spring water failed us, they knew it was I who suggested foregoing the harvest of the sap in the hopes that it would increase next year." She lowered her voice instinctively, as one always assumed the presence of eavesdroppers. "Your father was all for adulterating our balsam by mixing it with honey and selling it as pure *opobalsam*. They have no interest in our finances of course, but I think they appreciated that I stood up to him and went the honest way, though it cost us. This year, when we cut into the bark, the sap will gush out and overflow the horns our workers hold beneath to catch it, I promise you. And when we boil the branches you will see that they too will have been strengthened from the rest we gave the trees last year, they will produce twice the fragrance of Jericho trees!"

To Itamar, Rebecca was the same young girl who had walked into the family's courtyard years ago. Her figure had not thickened until her pregnancy had begun to burgeon, and the curls that insisted on escaping from beneath her veil were still luxuriant and dark. Neither had years dimmed the gleam of determination into those dark eyes whenever a task was to be performed. Itamar saw it there now. She was not asking his advice or permission, but announcing her decision. He could not know that in his acquiescence, he was deciding the future for everyone he knew.

And so, the next morning, Rebecca came to the balsam factory, over the stormy protests of her mother-in-law. It is more like the caldarium in here than in the bathhouse, Rebecca though wryly as she used the back of her hand to push away a curl that perspiration had glued to her forehead. Through the steam rising from the soaking pool that took up most of the nine-foot long wall, she could see that the branches of the thorny balsam bushes had already sunk to the bottom. The boiling water had forced their precious essence to rise to the top and spill over through a hole in the wall to the room on the other side where it was mixed with olive oil. From the great number of branches piled up under the watchful eye of the day-guards and still waiting to be processed, she knew she had made the right decision. The fat little shrubs that dotted the terraces above their community would not disappoint them this year.

Today was different from the previous ten in only one way – it was the last day of production. It was last time this season that the night guards would strain to see Rebecca walking toward them in the murky pre-dawn light, her appearance the signal to roll aside the stone that sealed the precious product within its thickly walled tower. At the same time, a small group of men descended from the caves to meet her – that day's labor cadre, chosen by lot from their fellows to work while the others remained in the caves to study Scripture. Theirs was a system that Rebecca knew better than to interfere with; they worked together in perfect unison, there was no talk and no wasted time. That was all that mattered. The sooner she could get their product to market, even if it was only one market day ahead of the Jericho plantations, the greater their profit. And with the amount that had to be shared with the conqueror – the real owner of the land they liked to call their own – the profit had to be great.

Once the stone was rolled away, Rebecca's opened one of the new pottery vessels containing the balsam sap harvested the day before, to see how the night's scant moisture and the settling of the liquid had effected it. She dipped her ladle into the fluid, and noted with satisfaction that the translucent golden liquid had not congealed. Next, she examined the level of the finished product, the oil-and-essence blend than had accumulated in the cooling vat on the other side of the wall from the ovens. She directed the waiting workmen to bring in the large clay jars into which they would pour the cooled liquid. When the light was better she would personally ladle the finished product, the balsam perfume, into the small bottles in which it would be sold.

After Emperor Vespasian had laid waste to Ein Gedi when he had finished ravaging Judea a half-century ago, he had displayed balsam branches cut from these very plantations in his victory parade in Rome. Ever since, the conqueror looked forward to the balsam harvest. Profits would be huge this year; the conqueror would be satisfied with his portion. So until the price was right, the gathering buyers could while away their time savoring the luxuries they would purchase with their gains.

Evening came. The fires were damped and the last of the jars had been filled and sealed. The light was once again as dim as it had been when she arrived that morning, and Rebecca could hardly see to aim the heavy key into the lock. The sun's last rays had turned the Asphalt Sea cobalt and cast a rubious glow on the mountains along the eastern shore. Rebecca was tired to her very bones, and her back ached with the burden of her unborn baby. As she turned to walk home, she looked downhill to see a line of lights bloom in the dusk, then bob and snake along the main road leading to the town. Tomorrow, the men who held them would be her first customers of the day.

Chapter 45

"The price will not fall tomorrow – you have nothing to gain by waiting," Rebecca's father-in-law curtly told the man on the other side of the counter in response to his inquiries. Surprise turned quickly to affront, and the man turned on his heel and walked away. Rebecca bit her lip not to show her impatience at this foolish slip. She had already let three or four buyers walk away without a word after courteously answering the usual opening questions about the cost of purchases in bulk. After that, even the lowliest shop apprentice knew that the next words must always be those of the buyer. The moment the seller responded out-of-turn, as her father-in-law had just done, the sale was lost.

She had seen it done every fall of her life since she could remember, back in Sepphoris when olive oil was the commodity sold to the wholesalers who came from miles around. The balsam trade was no different, the stakes were just much, much higher. She caught the look that passed between Itamar and Nathan, which told her that Ezra's bumbling efforts to exercise his authority had not gone unnoticed.

Rebecca sought somewhere to cast her own eyes to hide her annoyance at this early and unwanted incident so early in the trading. Suddenly she found them resting on the most beautifully decorated – and most enormous – girth she had ever seen. Pale Damascene silk dyed with murex purple that must have cost enough to feed the entire town of Ein Gedi for a month gleamed in the early morning sun through linen whose unmistakably delicate natural hue bespoke its origin in the flax fields of Egypt. Beginning a hand's span above the linen belt, straining under its burden, was a magnificent beard anointed with the very scent that rose from the pots before her. The beard began just below cheeks red as ripe pomegranate seeds with the effort their owner had made to climb the small hill from where his beasts of burden were tethered. A hawkish pair of nut-brown eyes concentrated on her.

Rebecca met his gaze steadily, a practiced move designed to conceal her efforts to recall whether this man had been among last year's buyers. Ezra bustled over the moment he caught sight of the affluent newcomer. The man motioned Ezra away imperiously before he had a chance to rise from his obsequious bow and utter his first unctuous words of welcome. Surreptitious glances were exchanged among the waiting merchants. It seemed there would be a story to tell by evening.

"There is not a home in the city of Ptolemais nor a manor house in the entire countryside, from the Plain of Sharon to the coast of Lebanon, that is not without your product, Madam," the man said to Rebecca. Beginning negotiations with a compliment? Many a lesser bargainer would have thought this the weakest possible opening gambit. Rebecca busily calculated the strategy behind it. But the man was not finished.

"Our ladies will neither anoint their skin, nor treat even their children's summer rashes with anything else."

"Nor dress their beautiful hair, I imagine," Rebecca responded lightly, with a pointed glance at the man's own glistening beard.

"Yes, well, of course. Dress their hair," he responded gruffly.

The man was thrown off balance by her bantering tone, just as Rebecca had intended.

"We do have the finest balsam available. Though our trees are not at all generous, considering the love and care we lavish on them. They grant us only the tiniest reward, which make them all the more precious to us," Rebecca said, getting down to business.

"My employers are well aware of the rarity of your product, and have instructed me accordingly," the man answered.

Silence. Rebecca folded her hands quietly over her belly and waited. She would certainly not be the first to mention a price. She would not risk naming a sum lower than the amount with which the demanding ladies of Ptolemais had supplied their purchasing agent. Too high, and she would risk losing the man's clearly significant business. She knew he would try to settle on a price lower than the amount he had been given, and pocket the difference. He had doused himself with the unguent, a tactical error had not escaped Rebecca. He would pay. But right up to the conclusion of their negotiations she would allow him to worry that the final sum would be no less than his employers had intended, and possibly more. She could wait until he named the price. Before the man knew what had happened, he found himself making the first offer.

"Fifty denarii for one *sextarius* of the pure sap," he said.

Rebecca let the offer hang there for just long enough to disabuse him of the notion that this transaction would be an easy one. Then:

"The price you offer is closer to the price of wheat than of the most precious commodity in the world."

"Madam, wheat at those prices must come in golden pithoi," he countered using the ridiculous analogy to show he was unfazed.

Rebecca knew the time had come for a demonstration of the value of her product. She reached for the glass vial she had prepared earlier, and slipped off the cap with a flourish. As the other merchants gathered around, she slowly, dramatically, let a tiny drop of the pure sap escape onto the back of her hand. The men all looked expectantly at the patch of viscous fluid. Would this peculiar woman dare leave it on long enough to dry into the brittle crust that would tell them it had been adulterated with gum? That would bring her price down in a hurry!

"What are you waiting for, gentlemen?" Rebecca called out gaily. "Our dry air has done as much as it can do," she said as she waved her hand in the air. The oil had been completely absorbed, leaving behind only its marvelous fragrance, demonstrating the high quality of her product. But Rebecca knew that the next phase of the bargaining had to be made privately, otherwise the stranger's honor – a commodity almost as important as profit – would be lost. With another lavish wave of her anointed hand she motioned him to the room behind the stand. Once inside, she lowered her head conspiratorially.

"The price of our pure balsam is as I said out there. However, I can let you have a *se'ah* of *xylobalsamum* for a mere six denarii a *libra*. It is of course not as fine as the pure product, but it will do nicely."

But the merchant remained adamant. "There is no one watching your performance now. Surely you do not believe I will pay more for your balsam than the family I serve receives for a month's rent of a single house on their land?" The man's laugh was caustic. "No more than I would pay for the pure stuff as much as it costs to clothe my lady for a year!" His hand went to the embroidered border of his cloak and he rocked his bulk confidently on his heels as he waited for her answer.

"I am sure your employer's customers will be prepared to pay this, and even more, as are most of the traders standing outside this room right now. It is, of course up to you."

Negotiation continued. Rebecca allowed the price to drop until the point she could sense that the man was not trying to set aside more than a fair profit for his own purse, but that the real limit of funds given him for this purpose had been reached. It was time to close the deal. "I believe the differences between us can be bridged. If you can provide payment in gold, I will accept five gold aurei per *se'ah*."

The man still hesitated. Rebecca pressed forward.

"With the money you have saved, you can purchase a fatted calf for a feast to celebrate your return to your wife and family," Rebecca suggested, her light tone returning.

"Done," said the man. The pair exited to the courtyard and resumed their positions on either side of the table. It was time to sweeten the deal. With the attention of the crowd still fixed on them, Rebecca presented the man with a delicate glass vial of balsam perfume, and a carved bone applicator. "To make your wife even lovelier than I am certain she already is." The man bowed his head in thanks, and Rebecca picked up the ladle that lay ready to transfer the balsam from its large jar to a smaller vessel sufficient to hold the man's purchase.

The show was over. Turning back to their own purses, people conjectured in low murmurs on how close to the enormous price the mistress had first named they would now have to pay. Concentrating on the task at hand, Rebecca thought she heard the man speak to her again. But his tone was so changed that she looked sharply at him to make sure she had not been mistaken. She was not.

"I say, your ladle has a crack in it, Madam."

She turned the ladle over, examining it closely. The man had to be mistaken. Before she set out the ladle yesterday, she examined it for defects that could be construed as an attempt at fraud. "... a crack ... your ladle has a crack ..." Blood roared in Rebecca's ears as she recognized these words from the last time they were spoken. It was when Samuel took leave of her sixteen years ago. After all this time, the coded message had finally come.

She grabbed the side of the table in a motion so sudden that Itamar, standing at her side at the beginning stages of a negotiation of his own, stopped in mid-sentence. "Some water for the lady," he shouted to a servant as he stepped toward her. "I knew that being here would be too much for you in your state," he admonished her more loudly than he had intended.

"No, I am well." Rebecca pushed him away gently without taking her eyes off the man standing before her. Those words. Samuel had said she would hear again someday, and as the years had passed she had all but forgotten them. Those words, which had always seemed to her too ordinary to serve as a battle cry.

The man's eyes never left her face. The woman had acknowledged his signal; he was now waiting for her composure to return. He had been assured that the woman to whom he was entrusting the fate of the entire community of Ein Gedi was equal to the task.

She was. Rebecca took a deep breath to steady herself. "I beg your pardon, sir. Please join me once again in the storage room, where you will inspect our ladles and choose whichever one you wish, and another vial of perfume as well."

Once again in the seclusion of the storeroom, it seemed that a different person stood before Rebecca. His girth no longer seemed ridiculous, but powerful and protective. His voice had lost the bluster and whine of the bargaining process and spoke in low urgent tones, wasting no words.

"The days of waiting are over. In Caesarea, the Romans have slain our beloved Rabbi Akiva. Our forces need to occupy Ein Gedi. With the town as our base, we will be able to make the eastern flank of Judea inaccessible to the conqueror."

"The warriors will take to the caves, as did our ancestors at Arbel?" Rebecca asked.

"No. We will only stay in the caves for as long as it takes for you to accomplish your mission. If our fighters remain in the caves now, the conqueror will take ten of your lives each day until we give ourselves up. Then he will do as King Herod did at Arbel: He will besiege us from the cliffs above until starvation kills us, and we will have accomplished nothing. We cannot enter the city until the people of the town are safely out of the way. And no one will obey our orders to leave; we are strangers, and they will surely suspect we are agents of Rome, lying in wait for the chance to take this town and its treasure. Your task is to get the people to leave the city, the sooner the better. They will trust you."

He watched Rebecca's eyes dart wildly around the room and wondered again, as he had when he caught his first glimpse of her, how this well-to-do matron, heavy with child, came to be selected for the task at hand.

Her honey-flecked eyes closed, and when they opened again, he knew the answer. He saw a calm there that he had seen before only in the eyes of the men who had fought alongside him in dozens skirmishes in years gone by. The look that came with complete readiness to carry out the final act of their lives, serene in the knowledge that this act would change the face of the future.

"By the new moon, the town will be yours," she said.

In one smooth motion, Rebecca swept a vial of balsam from its row in the wall niche, and stepped over the threshold back into the courtyard. A smile was now frozen on her face, the other merchants noticed. No doubt it was due to the awkwardness of the situation. "Even though a cracked ladle came close to foiling this first successful transaction of the season, the lady never lost her bearing," was the way things would be repeated from the kitchen to the synagogue. Rebecca handed the vial to the merchant with a flourish.

His facade restored, and with a bow so low over his girth that he threatened to tumble forward, he took his leave. He studied the knots on the woven bands holding the balsam jar firmly within its saddlebag, as if this were the most important thing he had done all day. At his signal, his servants began a comic series of pushes and pulls that finally landed his bulk atop a second donkey.

"We will look forward to your return next season," Rebecca called out lightly to the retreating caravan. "Go in peace."

Chapter 46

The exchange of gold and silver for the precious unguent continued throughout the week, until the storerooms were all but empty and the coffers full and closely guarded. By the eve of Sabbath the date stores, too, were depleted, as most of the hardest-driven bargains were sweetened with the promise of a generous basket of the dates, which remained succulent, it was said, all the way home to Alexandria or Tyre.

After the first day of trade, Ezra left the bargaining to his daughter-in-law, son and steward. All this frenzied activity was beneath his status as lord of the manor, he told his wife. But he assured her he was supervising every transaction from a distance so that no errors of judgment on the part of the younger people would end up costing them their hard-earned profit.

Rebecca had been unusually quiet since that first day. Itamar took her behavior to be a result of mounting fatigue with the burden of both her unborn child and the negotiations. Finally, at the end of preparation day for the Sabbath, the empty storeroom was closed. The next day Rebecca helped her mother-in-law super vise the finishing touches on their Sabbath meal.

Much later, as the silence of the Sabbath enveloped them, Itamar took his wife to him, her back cradled against him, his arms around her broad, tight belly. He felt the infant move within. God willing, at this time next year, a child would be sleeping next to their bed in its wooden cradle.

With her husband sleeping soundly, Rebecca spent the rest of the night formulated her plan. The next morning, she set it into motion.

Although the number of servants in their household could have freed her from the daily grinding of the flour, she rarely missed a morning at the task. It was one of the things that had endeared her to the household. This morning found her hard at work in the circle of women kneading the dough for the morning's baking. As one after another rose and clapped the remnants of coarse flour from hands and robes, so did Rebecca, albeit more heavily. "I will tend to mats and blankets this day... thankfully with work in the plantation done we can see to their repair," she informed her mother-in-law.

Zippora's head was bent in what she thought was an unobtrusive manner, as she concentrated on hearing what the servants were saying about the outcome of the latest quarrel at the house of her sister's son. She nodded absently, and Rebecca made her getaway.

She went straight for the bench in their room under which she and Itamar had placed their rolled sleep mats that morning. She moved them aside, pulling from their wall niche a few blankets and piling them atop the mats with which she would appear busy in case anyone walked in on her. She pulled the bench away from the wall. Nimble fingers ran over the plaster, smooth except where she had made the sign of the hiding place those long years ago. Firm hands wielding the awl taken from the basket of weaving tools pried aside the stone. Behind the stone was the hiding place, containing her grandmother's *get*. The document, rolled in its leather pouch, came out first, and Rebecca placed it into the folds of her belt, now tied well below the place where her waist once was. There was something more in the box: the coins. It was these she needed now.

Within the purse Rebecca withdrew from the box, a substantial fifty denarii were still left of the money that Samuel had given her with instructions that she hide it immediately. The purse went into the folds of the belt as well, and Rebecca hurried to restore the crumbling pieces of wall as best she could, and to move the bench back into its place.

Her arms piled high with blankets, Rebecca asked a passing serving woman to have Nathan meet her in the estate office. Dodging children and chickens as she walked, she set down her burden on the other side of the courtyard where the women were taking advantage of the shady morning hours to complete the day's weaving.

She had not planned what she would do if Ezra or Itamar were already at the office. But, the room was empty. Nathan appeared a moment later. "I must ask something of you now and I must also insist that you not ask the reason."

Nathan waited patiently for Rebecca to continue. From the moment she had come into their lives he sensed that there was more to this young girl from the north than anyone could guess. Over the years he wondered when he would find out. Now, it seemed, was the moment.

"Who in our household bears a grudge against Ezra great enough to betray us to the Romans in exchange for money?"

His expression remained impassive while he considered her question. "There is one man among us who would do such a deed. A man who has not always been of our household. His father owned the plantation at Einot Qaneh, where it is said the water is even sweeter than our own."

In their gossip-ridden rooms and courtyards, Rebecca could hardly imagine that there was a story she had not heard. Yet here it was. Nathan spoke to her of Ochran, the blacksmith, a man as indistinguishable from other men as one loom weight from another. She vaguely recalled that some years ago this Ochran had asked Ezra's approval to bring a wife to live at Ein Gedi. The woman had borne him five children in quick succession, some of whom Rebecca had probably shooed away not five minutes before as she crossed the courtyard. But there the similarity of his story with that of their forty other servants ended.

It was the same year that Rebecca's grandparents bought their olive grove at Beit Govrin. Ezra's father received permission from the

Romans to add Ochran's father's lucrative date plantation at Einot Qaneh, seven parasangs north of Ein Gedi, to his already extensive holdings. Much gold had crossed the outstretched palms of the conqueror's minions to facilitate this purchase – and not one bronze *issar* of it had reached Ochran's father, debt-plagued as were so many farmers in those terrible years after the Romans laid waste to Jerusalem. The same year that Rebecca's grandmother had begun to dig for scraps before the walls of Jerusalem, Ochran's father came to live at Ein Gedi as an indentured servant. He died there ten years later. Ochran was never able to earn enough to buy his own way out of servitude.

By all accounts, the man was an excellent blacksmith. Over the years, his eyes had become as hard as the iron tools he forged. But Rebecca could not know that. She had been brought up in the ways of the wealthy. She never looked a servant in the eye and they certainly did not look into hers.

But not this time. Curiosity had gotten the better of Nathan and he caught his mistress' burnished eyes with his own, trying to fathom the purpose of her query as he continued his recitation, but to no avail. "This is the man you seek," he finished finally.

"Send him to me, and tell him that if he breathes one word of my request, Ezra will release him from his servitude … and see to it that the only road open to him and his family will be the one to the southern wilderness."

Ochran appeared a few moments later. He had not bothered to remove his leather blacksmith's apron for the interview with his mistress, and it draped his muscular form casually. He was mocking her, Rebecca thought, as if he had been loath to stop work. She was no stranger to the vinegar stink of perspiration that entered the room with him. Even Itamar carried it, on every day but the Sabbath, when they all bathed. But the insolence of his bearing carried with it its own scent, a threatening one that entwined itself around Rebecca and dared her to go ahead with the speech she had planned for this moment.

"There are fifty denarii in there," Rebecca said, indicating the worn leather pouch on the stone table that stood against the wall. "They are yours, together with your freedom and that of your family, when you leave this place to deliver the message I will give you."

The mask went up that turned every servant, everywhere, into an actor.

"What message?"

Rebecca lowered her voice even further, and she gave Ochran the words to say and the name of the man who was to hear it. "Whether or not you repeat to others what I have told you is of no consequence to me. You will not be believed. You are never to return to this place," she finished. Ochran waited for her to hand him the pouch herself, but she merely stepped aside so he could pick it up from the table. A moment later he left Rebecca standing alone in the shadows.

Chapter 47

In the gleam of the full moon of the month of Av, the whitewashed houses of Ein Gedi glowed against the purple hillside. The shadows were unmoving and silent. Then, the terrible crunch-crunch of Roman hob-nailed boots against the pebbled paths and the rush of air past blazing torches aroused the sleeping community. Before women could reach for their robes and their children, and the men for anything that could be used as a weapon, they were set upon.

At the house of Ezra and Zippora, on the slope of the hill some distance from the road, the noises were heard only faintly behind the locked courtyard door. "In the name of the emperor, come out of your houses. Everyone out of your houses or we will burn them with you in them!"

Rebecca and Itamar opened their eyes at the same moment. At first, they heard only the barking of dogs. Then, the men's voices, in coarse Aramaic sifted through their native Latin. They were banging on door after door and repeating badly pronounced phrases clearly learned for the occasion. "Open your doors, in the name of the emperor."

Itamar thrust aside the curtain that was their only door, in time to see Ezra and Zippora standing on the wooden staircase of the tower, confusion in their faces. Nathan appeared from the shadows and strode to the bottom step, holding a torch that he had lit so quickly that it smoked more than it illuminated. The servants had run from their rooms and came to a standstill as the unfamiliar sounds swirled around them.

"Leave house now and come to town gate." This time the voice was at their courtyard door, and it had a face and form. It was a *pedes*, his battered armor dully catching the torchlight, his small black eyes darting around the courtyard seeking the head of this family, barking out his orders. Finally, the eyes found Ezra. "All," he said, looking straight at the lord of the manor before leaving to head up the street to the next house.

As the family and the servants fled the house for the street, they joined a stream of their neighbors flowing down toward the square and the entrance to the town. Bewilderment and fear churned the crowd. Everyone knew the results of roustings such as these. Ezra was shaking from head to foot and Itamar led him to a shadow-cast corner of the square where his fear would not shame him further. Zippora's haughtiness, however did not fail her even now, and she stepped up to the centurion. "I demand to know the meaning of this!"

"What grandmother comes calling on me at this late hour?" the centurion asked his juniors lightly, tilting his head toward the little old Judean woman.

The unmistakable grind of his mother's voice brought Itamar running across the square toward the source. There she stood, arms akimbo and although her upturned face barely reached midway up the officer's cuirass, her eyes flashing with an anger that silenced the laughter. Sicas had been known to emerge even from beneath the robes of old Judean grandmothers, ending up in the gut of more than one unsuspecting officer or legionary.

Itamar staved off the confrontation as if distracting a bear in the arena. "Centurion!" he shouted, not sure what would actually come next. But at least the moment of danger for Zippora had passed. The centurion pushed Zippora aside and moved toward a new subject on whom to prey: Itamar.

"We should have established a better working relationship when first we met sixteen years ago," said the centurion.

"I do not understand your meaning," Itamar replied steadily. But he remembered very well that day in the courtyard, the day Rebecca had come, when he had first met this man. In the interim they had seen each other from time to time, but in the dark, even with the centurion in full battle dress, Itamar could see that his years of milking taxes from Judean farmers had added layers of girth and jowl.

"Your own people are your downfall, you know," the centurion spit out the words. "I have been reliably informed that the emperor is not receiving his due from Ein Gedi's date groves and balsam plantations. Thanks to Jewish eyes, full storerooms have been seen that have escaped Roman assessors. You are to keep the people here and at first light we will begin, shall we say, to readjust the account of taxes due."

All that day troops moved from one house to another. Behind most of the locked doors they broke down were prized possessions, garments of purple and gleaming white, a cherished set of red-slipped dishes. A silver broach, even one matron's golden Crown of Jerusalem, the pride of her Sabbath attire, disappeared into a sack at the searcher's belt, despite their commander's instructions to seek out only secret storerooms.

And sure enough, the trapdoor leading to the underground room where part of their balsam stock had been secreted far from prying eyes was quickly discovered in Ezra's home and in several others. These Judeans were expert cheats – for decades no way had been found to stop it. These days it had become even harder, as the one whom the Jews called the Son of a Star – at least the name was appropriate, he had appeared out of nowhere like a shooting star – had taught them how to hide not only goods, but people. Every nook and cranny, the remote rocky places of the wilderness seemed to leach these people out when they were least expected. The centurion knew many who had lost their commands, not because of the number of foot soldiers killed on such raids, but because of their failure to root out the rebels. But he would not be among them. He must remember to thank the traitor this town never knew it had, before ordering him strangled. It would be a respectable ending to his sixteen-year sentence with these barbarian Judeans. And then, finally, he would move up in the world.

Finally, the soldiers departed. Rebecca and Itamar were exhausted like the rest of the townspeople from the day spent sitting helpless under a broiling sun, begging permission from their guards to move the aged and the infants to the shade. Rebecca thought she had begun to feel the pangs the women had told her to expect before the onslaught of the birth. The younger couple helped Ezra and Zippora to stand and shepherded them back to the house. There had never been a day like this. No fires had been lit, no bread had been baked. With none to tell them otherwise, some of the bewildered servants made for their quarters, pausing only long enough to stand silently in line to fill pitchers from the courtyard water jars. Some then fell to their pallets drained; others managed to feed their children a bit of dried fruit.

Itamar was burning with the humiliation of the day. "This is not the end," he whispered to Rebecca. "They have no reason to stop at this. They will be back tomorrow or the next day to strip Ein Gedi of everything we own, everything we have worked for. We will not let this happen. We will do as others have done. We will take to the caves. Let the Romans try to dig us out."

Itamar could not know that these words were repeated in every one of the town's hundred homes. And he would never know that the single-minded decision the entire town came to was set in motion by his own wife.

Chapter 48

Once again, the townspeople left their home. But this time no Roman soldiers prodded them and they passed right by the town square, heading west to the mountains. This time there was neither shouting nor confusion. "We'll be back," some said, not in words, but in the wooden-knobbed elbow keys several had inserted in their belts, freeing their hands to carry other possessions, or their babies. The leaders of the column had already passed the last houses of Ein Gedi, then the seasonal workers' empty huts. Spice plants crushed underfoot released their pungent aroma. Breathing grew labored as the climb to the caves above the town grew steeper. Hand over hand, hand helping hand.

Zippora wailed and shed copious tears as she digested the bizarre turn her life had taken in the last twenty-four hours. She had not been unaware of the growing chaos threatening them over the past years. She could not help but know that Judea was up in arms again. That one, The Star or Son of the Star, or some such name, had taken most of their best young men. The sons of some of her friends had left to join him and had not been heard of for three long years. Thankfully, her Itamar was not one of them. Thankfully, Rebecca had kept Itamar close to home, even when it seemed she would never give him an heir. Their lives had prospered, she admitted, because of her daughter-in-law. And now, what of the grandson she was to have seen born in a few weeks' time? What of her life?

Now, Rebecca was here to take her away. They had told her to take nothing, but she would not hear of it. In her hands, Zippora cradled the magnificent glass serving dish, created in the marvelous workshops of Sidon, which she had brought to her husband's home with her dowry. Zippora had once served the governor himself from this dish, before the troubles. Each of the few times Rebecca had seen it come out of its palm-heart wrappings, Zippora would sing out cheerfully, "The governor himself has eaten roast lamb with hot mint sauce from this very plate." Rebecca saw what Zippora had laid on the table to take with her and words failed her: a copper mirror, a tiny ivory box of kohl and three applicators for the eye color. When Zippora saw her approach, she leaned forward, hugging the plate defiantly. Her hands fluttered over the table, and seizing the objects, she hastily stuffed them beneath her robe.

Rebecca pretended not to see. Her own treasure – the scroll, all that could prove the existence of her grandmother and the roots of her mission, was secreted in the folds of her own robe. "Come," was all she said, and gently she led her mother-in-law out of the room, down the tower stairs, and out to the street. By this time the others were all far ahead. Rebecca and Itamar, Ezra, Zippora, and Nathan joined their neighbors in the trudge up the path to where the caves punctured the escarpment above.

Days were spent in near darkness, nights blacker than pitch from the Asphalt Sea below. Early on, they had moved from the caves above the town to another, higher valley, to the north. The children quickly lost their fear of the darkness, comforted by the murmuring of their parents and neighbors as they crawled endlessly back and forth along tunnels that penetrated the depths of the mountain. The adults took turns sitting at the entrance to the cave or on the ledge outside. When Rebecca's turn came to sit in the light, she took to watching the ibex she spied nearby, in a vain attempt to help her forget the constant pressure of her infant on her lower back. At first the wild goats were skittish at the human intruders, but eventually the animals ignored them and returned to their daily routine, moving between the high, safe haven of the crags to drink at the spring and to forage in the valley floor below. They scampered down the cliff, fearless for themselves, but diligently protecting their young, even blocking off danger with their bodies where the rock face sheared away to the gorge.

A pair of vultures had built a nest on the edge of a spur that stretched out below them. Soon it cradled their featherless, teetering offspring, and Rebecca sometimes saw the parents taking turns bringing it prey, which it gobbled down hungrily, its body growing more powerful, its wings flapping more determinedly each day that passed. Soon, she thought, its devoted parents seemed to be telling it, very soon, be patient, you will soar. She took to singing the words softly, under her breath, to her unborn baby.

In the darkness of the cave or in the sunlight on the ledge, Rebecca's fellow refugees spoke to each other of one thing only: the day the Son of the Star would lure the conqueror into the desert, secure the town, and beat back the tyrant from their doors. They would return to their homes that very day, they said to each other. That very day.

Some of the younger men, against the instructions of the elders, sneaked back to Ein Gedi. They returned to report that blackened stumps were all that remained of the date groves. The balsam plants had been ripped from the soil and the slopes lay desolate. Jewish warriors were nowhere to be seen, they reported.

At least, the elders told everyone, we are safe here. Our store of food will last long enough for us to be certain that the conqueror has seized his fill, and we will return home to rebuild. Of that much they were certain, they said.

Rebecca despaired as she saw people nodding and murmuring in assent. Finally, she brought Itamar into her world: "Long ago, a man told me that he had witnessed the death of my grandmother at the walls of Jerusalem. The man turned her death into something noble. I embraced the burden he placed upon me. "

"What do you mean he *turned* her death into something noble?" Itamar said. "You used to say your grandmother's death *was* noble. She worked her entire life for the freedom of our people, you said. She died heroically! We could not have survived this long without the spirits of those like her to guide us."

The sun rose higher in the sky, taking with it most of their daily portion of light. Itamar could not see the bitter smile that broke open Rebecca's dry lips as she heard Samuel's lies in Itamar's voice. She licked absently at the drops of blood that oozed from the cracked skin.

"We are not alone," Itamar persisted. "You taught me that. Everyone who came before us who fought tyranny is here with us now. For their sake, we must continue the struggle. We will find the way to leave this cave and when we do, we will resist until we gain our freedom."

Rebecca had no strength to reply. Yes, they would continue to fight, she thought. To fight the last battle in a war already lost. She felt her eyes burning with the tears her eyes were too dry to shed. Then her body convulsed as her baby began to fight its way into the world.

Chapter 49

The sounds from the plateau above them were at first of no particular concern. It wouldn't have been the first time, some said, that a leopard had come slinking around to investigate the unfamiliar odor of human proximity. But the sounds refused to abate. They were constant now, and the scouts once again risked their lives, edging out almost half a parasang along the stone ledge that fronted the cave, where the ledge rose higher than the cave, but thinned out to nearly nothing.

When they returned, their faces had gone from sun-deprived pale to ashen. The rest of the men followed the scouts to the back of the rocky chamber where their murmurs would be inaudible despite the cramped quarters. When Itamar went back to Rebecca, at first he could not speak or even look at her, or at the bundle in her arms.

"The scouts have reported that there are Romans above us on the mountain. If we leave the cave, even to sit on the ledge, they can see us. Their marksmen are at the ready. We must find a way to make sure this cave does not become our tomb."

"What is it, son?" Zippora's cracked voice came from the darkness. "Soon? Did you say soon? Will we be going back home soon?"

"Yes, Mother, soon," Itamar soothed her, not taking his eyes off Rebecca.

"That's wonderful," Zippora called back. Then we can bring that baby of ours into the covenant of Abraham our Patriarch and have a celebration the likes of which this town has never seen! The neighbors will die of envy!"

Rebecca met Itamar's gaze. Zippora knew the infant had come into the world, for its howling had filled the cave yesterday. But although Itamar and Ezra had tried to tell her, she could not remember that the tiny, wrinkled baby was a girl.

Muffled cries and soft weeping rose from each family group huddled together in the darkness as their men delivered the news. Then, slowly, silence descended. No one could say whether minutes or hours had passed, when Abraham the carpenter rose and, with a speed that denied the toll of starvation, he clamored over the tangle of bodies. He stepped outside on the ledge. For a moment, his skeletal silhouette, hands raised, was framed by the jagged edges of the cave entrance. Until his scream sliced the air. Its echo lived longer than he did after the arrow cleaved his skull in two. The hideous sound faded only when he toppled from view into the bottomless gorge.

Silence became the closest companion of all but those, like Itamar's mother, who had disconnected themselves from their surroundings. Those lucky souls sang or mumbled to themselves; but finally, most of them fell silent as well. The children now no longer had to be shushed by their elders. In the week that followed, a few more people shook off restraining hands and tried to make their way up the ledge to the conqueror, whose arrows never missed these easy targets. This time, the tyrant cared neither about surrender or captives.

It had been days since Rebecca had even bothered to stand up. The day that Abraham the carpenter had died she had been thirsty, and perhaps the next day as well, as far as she could discern the passage of time. When the baby whimpered, she put it to her breast; it suckled and went silent. But Rebecca could not tell whether her emaciated body had any sustenance to offer, or whether her tiny daughter, too, was about to breathe her last.

Then, even thirst abandoned her, replaced with pain that gripped every fiber of her being. Finally, the pain, too, was gone. Suddenly, her father and mother appeared. She urged them to return home to Sepphoris before it was too late. To take up the threads of their lives, to make sure they survived, even under the heel of the conqueror.

She grew colder. Itamar held her close but his vital heat was waning, too. Until the end, he managed each day to bring her to the cave entrance, where she could see blue sky above and the spur below, with the pair of vultures coming and going to their nest.

Then came the day when Rebecca knew that Itamar was dead and she and her infant daughter were the only ones left. That was when she took the scroll from her belt.

She opened the frayed swaddling cloth around the sleeping baby and placed the scroll next to the infant's parched skin, watching it rise and fall with the frail beating of the baby's heart. She cupped her hand over the baby and the scroll, and her grandmother came to her.

"Will anyone know that we lived, Grandmother? Will they learn the lesson of my life, though only now I have learned the lesson of yours?" Rebecca asked. The grandmother she never met did not speak. But she took Rebecca's cold hands firmly in her two warm ones and Rebecca rose to greet her.

Before she closed her eyes for the last time, she saw the fledged young raptor streak across the sky.

Epilogue

The tent flaps framed the brightening eastern sky. The sour smell of wine and vomit hung heavy within, as the girl pushed her heavy, dark hair away from her face. Covering her nakedness with her tunic, she gingerly disentangled her smooth limbs from those of the snoring, stinking man who had been the last to take her in the drunken revelry of the night before.

There had been no sound or movement for days from the cave below where her neighbors had been hiding. The soldiers who were set the unenviable task of climbing down to what she had heard them call "the scorpions' nest" hurried back to report that they saw nothing but dead, skeletal bodies. And so, even though official orders that they could leave this hellish place would arrive only days from now, the men had been given leave to drink themselves into a stupor and keep the women until dawn, after the officers had had their fill.

Fourteen-year-old Judith had awakened again in the gloom of night, imbued with the suffocating sadness she had felt since the day the Roman soldiers had stolen her from her home in Ein Gedi. It was as if she were living inside the blackness of the rock-cut tomb to which she had begun accompanying her mother last year to help anoint the bodies of the dead. She could not forget what it was like to breathe the choking air while shadows leaped at her frightfully in the flickering lamplight. This was what it was like.

She had learned on that first day of incessant assault on her body and her soul that tears led to more abuse. And so she turned her pain inward, the pang of every waking moment bringing her back to her lost family, her girlhood, her village. She had not spoken a word since that day, neither to her captors nor to the girls that shared her fate.

When the men left her alone and she was allowed a few hours' sleep, she dreamt she was home again in Ein Gedi, rocked by the gentle waves that lapped against the ferryboat with which her father had made a fine living plying the Salt Sea, which he had taught her to row even better than her brothers. She dreamed of the little raft he had begun helping her build when she was hardly old enough to stand at her mother's loom. She saw herself once again lashing sections of palm trunk together that were as tall as she was, and how he had taught her to steer a straight course and keep her oars from splashing the bitter water into her eyes and mouth.

Her silence had earned her the exclusion of the three other girls who had been taken with her to serve the soldiers; they no longer even glanced at her when, in the rare moments they spent alone together, they tried to remind each other of who they had been. They spoke longingly of Ein Gedi, whose balsam orchards they thought they could still see greening on the dun desert slope to the south. The other girls also talked about things that had gone unspoken at home. Of fathers, uncles and grandfathers who had kept the conqueror's minions happy with a regular supply of their precious balsam. Surely they would have been allowed to escape the sorry procession that fled to the caves. Each of the girls boasted of a relative closer to the conqueror than her friends had. He had doubtless already reported his missing daughter, granddaughter or niece. She would be redeemed any moment now and the soldiers would be punished for their excesses.

The other girls dreamed of going home; Judith would do it, she thought. Now.

She threw on her hooded cloak and emerged soundlessly from the tent.

Outside, every sentry she spied was snoring at his post. She had seen that before; had watched them escape a flogging by snapping alert at the first faint clank of the armor of an approaching officer. But the fleet-footed young girl in her silent, simple sandals darted past them without disturbing their drunken slumber. She made straight for the cliff edge, where every day since she had been brought to the camp, she had watched the archers, bow and arrow in hand, poised to pick off any of the cave-dwellers below who dared venture out into their deadly range.

There was no one there now. Soon, she was out of sight of the camp, picking her way down the cliff by one of the dozens of wild-goat paths that snaked down to the cave and the gorge below.

Since being brought to the conqueror's camp, she had numbed herself against any one of a dozen fetid smells for which nothing her young life in the prosperous oasis town could have prepared her. But the stench that wafted out from the cave made her gag as she had not done since that horrific first day in captivity. She forced herself to place one foot in front of the other, then another, clinging with both hands to the rock face. It seemed like hours, but the sun had not yet fully burned off the morning coolness when she arrived at the ledge that fronted the cave. She ducked inside. Her hand flew instinctively over her nose and mouth as the grey light mercilessly illuminated heaps of what were once human beings, as far back as she could see.

But the welcome, swirling darkness that had crept up to embrace her from the deadly silence now slunk back, chased away by a muffled rasping. Judith looked down to see a pile of rags stirring at her feet. She knelt to move them aside, and her mouth dropped open to find the wizened face of an infant staring up at her. She scooped up the tiny, struggling form. Grasping it to her, she felt her legs lead her out of the death-filled cavern back into the light.

Who was the mother of this infant, she thought; who was its father, its neighbor? No, she pushed the thought away as she had taught herself to do these past weeks. The only thing that mattered was to flee for her life and now, to fight for the flickering soul of this being in her arms. She headed in the only direction she knew. Home.

The sun rose higher in the sky as she inched along the switchbacks down toward the Salt Sea shore. Her progress was painfully slow. But this was the only safe way to navigate with her burden, and inexorably, Ein Gedi drew closer. She reached it only as the sun dipped behind the mountains in the west. The baby had not stirred for hours.

No lights were glowing from the high windows of the town's clustered houses. Perhaps, she thought, it was still too early for the more frugal of her neighbors to light their oil lamps. She pushed open the wooden door of the first home she came to – Isaac the tanner's. She headed straight through the empty front room to the courtyard and its huge water jars. Laying the too-still baby down, she removed the lid, thrust her hand inside and brought a little of the life-giving liquid to her mouth.

A moment later she turned to the infant. Unwrapping its swaddling cloths, she dipped her whole arm into the jar again, then withdrew her soaking sleeve and placed a corner gently against the baby's lips. It sucked, feebly, but soon the sleeve was dry. She dipped it into the jar again and placed it once more against the tiny mouth. Then she pressed it gently over the baby's face, neck and chest. Before wrapping the infant again against the chill of oncoming dusk, she noticed it was a girl. And then, she noticed something else. A scroll lay among the folds of the swaddling cloth. Puzzled, she lifted it out, cradling it in her lap. In the last light, she saw it bore script. She could not read it; even her father had needed a scribe to write and read out the contract that had purchased his boat. But he had guarded that contract carefully in a little jar on a shelf in their wall niche, and the whole family knew how important it was. So this scroll, whatever it was, must be very important, she knew. She placed it in the folds of her belt, and before she could think further, exhaustion overtook her.

It seemed as if Judith had only closed her eyes for a moment when the baby's mewling woke her. She knew the little one had to have sustenance right away, or the death it had escaped in the cave would find it within hours. She had never been inside Isaac the tanner's home – the smells that still hung over it, although his vats had been empty for weeks – had usually kept most of the townspeople away. But glancing around, she could see it was not much different than her own. She quickly found a piece of cloth to place beneath the baby and another to replace its soiled swaddling, and, leaving the main room, she crossed the courtyard to a small enclosure where six skinny, thirsty goats were huddled.

Opening the gate, she shooed four of them out to find their way to the streambed and whatever they could forage. At the same time she blocked the way of a female and its kid. Grabbing a jug from a nearby shelf, she milked the goat until the jar frothed full and brought it back to her tiny charge. The baby sucked weakly but steadily on the milk-soaked cloth, and fell asleep on her lap.

There was no time to spare. The silence in the village told her there was no living soul about, and she feared that any moment now she would hear the conqueror's dark voices on the street outside. Judith lay the baby down while she quickly surveyed the tanner's house again. She grabbed the cloth sling she spied in the wall niche and filled it with dried dates and the hard, white goat cheese she found in the corner of the courtyard, where a leather water skin hung on the wall. She tossed the skin by its strap into the courtyard water jar. As she pulled it up, full and dripping, she pushed away the thought of where she and the baby might be when it ran dry.

Fashioning a sling out of the loose cloth in the front of her robe, she cradled the baby in it, and hoisting the water onto her back, she emerged from the courtyard, her mind working quickly. In better times, her parents had taken the family to see the sages, all the way to Yavne on the coast, within sight of the Great Sea. She marshaled every instinct, all the oft-repeated stories at family gatherings, recalling that the first part of the journey had been made by her father's own ferry-boat along the coast. But even if she could find it at the port, which the conqueror had no doubt destroyed, she could never manage the oars alone. And so she headed northward along the impossibly narrow belt of salt-suffused flatlands between the towering cliffs to the west and the Salt Sea.

All day long she trudged, hardly lifting her eyes. The infant had been as still as death almost the entire time. Judith had stopped as often as she dared to drip water into its mouth, and now it was too late to go further. She raised her hand to shade her eyes from the afternoon sun, and there it was. There was no mistaking the great canyon – "The Steps" as her townspeople called it.

The tiny creature hung heavily against her, its feet pressed against the scroll tucked into her belt. But it had been hours since the baby had even opened her eyes. Judith would have to wait until tomorrow for the hardest part of the journey, the climb up The Steps.

And so she stopped and fell, exhausted, against the trunk of an acacia tree. The baby stirred almost imperceptibly when she laid her on the ground. How can she possibly have survived so long, Judith thought, looking down at her. It never entered her mind that she should be asking the same question about herself.

She pulled out a small chunk of the hard cheese, and placed it on a flat piece of rock. Pouring some of her precious water over it she poked at it with a small stone until it turned into watery chunks that she slipped into the baby's mouth, one tiny bit at a time.

After sunset, the howl and yip of jackals floated to her on the night breeze. She knew the sound well. Growing up, she had barely heard it through the stout stone walls of her home, surrounded by her sleeping family. But she knew enough to realize a pack of these scavengers could carry off this little one as easily as they did the occasional newborn lamb or goat from the night pasture. And so, at the first sign of dawn, she stood, picked up the baby, and began walking west up The Steps.

The sun was well up in the sky when Judith saw four tiny figures walking along the ledge above her in the distance. They stopped in their tracks; so did she. Is this where it would end? After all this, to fall straight into the hands of the conqueror again? But she was almost beyond caring. She could see huge caves up the canyon, but they were too far ahead for her to reach; the men who were now making straight for her had emerged from one of them. She leaned heavily against the canyon wall and waited for the inevitable.

They were talking among themselves, gesturing, their voices infused with uncertainty. They were talking about her, Judith realized; she could understand every word they said. Then, one of them called out.

"Who are you?"

"Who are *you*?" she heard herself reply.

No answer.

By this time she could clearly see the little knot of four men ahead of her now on the path. They were looking at each other, then at her, nonplussed at the brashness of her reply, belying the youth and weakness of the barely audible voice.

They could not believe their eyes. A girl, an empty water-skin on her back, her hands protectively cradling a tiny bundle slung across her breast.

"Don't be afraid," one of them said, and stepped out ahead of the other three.

Although she immediately spied the Roman dagger at his waist, she was not afraid. As if the man's rough highland Aramaic was not enough, his short stature, plain, thin-soled leather sandals and peasant's tunic barely covering his knees told her what she needed to know, even before she spied the unkempt side-locks hanging from his short-cropped hair down to his thickly bearded face. Jews.

So she and the girl-child she carried were not the last of her people. She thought she had uttered the words aloud, but then realized she had not. The man in the lead repeated his question. She sensed the suspicion in his voice, and forced herself to speak.

"I am Judith, of Ein Gedi," she said.

The men were visibly shaken by her response.

"But there is no one left in Ein Gedi. They all died in the caves, ben Galgoula," one of the other men offered hesitantly to the man who had spoken to her first.

"We only know what we saw in the town, and the encampment the Romans stationed near the cliff edge to the south," the man called ben Galgoula, clearly their leader, answered, without taking his eyes off the girl. Then he added, as if to himself: "Now we see someone has survived after all."

At that, another man now spoke, using ben Galgoula's first name. "Careful, Yeshua, he said. I know exactly what you are thinking. Remember the letter Ben Cosiba sent you – we are not to shelter strangers."

"You speak too freely since you married my sister, John," ben Galgoula shot back. "Of all our commander's letters – that's the one you remember, written so many years ago? In any case, that letter referred only to the Tekoans and the Galileans. We cannot leave a young woman here to die, when we can give her shelter," ben Galgoula said.

"Besides," he added, "you know as well as I do, someone must be left behind to tell our story."

John did not respond. He did not have to. This was not the first time they had uttered the words for which their supreme commander Ben Cosiba would execute them if he heard. Ben Galgoula's words were true, and he knew it.

Ben Galgoula motioned to one of the other men to hand the full water jug at his waist to the girl, who reached out eagerly for it. The men were amazed to see her open her makeshift sling to reveal an infant, whose still lips she wet before taking a long drink herself. When she raised her arms to drink and her outer robe fell away, John and ben Galgoula both saw the tip of the scroll over the top of her belt. The glances the comrades exchanged, with their years of experience in the wordless communication on which their lives depended, said everything the other needed to know. John's look warned that the girl could be a spy, forced or otherwise, into Roman service. Ben Galgoula's told his subordinate there would be time to solve this new mystery when they reached their hideout.

"Follow us," the man called John said brusquely to the girl.

Judith fell in behind the men, and all turned and paced single-file along the cliff edge.

She could see their destination – up ahead where the goat path widened to a ledge where three people could stand abreast, was a huge cave opening. Two men stood guard at the entrance. They had seen enough in their years as wilderness warriors that nothing surprised them, so the only response to the presence of the contingent's unlikely new members was for one of them to duck inside. A moment later he reappeared with an older woman who walked toward the small group and fell in wordlessly beside Judith, placing a hand lightly at the small of her back. Judith had not realized how exhausted and alone she had been until that hand, resting against her, reminded her of the blessing of such a simple, caring, human gesture. Her eyes filled with tears for the first time since her abduction by the legionaries, a lifetime ago.

At the cave's entrance, the woman, who had still not said a word to her, merely pressed her hand a little more firmly against Judith's back, and the little group stepped inside. Judith welcomed the cool darkness, but with her first breath came the sour smell of closely packed humans. As her vision adjusted slowly to the dim interior, she saw several pairs of eyes directed at her. Children and adults, all with eyes milky and sunken in faces scarred by sorrow-filled years.

The older woman took the baby gently and handed it to a girl not much older than Judith. A look passed between the two cave-dwellers, and unquestioningly, the girl placed the baby she had been holding into the hands of the woman sitting next to her, and put the newcomer's infant to her breast. The baby suckled, at first weakly, then hungrily, oblivious to the world.

During the next few hours, the cave people revealed their story to Judith. Refugees from Bethlehem and other, smaller villages, even some from Jerusalem, had gathered here after trudging through the wilderness from King Herod's old fortress where they had lived underground until the Romans had finally unearthed them. The women and children had fled the fortress with the small escort under the command of ben Galgoula and his brother-in-law, leaving husbands and brothers behind to defend the mountain, heading eastward, seeking another refuge until the Romans finally surrendered and accepted Ben Cosiba's inevitable, God-given victory.

Now, though no one said so openly, Ben Cosiba's absent presence no longer held them in thrall. The adults knew there was to be no "until." Judith then told them her story, and offered ben Galgoula the scroll. Moving to the light at the entrance to the cave, he unrolled it carefully, hunkered down and perused it, his eyes slowly widening as he realized what it was. He cocked his head at his lieutenants to follow him outside.

The men's murmuring voices ceased after a few short minutes, and they reentered the cave, the scroll tightly re-rolled in ben Galgoula's hands. He turned to Judith. "We are too many to take the path back up the mountains," he told her. "We will continue down to Ein Gedi. The Romans are gone, he said, the confidence in his tone now no more than code for precisely the opposite emotion, when he realized everyone in the group was listening closely.

"But you will go up," he said. "We will give you enough water and food for the two days it will take you and the babe to reach the mountaintops, and tomorrow at dawn, you will go your way and we will go ours. This valley leads directly to King Herod's fortress. You will see it in the distance, but do not stop there." Ben Galgoula and his lieutenants needed no pigeon-borne message to tell him the fortress must be in Roman hands by now.

"As soon as you reach the first grazing flocks, take the valley's northern fork. It will take you to Jerusalem – but do not stop there either. Continue north until you reach Galilee, where you will be safe from the wrath of Edom," he said, using the code word people used for the conqueror. "There, the Jews will take you in, and you can begin life anew," he finished.

He saw the young woman's eyes stray to the scroll he still held. "This, you must leave here. It is better for you not even to know what it contains. I will tell you only that the conqueror so hates the place it mentions, that they neither utter nor write its name. To them, it would be proof you are part of the rebellion and they would torture and kill you and the infant as soon as they realized what it says. Ben Galgoula turned away and did not speak to her again. The older woman led Judith and the baby to where the women and children were preparing for the night.

The next day, as the sun rose over the mountains of Moab, Judith emerged from the cave, turned, and headed upward.

Glossary

Distances

1 parasang equals approximately 4 miles (6 km)

"Mile": The Roman mile was approximately 960 meters (960 yards)

Weights, measures, and coinage

1 *se'ah*: a unit of measure equal to about 2 gallons

1 *qav*: 1/6 *se'ah*

1 *sextarius* = .547 liters

Aureus: a gold coin

Denarius: a small silver coin

1 cubit: one-half meter (19 inches)

Pithoi: huge pots

Plithar: a spatial measure equal to slightly under 1 modern acre

Roman military terms

Eques – Roman cavalryman

Pedes – Roman foot soldier

Terms from Jewish life

Ebionites – an early Christian sect

Minim – Sectarians. It is commonly understood that they later became known as Christians.

Hazan – prayer leader; in modern Hebrew, a cantor

Tallitot – prayer shawls

Gabbai – sexton

About the Author

Miriam Feinberg Vamosh grew up in Trenton, New Jersey, and has lived in Israel since 1970. An author, editor and translator, Miriam started her love affair with the Bible and ancient sources as a tour educator in 1975, when she began specializing in weaving together Jewish literary sources, traditions and beliefs with the origins of Christianity, and teaching about them on-site throughout Israel. Miriam's books include *Daily Life at the Time of Jesus* (Palphot), an illustrated, lively, wide-ranging exploration of everyday life during Second Temple times, which has been translated into thirty-two languages. She has also authored *Food at the Time of the Bible,* and *Women at the Time of the Bible* (Palphot) and *Teach It to Your Children: How Kids Lived in Bible Days* (Avimedia). Together with Eva Marie Everson, she wrote the award-winning *Reflections of God's Holy Land: A Personal Journey through Israel* (Thomas Nelson). Other works include *Israel, Land of the Bible* (Palphot), and *Pathways through the Land of the Hart* (Gefen). Miriam, who has an M.A. in Archaeology and Heritage, is on the editorial staff of the English edition of the Israeli daily *Haaretz.* She is married to Arik, has two married daughters and five grandchildren, and lives near Jerusalem.

The fonts used in this book are from the Arno family